I0611920

CLASSICAL FRENCH DRAMA AND COMEDY

Chief editor – Vladimir Orel

CORNEILLE

✺

RACINE

✺

MOLIÈRE

Polyeucte
PIERRE CORNEILLE

CHARACTERS

FELIX, Governor of Armenia
POLYEUCTE, an Armenian noble, son-in-law to Felix
SEVERUS, a Roman Knight, favourite of the Emperor Decius
NEARCHUS, an Armenian noble, friend to Polyeucte
PAULINE, daughter to Felix, wife to Polyeucte
STRATONICE, companion to Pauline
ALBIN, friend to Felix
FABIAN, servant to Severus
FABIAN, friend to Felix
Three Guards

The Scene is at Melitena, capital of Armenia. The action takes place in
the Palace of FELIX

ACT I
POLYEUCTE, NEARCHUS

NEARCHUS
Shall woman's dream of terror hurl the dart?
Oh, feeble weapon 'gainst so great a heart!
Must courage proved a thousand times in arms
Bow to a peril forged by vain alarms?

POLY.
I know that dreams are born to fade away,
And melt in air before the light of day;
I know that misty vapours of the night
Dissolve and fly before the morning bright.
The dream is naught — but the dear dreamer — all!

She has my soul, Nearchus, fast in thrall;
Who holds the marriage torch — august, divine,
Bids me to her sweet voice my will resign.
She fears my death — tho' baseless this her fright,
Pauline is wrung with fear — by day — by night;
My road to duty hampered by her fears,
How can I go when all undried her tears?
Her terror I disown — and all alarms,
Yet pity holds me in her loving arms:
No bolts or bars imprison, — yet her sighs
My fetters are — my conquerors, her eyes!
Say, kind Nearchus, is the cause you press
Such as to make me deaf to her distress?
The bonds I slacken I would not unloose
Nothing I yield — yet grant a timely truce.

NEAR.
How grant you know not what? Are you assured
Of constancy? — as one who has endured?
God claims your soul for Him! — Now! Now! To-day!
The fruit to-morrow yields — oh, who shall say?
Our God is just, but do His grace and power
Descend on recreants with equal shower?
On darkened souls His flame of light He turns,
Yet flame neglected soon but faintly burns,
And dying embers fade to ashes cold
If we the heart His spirit wooes withhold.
Great Heaven retains the fire no longer sought,
While ashes turn to dust, and dust to naught.
His holy baptism He bids thee seek,
Neglect the call, and the desire grows weak.
Ah! whilst from woman's breast thou heedst the sighs,
The flame first flickers, then, untended — dies!

POLY.
You know me ill, — 'tis mine, that holy fire,

Fed, not extinguished, by unslaked desire
Her tears — I view them with a lover's eye;
And yet your Christ is mine — a Christian I!
The healing, cleansing flood o'er me shall flow,
I would efface the stain from birth I owe;
I would be pure — my sealed eyes would see!
The birthright Adam lost restored to me
This, this, the unfading crown! For this I yearn,
For that exhaustless fount I thirst, I burn.
Then, since my heart is true, Nearchus, say —
Shall I not grant to pity this delay?

NEAR.
So doth the ghostly foe our souls abuse,
And all beyond his force he gains by ruse;
He hates the purpose fast he cannot foil, —
Then he retreats — retreats but to recoil!
In endless barricade obstruction piles,
To-day 'tis tears impede, to-morrow — smiles!
And this poor dream — his coinage of the night
Gives place to other lures, all falsely bright:
All tricks he knows and uses — threats and prayers
Attacks in parley — as the Parthian dares.
In chain unheeded weakest link must fail,
So fortress yet unwon he'll mount and scale.
O break his bonds! Let feeble woman weep!
The heart that God has touched 'tis God must keep!
Who looks behind to dally with his choice
When Heaven demands — obeys another voice!

POLY.
Who loves thy Christ — say, must he love no other?

NEAR.
He may — he must! 'Tis Christ says, "Love thy brother,"
Yet on the altar of the Heavenly King

No rival place, no alien incense fling!
Through Him — by Him — for Him — all goodness know!
'Tis from the source alone each stream must flow.
To please Him, wife, and wealth, and rank, and state
Must be forsaken — strait the heavenly gate.
Poor silly sheep! afar you err and stray
From Him who is The Life, The Truth, The Way!
My grief chokes utterance! I see your fate,
As round the fold the hungry wolves of hate
Closer and fiercer rage: from sword and flame
One shelter for His flock — one only Name!
The Cross alone our victor over fears,
Not this thy strength, — thy plea — a woman's tears!

POLY.
I know thy heart! It is mine own — the tear
My pity drops hath ne'er a taint of fear!
Who dreads not torture, yet — to give relief
To her he loves, perforce must ease her grief!
If Heaven should claim my life, my death, my all,
Then Heaven will give the strength to heed the call.
The shepherd guides me surely to the fold,
There, safe with Him, 'tis He will make me bold!

NEAR.
Be bold! O come!

POLY.
Yes, let thy faith be mine!
There — at his feet — do I my life resign
If but Pauline — my love — would give consent!
Else heaven were hell, and home but banishment!

NEAR.
Come! — to return. Thrice welcome to her sight,
To see thee safe will double her delight:

As the pierced cloud unveils a brighter sun,
So is her joy enhanced — thy glory won!
O come, they wait!

POLY.
Appease her fear! Ah, this
Alone will give her rest — her lover bliss.
She comes!

NEAR.
Then fly!

POLY.
I cannot!

NEAR.
To deny would yield thine enemy the victory!
He loves to kill, and knows his deadliest dart
Finds friend within the fort — thy traitor heart!

Enter Pauline and Stratonice

POLY.
I needs must go, Pauline! My love, good-bye!
I go but to return — for thine am I!

PAUL.
Oh, why this haste to leave a loving wife?
Doth honour call? — or fear'st thou for thy life?

POLY.
For more, a thousandfold!

PAUL.
Great Gods above!

POLY.
Thou hast my heart! Let this content thy love!

PAUL.
You love and yet you leave me. What am I?
Not mine to solve the dreary mystery!

POLY.
I love thee more than self — than life — than fame
But — —

PAUL.
There is something that thou dar'st not name.
Oh, on my knees I supplicate, I pray,
Remove my darkness! — turn my night to day!

POLY.
Oh, dreams are naught!

PAUL.
Yet, when they tell of thee,
I needs must listen, for I love! Ah, me!

POLY.
Take courage, dear one, 'tis but for an hour,
Thy love must draw me back, for love hath power
O'er all in earth and heaven. My soul's delight,
I can no more! My only safety — flight!

(Exeunt POLYEYCTE and NEARCHUS)

PAUL.
Yes, go, despise my prayer — my agony;
Go, ruthless — meet thy fate — forewarned by me;
Chase thy pursuer, herald thine own doom;
Go, kiss the murderer's hand, and hail the tomb!

Ah, Stratonice! for our boasted power
As sovereigns o'er man's heart! Poor regents of an hour!
Faint, helpless, moonbeam — light was all I gave,
The sun breaks forth — his queen becomes his slave!
Wooed? Yes; as other queens I held my court
Won — but to lose my crown, and be the sport
Of proud, absorbing and imperious man!

STRAT.
Ah, man does what he wills — we, what we can;
He loves thee, lady!

PAUL.
Love should mate with trusts;
He leaves me!

STRAT.
Lady, 'tis because he must!
He loves thee with a love will never die,
Then, if he leave thee, reason not the why:
Give him thy trust! Oh, thou shalt have reward,
For thee he hides the secret! Let him guard
Thy life beloved — in fullest liberty.
The wife who wholly trusts alone is free!
One heart for thee and him — one purpose sure,
Yet this heart beats to dare — and to endure.
The wife's true heart must o'er the peril sigh
Which meets his heart moved but to purpose high;
Thy pain his pain, but not his terror thine:
He is Armenian, thou of Roman line.
We, of Armenia, mock thy dreams to scorn,
For they are born of night, as truth of morn;
While Romans hold that dreams are heaven-sent,
And spring from Jove for man's admonishment.

PAUL.

Though this thy faith — if thou my dream shouldst hear —
My grief must needs be thine, thy fear my fear,
And, that the horror thou may'st fully prove,
Know that I — his dear wife — did once another love!
Nay, start not, shrink not, 'tis no tale of shame,
For though in other years the heavenly flame
Descended, kindled, scorched — it left me pure
With courage to resign — with strength to endure.
He touched my heart, but never stained the soul
That gained this hardest conquest — self-control.
At Rome — where I was born — a soldier's eye
Marked this poor face, from which must Polyeucte fly;
Severus was his name: — Ah! memory
May spare love linked with death a tear, a sigh!

STRAT.

Say, is it he who, at the risk of life,
Saved Decius from his foes and endless strife?
Who, dying, dealt to Persia stroke of death,
And shouted 'Victory!' with his latest breath?
His whitening bones, amid the nameless brave,
Lie still unfound, unknown, without a grave;
Unburied lies his dust amid the slain,
While Decius rears an empty urn in vain!

PAUL.

Alas! 'tis he; all Rome attests his worth,
Hide not his memory, kindly Mother Earth!
'Tis but his memory that I adore
The past is past — and I can say no more.
All gifts save one had he — yes, Fortune held her hand,
And I, as Fortune's slave, obeyed my sire's command.

STRAT.

Ah! I must wish that love the day had won!

PAUL.
Which duty lost — then had I been undone;
Though duty gave, yet duty healed, my pain;
Yet say not that my love was weak or vain!
Our tears fell fast, yet ne'er bore our distress
The fatal fruit of strife and bitterness.
Then, then, I left my hero, hope and Rome,
And, far from him, I found another home;
While he, in his despair, sought sure relief
In death, the only end to life's long grief!
You know the rest: — you know that Polyeucte's eye
Was caught, — his fancy pleased; his wife am I.
Once more by counsel of my father led,
To Armenia's greatest noble am I wed;
Ambition, prudence, policy his guide
Yet only duty made Pauline his bride;
Love might have bound me to Severus' heart,
Had duty not enforced a sterner part.
Yes, let these fears attest, all trembling for his life,
That I am his for aye — his faithful, loving wife.

STRAT.
Thy new love true and tender as the old: —
But this thy dream? No more thy tale withhold!

PAUL.
Last night I saw Severus: but his eye
With anger blazed; his port was proud and high,
No suppliant he — no feeble, formless shade,
With dim, averted eye; no sword had made
My hero lifeless ghost. Nor wound, nor scar
Marked death his only conqueror in war.
Nor spoil of death, nor memory's child was he,
His mien triumphant, full of majesty!
So might victorious Caesar near his home

To claim the key to every heart in Rome!
He spoke: in nameless awe I heard his voice, —
'Give love, that is my due, to him — thy choice, —
But know, oh faithless one, ere day expires,
All vain these tears for him thy heart desires!'
Anon a Christian band (an impious horde),
With shameful cross in hand, attest his word;
They vouch Severus' truth — and, to complete
My doom, hurl Polyeucte beneath his feet!
I cried, 'O father, timely succour bear!'
He heard, he came, my grief was now despair!
He drew his dagger — plunged it in the breast
Of him, my husband, late his honoured guest!
Relief came but from agony supreme —
I shrieked — I writhed — I woke — it was a dream!
And yet my dream is true!

STRAT.
'Tis true your dream is sad,
But now you are awake, 'tis but a dream you had!
For horror's prey in darkness of the night
Is but our reason's sport in morning light.
How can you dread a shade? How a fond father fear,
Who as a son regards the man you hold so dear?
To phantom of the night no credence yield;
For him and you he chose thy strength and shield.

PAUL.
You say *his* words: at all my fears he smiles,
But I must dread these Christians and their wiles!
I dread their vengeance, wreaked upon my lord,
For Christian blood my father has outpoured!

STRAT.
Their sect is impious, mad, absurd and vain,
Their rites repulsive, as their cult profane.

Deride their altar, their weak frenzy ban,
Yet do they war with gods and not with man!
Relentless wills our law that they must die:
Their joy — endurance; death — their ecstasy;
Judged — by decree, the foes of human race,
Meekly their heads they bow — to court disgrace!

PAUL.
My father comes — oh, peace!

(Enter Felix and Albin)

FELIX
Nay, peace is flown!
Thy dream begets dull fears, till now unknown;
In part this dream is true, and for the rest — —

PAUL.
By what new fear, say, is thy heart opprest?

FELIX
Severus lives!

PAUL.
Ah! this no cause for fear!

FELIX
At Decius' court, he, held in honour dear,
Risked life to save his Emperor from his foes,
'Tis to his saviour Decius honour shows!

PAUL.
Thus fickle Fortune bows her head to fate,
And pays the honour due, though all too late!

FELIX
He comes! Is near — —

PAUL.
The gods — —

FELIX
Do all things well.

PAUL.
My dream fulfilled! But how? O father, tell!

FELIX
Let Albin speak, who saw him face to face
With tribe of courtiers; all to him give place;
Unscathed in battle, all extol his fame,
Unstained, undimmed, his glory, life and name!

ALBIN
You know the issue of that glorious fight:
The crowning glory his — who, in despite
Of danger sore to life and liberty,
Became a slave to set his Emperor free:
Rome gave her honours to Severus' shade,
Whilst he, her ransomer, in a dungeon stayed.
His death they mourned above ten thousand slain,
While Persia held him — yes, their tears were vain,
But not in vain his noble sacrifice!
The king released him: Rome grudged not the price;
No Persian bribe could tempt him from his home.
When Decius cried — 'Fight once again for Rome!'
Again he fights — he leads — all others hope resign;
But from despair's deep breast he plucks a star benign,
This — hope's fair fruit, contentment, plenty, ease,
Brings joy from grief, to crown a lasting peace.
The Emperor holds him as his dearest friend,

And doth Severus to Armenia send —
To offer up to Mars, and mighty Jove,
'Mid feast and sacrifice, his thanks and love.

FELIX
Ah, Fortune, turn thy wheel, else I misfortune meet!

ALBIN
This news I learn'd from one of great Severus' suite:
Thence, swiftly here, the tale to tell I sped.

FELIX
He who once vainly wooed, hopes now to wed.
The sacrifice, the offering, all are feigned,
All but the suit, which lightly I disdained.

PAUL.
Yes, this may be, for ah! he loved me well!

FELIX
What room for hope? Such wrath is child of hell.
Before his righteous ire I shrink, I cower;
Revenge I dread — and vengeance linked with power
Unnerves me quite.

PAUL.
Fear not, his soul is great.

FELIX
Thy comfort, oh my daughter, comes too late.
The thought to crush me down, to turn my heart to stone,
This, that I prized not worth for worth's dear sake alone!
Too well, Pauline, thou hast thy sire obeyed;
Thy heart was fond, but duty love betrayed.
How surely thy revolt had safety won!
'Tis thine obedience leaves us all undone.

In thee, in thee alone, one hope remains,
Love held him fast, relax not thou love's chains.
O Love, my sometime foe, forgive, be mine ally,
And let the dart that slew now bring the remedy!

PAUL.
Forbid it, Heaven! One good yet mine, — *my will*,
The dart that wounded has the power to kill.
One lesson woman learns — her feebleness;
Shame is the only grief without redress.
The traitor heart shall still a prisoner be;
For freedom were disgrace to thee and me!
I will not see him!

FELIX
But one word! Be kind!

PAUL.
I will not, for I love! — and love is blind.
Before his kingly eye my soul to unveil
Were shame and failure: and I will not fail:
I will not see him!

FELIX
One word more — 'Obey!'
Wouldst thou thy father and his weal betray?

PAUL.
I yield! Come woe! — come shame! — come every ill!
My father thou! — and I thy daughter still!

FELIX
I know thee pure.

PAUL.
And pure I will remain,

But, crushed and bruised, the flower no guilt shall stain.
I fear the combat that I may not fly,
Hard-won the fight, and dear the victory.
Here, love, my curse! Here, dearest friend, my foe!
Yet will I arm me! Father, I would go
To steel my heart — all weapons to embrace!

FELIX
I too will go, the conqueror's march to grace!
Restore thy strength, ere yet it be too late,
And know that in thy hands thou hold'st our fate!

PAUL.
Go, broken heart, to probe thy wound; cut deep and do not spare!
Herself — the crowning sacrifice — the victim shall prepare!

ACT II — SEVERUS. FABIAN

SEV.
Let Felix bow to Jove and incense pour,
I seek a dearer shrine, for I adore
Nor Jove, nor Mars, nor Fortune — but Pauline.
This fruit now ripening late my hand would glean:
You know, my friend, the god who wings my way,
You know the only goddess I obey:
What reck the gods on high our sacrifice and prayer?
An earthly worship mine, sole refuge from despair!

FABIAN
Ah! You may see her — —

SEV.
Blessed be thy tongue!
O magic word, that turns my grief to song!
Yet, if she now forget each fair, fond vow?
She loved me once, — but does she love me now?
On that sweet face shall I but trouble see
Who hope for love undimmed, for ecstasy?
Great Decius gives her hand, but if her heart
Be mine no more — than let vain hope depart!
This mandate binds her father only; she
Shall give no captive hand — her heart is free:
No promise wrung, no king's command be mine to claim,
Her love the boon I crave; all else an empty name!

FABIAN
Yes, — you may — see her — *see* her — this you may —

SEV.
Thy speech is halting — odious thy delay!
She loves no more? I grope! O give me light!

FABIAN
O see her not, for painful were the sight!
In Rome each matron's kind! In Rome all maids are fair!
Let lips meet other lips — seek for caresses there!
No stately Claudia will refuse — no Julia proud disdain;
A hero captures every heart, from Antioch to Spain!

SEV.
To wed a queen — an empress — were only loss and shame;
One heart for me — Pauline's! One boast — that dearest name!
Her love was virgin gold! O ne'er shall baser metal ring
From mine, who live her name to bless! her peerless praise to sing!
O, words are naught, till that I see her face,
Then doubly naught till I my love embrace.
In every war my hope was placed in death,
Her name upon my lips at every breath:
My rank, my fame, now hers and hers alone,
What is not hers, hers only — I disown!

FABIAN
Once more, oh see her not, 'twere for thy peace!

SEV.
Thy meaning, knave, or let this babble cease!
Say, was she cold? My love! My only life!

FABIAN
No — but — my lord — —

SEV.
Say on!

FABIAN
Another's wife!

SEV.
(Reels.)
Help! — No, I will not blench — ah, say you lie!
If this be true! — ye gods — can I be I?

FABIAN
No, thou art changed. Where is thy courage fled?

SEV.
I know not, FABIAN Lost! Gone! Vanished! Dead!
I thought my strength was oak — 'tis but a reed!
Pauline is wed, then am I lost indeed!
Hope hid beyond the cloud, yet still fond hope was there:
But now all hope is dead, lives only black despair!
Pauline another's wife?

FABIAN
Yes, Polyeucte is her lord.
He came, he saw, he conquered thine adored.

SEV.
Her choice is not unworthy — his a name
Illustrious, from a line of kings he came
Cold comfort for a wound no cure can heal!
My cause is lost, — foredoomed without appeal!
Malignant Jove, to drag me back to-day!
Relentless Fate, to quench hope's dawning ray!
Take back your gifts! One boon alone I crave,
That only boon to none denied — the grave.
Yet would I see her, breathe one last good-bye,
Would hear once more that voice before I die!
My latest breath would still my homage pay,
That memory mine, when lost to realms of day.

FABIAN
Yet think, my lord —

SEV.
Oh, I have thought of all;
What worser ill can dull despair befall?
She will not see me?

FABIAN
Yes, my lord, but —

SEV.
Cease!

FABIAN
'Twill but enhance the grief I would appease.

SEV.
For hopeless ill, good friend, I seek no cure.
Who welcomes death can life's short pain endure!

FABIAN
O lost indeed, if round her fatal light you hover! —
The lover, losing all, speaks hardly like a lover!
While passion still is lord — the passion-swept is slave —
From this last bitterness would I Severus save!

SEV.
That word, my friend, unsay; tho' grief this bosom tear,
The hand that wounds I kiss — love vanquishes despair;
Fate only, not Pauline, the foe that I accuse,
No plighted faith she breaks who did this hand refuse.
Duty — her father — Fate — these willed, she but obeyed;
Not hers the woe, the strife that envious Ate made!
Untimely, Fortune's shower must drown me, not revive;
Too lavish and too late her fatal gifts arrive.
The golden apple falls, the gold is turned to dross:
When Fate at Fortune mocks, all gain is only loss!

FABIAN

Yes, I will go to tell her thou hast drained
To the last drop the cup that Fate ordained.
She knows thee hero, but she feared that pain
Might prove thee also man — by passion slain.
She feared Despair, who gains the victory
O'er other men, might e'en thy master be!

SEV.

Peace! Peace! She comes!

FABIAN

To thine own self be true!

SEV.

Nay! True to her! Shall I her life undo?
She loves the Armenian!

Enter Pauline

PAUL.

Yes, that debt I pay,
Hard — wrung, acquitted, — his my love alway!
Who has my hand, he holds — shall hold — my heart!
Truth is my guide, — let sophistry depart!
Had Fate been kind, then had Pauline been thine,
Heart, faith and duty, linked with bliss divine.
In vain had fickle Fortune barred the way,
Want had been wealth with thee, my guide, my stay,
And poverty had fallen from the wings
Of soaring love, who mocks the wealth of kings!
Not mine to choose, for he — my father's choice —
Must needs be mine; yes, when I heard his voice,
Duty must echo be: if thou couldst cast
Before my feet an emperor's crown, — a past

By worth and glory lit — beloved, adored —
Yet at my father's word, 'Not this thy lord;
Take one despised — nay, loathed — to share thy bed,' —
Him, and not thee, beloved, would I wed.
Duty, obedience, must have been the part
Of me, who own their sway, e'en with a broken heart!

SEV.
O happy thou! O easy remedy!
One poor faint sigh cures love's infirmity!
Thy heart thy tool, o'er every passion queen,
Beyond all change and chance thou sit'st serene!
In easy flow can pass thy love new-born
From cold indifference to colder scorn;
Such resolution is the equal mate
Of god or monster, love, aversion, hate.
This fine-spun adamant Ithuriel's spear
Could never pierce: for other stuff is here!
(Points to himself.)
No faint 'Alas!' no swift-repented sigh
Can heal the cureless wound from which I die.
Sure, reason finds that love his easy prey
With Lethe aye at hand to point the way;
With ordered fires like thine, I too could smother
A heart in leash, find solace in another.
Too fair, too dear — from whom the Fates me sever!
Thou hast no heart to give — thou lov'dst me never!

PAUL.
Too plain, Severus, I my torture show, —
Tho' flame leap up no more, the embers glow;
Far other speech and voice, and mien were mine,
Could I forget that once thou call'dst me thine!
Tho' reason rules, yes, gains the mastery
No queen benignant, but a tyrant she!
Oh, if I conquer — if the strife I gain,

Yet memory for aye is linked with pain!
I feel the charm that binds me still to thee;
If duty great, yet great thy worth to me:
I see thee still the same, who waked the fire
Which waked in me ineffable desire.
Begirt by crown of everlasting fame
Thou art more glorious — yet art still the same.
I know thy valour's worth, — well hast thou justified
That bounding hope of mine, though fruitage was denied,
Yet this same fate which did our union ban
Hath made me, fated — wed another man.
Let Duty still be queen! Yea, let her break
The heart she pierces, yet can never shake.
The virtue, once thy pride in days gone by
Doth that same worth now merit blasphemy?
Bewail her bitter fruit — but praised be
The rights that triumph over thee and me!

SEV.
Forgive, Pauline, forgive; ah! grief hath made me blind
To all but grief's excess, and fortune most unkind.
Forgive that I mistook — nay, treated as a crime
Thy constancy of soul, unequalled and sublime;
In pity for my life forlorn, my peace denied,
Ah! show thyself less fair, — one least perfection hide!
Let some alloy be seen, some saving weakness left,
Take pity on a heart of thee and Heaven bereft!
One faintest flaw reveal, to give my soul relief!
Else, how to bear the love that only mates with grief?

PAUL.
Alas! the rents in armour donned and proved
Too well my fight proclaim; yes, I have loved;
The traitor sigh, the tear unbid, attest
The combat fierce — the warrior sore distrest.
Say, who can stanch these wounds, that armour mend?

Thou who hast pierced, thou, thou alone defend!
Ah, if thou honourest my victory
Depart, that thou may'st still defender be!
So dry the tears that, to my shame, still flow —
So quench the fire would work my overthrow!
Yes, go, my only friend, with me combine
To end my torture, for thy pain is mine!

SEV.
This last poor drop of comfort may not be?

PAUL.
The cup is poisoned both for me and thee!

SEV.
The flower is gone — I cherish but the root!

PAUL.
Untimely blossom bears a fated fruit!

SEV.
My grief be mine! Let memory remain!

PAUL.
That grief might hope beget, so leave a stain!

SEV.
Not mine to stain what Heaven hath made so pure!
For me one offering left: 'tis this: Endure!
Thy glory shall be mine, my load I bear,
So, spotless, thou thy peerless crown shalt wear!
Farewell, my love, farewell; I go to prove my faith,
To bless, to save thy life, so will I mate with death!
If prostrate from the blow, there yet remains of life
Enough to summon death, and end the piteous strife!

PAUL.
My grief, too deep for voice, shall silent be,
There, in my chamber, will I pray for thee!
When thou art gone, great Heaven shall hear my cry;
Grief's fruit for thee be hope — death — immortality!

SEV.
Now with my loss alone let Fate contented be.
May Heaven shower bliss and peace on Polyeucte and thee!

PAUL.
Stern Fate obeyed, end, Death, his agony,
And Jove receive my hero — to the sky!

SEV.
Thou wast my heaven!

PAUL.
My father I obeyed —

SEV.
O victim pure, obedient, undismayed!
Pauline — too fair — too dear — I can no more!

PAUL.
So must I say — depart — where I adore!

(Exit Severus.)

STRAT.
Yes, it is hard — most sad — behold my tears!
But now, at least, there is no cause for fears:
Thy dream is but a dream — is naught, is vain;
Severus pardons. Gone that cause for pain!

PAUL.
Oh, if from pity start thy easy tear,
Add not that other woe — forgotten fear!
Ah! let me breathe, some respite give from trouble,
Those fears, half-dead, thou dost revive, redouble!

STRAT.
What dost thou dread?

PAUL.
Heaven — hell — earth — empty air!
All, all is food for dread to my despair,
As thou unveil'st, begirt in lurid light,
The pallid ghost that slew me in the night!

STRAT.
Severus he by name, yet noble in his heart!

PAUL.
Ah, Polyeucte bathed in blood! Depart! depart!

STRAT.
For Polyeucte's welfare did Severus pray!

PAUL.
Yes, yes, his heart is great; be that my stay!
Yet, tho' his truth, his faith, well-proved be,
Most baleful is his presence here to me;
Yea, tho' he would all ill for me undo
Yet he hath power, he loves — he came to woo.

(Enter Polyeucte and NEARCHUS)

POLY.
The source of tears is dry, oh, weep no more,
Thy grief lay down, thy fearful heart restore!

Let night's dark dream with superstition die,
The dream is past, for here in life am I!

PAUL.
The day is young, and oh, the day is long, —
And half the dream is true, and Fate is strong;
Severus have I seen, who thought him dead!

POLY.
I know it! Let no tear for this be shed!
Secure with thee am I! Tho' great the knight,
Thy father will command to do me right;
The general is a man of honour, — he
Would ne'er that honour dim by treachery!
He comes in amity, our friend, our guest;
To greet his worth and valour now my quest.

PAUL.
Radiant he came, who left me hopeless, sad,
But he will come no more, — this grace I had.

POLY.
What? Thinkest thou that I can jealous be?

PAUL.
An outrage this on him, on thee, on me!
He came in peace, who all my peace hath marred.
Who would run safely, every step must guard;
The wife who danger courts but courts her fall
My husband, aid me! — I would tell thee all!
His worth, his charm, do my weak hearth enflame
A traitor here! And he is aye the same!
If I should gaze, and long — 'gainst virtue, honour, sense,
The citadel I yield, and mine my own defence!
I know my virtues sure, and fair my fame,
But struggle is defeat, — and combat shame!

POLY.
Oh, true thy shield, thy victory is won,
He only who has lost thee is undone;
His noble grief the cost of all my bliss,
Ah, Cleopatra's pearl was naught to this!
The more my faults I see, the more thy truth I learn,
The more do I admire — —

(Enter FABIAN.)

FABIAN.
My lord, the altars burn
With holy fire. The victim they prepare;
On thee alone they wait, our rites to share.

POLY.
Go, we do follow thee!

PAUL.
I cannot go;
Severus flies my sight; to him I owe
My absence — not, alas! to him alone!
Go thou, and oh, remember he is great;
In his sole hands Severus holds thy fate!

POLY.
A foe so great, so noble, is a friend,
Oh, not from him the lance that Heaven will send!

Exeunt Pauline, Stratonice and FABIAN.

NEAR.
Where go'st thou?

POLY.
To the temple is the call.

NEAR.
What! Wouldst thou mingle in their heathen brawl?
Thou art a Christian, and canst thou forget?

POLY.
Canst *thou*, who fore mine eyes the cross didst set?

NEAR.
Not mine their gods!

POLY.
He calls me! I must go!

NEAR.
I fly their altars!

POLY.
I would overthrow!
Not mine to fly a worship I disown,
By me Jehovah, King of kings, be known!
Not mine to tremble as I kiss the rod!
I conquer by the Cross, I fight for God!
Thou wouldst abstain! For me another course
From Heaven the call, and Heaven will give the force!
What! Yield to evil! His Cross on my brow!
His freemen we! O fight, Nearchus, now!
For us our Lord was scourged, pierced, tortured, slain!
For us He bled! Say, has He died in vain?

NEAR.
Let timely moderation temper zeal!

POLY.
His — His alone am I! His woe my weal!

NEAR.
In love with death?

POLY.
For Him I love I die!
He died for me! So death is victory!

NEAR.
Thy flesh is weak!

POLY.
Yet He will make me bold!

NEAR.
And if thou waver?

POLY.
He will me uphold!

NEAR.
To tempt the Lord thy God were an offence.

POLY.
He is my shield — hence! cursed tempter, hence!

NEAR.
In time of need the faith must be confessed.

POLY.
The offering grudged is sacrifice unblessed.

NEAR.
Seek thou the death thine own self-will prepares!

POLY.
A crown I seek, which every martyr shares!

NEAR.
A life of duty well that crown can win.

POLY.
The purest life on earth is stained with sin.
Why yield to time and chance what death assures?
Death but the gate of life that aye endures.
If I be His — let me be His alone!
The faith that soars shall full fruition own;
Who trusts, yet fears and doubts, his faith is dead!

NEAR.
Not death the Christian's prayer, but daily bread.
Live to protect the flock, so sore oppressed.

POLY.
Example be their friend, most sure, most blessed!

NEAR.
Thou woo'st thy death!

POLY.
Is this poor life so dear?

NEAR.
Ah, I must own my heart is slave to fear.
The rack! The cross! I might my Lord disown!

POLY.
From Him our help, our strength, from Him alone!
Who fears denial does at heart deny;
Who doubts the power of faith makes faith a lie!

NEAR.
Who leans upon a reed shall find distress.

POLY.
His staff will guide, support my feebleness.
Thou wert my staff, to show the Truth, the Way,
Must I now urge thee to the realms of day?
Thou fearest death?

NEAR.
The Christ once feared to die!

POLY.
Yet drained the bitter cup of agony!
The way that thou hast shown — that way He trod;
His way be ours to lead man's soul to God —
For heathen shrine — to rear His altar fair, —
The deathless hope alone can kill despair!
Thou said'st: 'If Him thou wilt for pattern take,
Then leave wife, wealth, home, all for His dear sake!'
Alas, that love of thine, now weak and poor,
Glows yet within my breast — and shall endure;
Ah, must the dawn of this my perfect day
Find thy full light beclouded, dimmed, astray?

NEAR.
Baptismal waters yet bedew thy brow;
The grace that once was mine, that grace hast thou.
No worldly thought has checked the flow, no guilty act has
stained;
Thy wings are strong, while mine are weak; thy love is fresh,
ungeigned, —
To these, thy heights, I cannot soar, held down by sense and sin,
How can I storm the citadel? — the traitor lurks within!
Forsake me not, my God! Thy spirit pour!

Oh, make me true to Him whom I adore!
With Thee I rise, — the flesh, the world, defy,
Thou, who hast died for me, for Thee I die!
Yes, I will go! With heaven-born zeal I burn,
I will be free, — all Satan's lures I spurn;
Death, torture, outrage, these will I embrace,
To nerve my heart and arm, Heaven grant me grace!

POLY.
On eagle wings of faith and hope ascend!
I hail my master — recognize my friend;
The old faith wanes, — we light her funeral pyre,
Her ashes fall before our holy fire;
Come, trample under foot the gods that men have wrought;
The rotten, helpless staff is broke, is gone — is naught.
Their darkness felt they own, but let them see the light!
Their gods of stone, of clay, but vampires of the night!
Their dust shall turn to dust, — shall moulder with the sod,
Ours for His name to fight: — the issue is with God.

NEAR.
The cause is just, is true — O coward heart, be still!
I lived to doubt His word — I die to do His Will!

ACT III — PAULINE

PAUL.
Cares — clouded and confused — oppress, obscure
In changeful forms, my eye, my heart, my mind:
My soul finds room for every guest save one;
Fair hope has flown, — no star can pierce my night:
Each tyrant rages 'gainst opposing foe
In deadly fight — yet brings to light no friend:
In travail sore hope comes not to the birth —
Fear hydra-headed terror still begets; —
All fancies grim I see, and straight embrace,
At hope I clutch, who still eludes my grasp;
Her rainbow hues adored are but a frame
That serve by contrast to make fear more dark.
Severus haunts me — oh, I know his love,
Yet hopeless love must mate with jealousy, —
While Polyeucte, who has won what he has lost,
Can meet no rival with an equal eye.
The fruit of rivalry is ever hate
And envy; both must still engender strife:
One sees that rival hand has grasped his prize,
The other yearns for prize himself has missed.
Weak reason naught, when headlong passion reigns,
For valour seeks a sword, and love — revenge.
One fears to see the prize he gained impaired,
The other would that wrested prize regain;
While patience, duty, conscience, vail their heads
'Fore obstinate defence and fierce attack.
Such steeds no charioteer controls — for they
Mistake both curb and reign for maddening whip.
Ah! what a base, unworthy fear is mine!
How ill I read these fair, these noble souls,
Whose virtue must all common snares o'erleap!
Their gold unstained by dross or mean alloy!
As generous foes so will they — must they meet!

Yet are they rivals — this the thought that kills!
Not even here — at home — is Polyeucte safe,
The eagle wings of Rome reach over all.
Oh, if my father bow to Roman might,
If he repent the choice that he hath made, —
At this one thought hope's flame leaps up to die!
Or — if new-born — dies ere she see the light.
Hope but deceived, — my fear alone I trust,
Heaven grant such confidence be false — be vain!

(Enter Stratonice.)

Nay, let me know the worst! What, girl! — no word?
The rites are o'er? What hast thou seen — what heard?
They met in amity? — In peace they part?

STRAT.
Alas! Alas!

PAUL.
Nay, soothe my aching heart!
I would have comfort, — but this face of woe —
A quarrel?

STRAT.
Polyeucte — Nearchus — go —
The Christians —

PAUL.
What of them?

STRAT.
Ah, how to speak —

PAUL.
They on my father would their vengeance wreak?

STRAT.
Oh, fear whate'er thou wilt — that fear too small!

PAUL.
The Christians rise?

STRAT.
Oh, would that this were all!
Thy dream, Pauline, is true; Polyeucte is — —

PAUL.
Dead?

STRAT.
Ah, no, he lives — yet every hope is fled;
That courage once so high, that noble name
Sunk in the mire of everlasting shame!
He lives, — who once was lovely in thy sight —
As monster foul — his every breath a blight;
The foe of Heaven, of Jove, of all our race,
His kisses poison, and his love — disgrace!
Wretch, coward, miscreant, steeped in infamy,
O worse than every name! — a Christian he!

PAUL.
Nay, that one word's enough! There needed not abuse.

STRAT.
My words fit well their guilt; — with evil make no truce.

PAUL.
If *he* be *Nazarene* — he must an outcast be!
But insult to my lord is insult unto me!

STRAT.
Think only that he hails the Cross, the badge of shame.

PAUL.
My plighted faith, my troth, my duty still the same!

STRAT.
When twined about thy breast, the hideous serpent slay!
Who mocks the Gods on high will his own wife betray!

PAUL.
If he be false, yet I will still be true,
The ties that bind me I will ne'er undo:
Let fate — Severus — passion — all combine
Against him! — I am his, and he is mine.
Yes, mine to guide, lead, win, forgive, and save!
I seek his honour tho' he court the grave.
Let Polyeucte be Christ's slave! — For woe, for weal,
He is my lord; the bond I owe I seal;
I fear my father, — all his vengeance, dread.

STRAT.
Fierce burns his rage o'er that devoted head;
Yet embers of old love still faintly glow,
And through his wrath some weak compassion show;
'Gainst Polyeucte biting words alone he speaks
But on Nearchus fullest vengeance wreaks!

PAUL.
Nearchus lured him on?

STRAT.
The tempter he;
Such friendship leads to death, or infamy.
Oh, cursed friend, who, in dear love's despite,
Has torn him from thine arms — his neophyte!

He dragged him to the front; — baptized, annealed —
He fights for Christ! — The secret is revealed.

PAUL.
Which I would know — and straightway had thy blame!

STRAT.
Ah! I foresaw not this — their deed of shame!

PAUL.
Ere dull despair o'ermaster all my fears,
Oh, let me gauge the worth of woman's tears!
For, if the daughter lose, the wife may gain, —
Or Felix may relent, if Polyeucte mock my pain;
If both are adamant unto my prayer,
Then — then alone — take counsel from despair!
How passed the temple sacrifice? Hide naught, my friend, tell all!

STRAT.
The horror and the sacrilege must I, perforce, recall?
To say the words, to think the thoughts, seems blasphemy and
shame;
Yet will I tell their infamy, — their deed without a name.
To silence hushed, the people knelt, and turned them to the East;
Then impious Polyeucte and his friend mock sacrifice and priest.
They every holy name invoked jeer with unbridled tongue,
To laughter vile the incense rose — 'tis thus our hymn was sung;
Both loud and deep the murmurs rang, and Felix' face grew pale,
Then Polyeucte mad defiance hurls, while all the people quail.
'Vain are your gods of wood and stone!' his voice was stern
and high —
'Vain every rite, prayer, sacrifice' so ran his blasphemy.
'Your Jupiter is parricide, adulterer, demon, knave,
'He cannot listen to your cry, not his to bless or save.
'One God — Jehovah — rules alone, supreme o'er earth and
heaven,

'And ye are His — yes, only His — to Him your prayers be given!
'He is our source, our life, our end, — no other god adore,
'To Him alone all prayer is due, then serve Him evermore!
'Who kneels before a meaner shrine, by devil's power enticed,
'Denies his Maker and his King, denies the Saviour Christ.
'He is our source, our guide, our end, our prophet, priest and king;
''Twas He that nerved Severus' arm, — His praise let Decius sing.
'Jehovah rules the battle-field ye call the field of Mars,
'He only grants a glorious peace, 'tis He guides all our wars.
'He casts the mighty from his seat, He doth the proud abase, —
'They only peace and blessing know who love and seek His face.
'His sword alone is strong to strike, His shield our only guard.
'He will His bleeding saints avenge, He is their sure reward.
'In vain to Jove and feeble Mars your full libations pour —
'Oh, kneel before the might ye spurn, the God ye mock — adore!'
Then Polyeucte the shrine o'erthrows, the holy vessels breaks,
Nor wrath of Jove, nor Felix' ire, his fatal purpose shakes.
Foredoomed by Fate, the Furies' prey — they rush, they rend, they tear,
The vessels all to fragments fly — all prone the offerings fair;
And on the front of awful Jove they set their impious feet,
And order fair to chaos turn, and thus their work complete.
Our hallowed mysteries disturbed, our temple dear profaned,
Mad flight and tumult dire let loose, proclaim a God disdained.
Thus pallid fear broods over all, presaging wrath to come,
While Felix — but I mark his step! — 'tis he shall speak the doom.

PAUL.
How threatening, how dark his mien! How lightning-fraught his eye!
Where wrath and grief, revenge and pain, do strive for mastery!

(Enter FELIX)

FELIX
O insolence undreamed! — Before my very eyes! —
Before the people's gaze! It is too much! — he dies!

PAUL.
O father! — on my knees!
(Kneels.)
Unsay that word!

FELIX
Nearchus' doom I speak, — not his, thy lord.
Though all unworthy he to be my son,
Yet still he bears the name that he hath won;
Nor crime of his nor wrath of mine shall ever move
Thy father's heart to hate the man thou crown'st with love!

PAUL.
Ne'er vainly have I sued for pity from my sire!

FELIX
And yet meet food were he for righteous ire!
To recount an act so fell my feeble words too weak,
But thou has heard the tale my lips refuse to speak
From her, thy maiden; she hath told thee all.

PAUL.
Nearchus goaded — planned — and he shall fall!

FELIX
So taught by torture of his vilest friend,
Shall Polyeucte mark of guilt the certain end,
When of the frenzied race he sees the goal,
The dread of torture shall subdue his soul!
Who mocked the thought of death, when death he views,
Will choose an easier mate — and rightly choose.

That shadowy guest, that doth his soul entice,
Once master, glues all ardour into ice,
And that proud heart, which never meekness knew,
When face to face with Death — will learn to sue!

PAUL.
What! Thinkest thou his soul can ever blench?

FELIX
Death's mighty flood must every furnace quench!

PAUL.
It might! It may! — I know such things can be!
A Polyeucte changed — debased — forsworn I see!
O, changeful Fortune! changeless Polyeucte move,
And grant a boon denied by father's love!

FELIX
My love too plain — myself too weakly kind,
Let him repent and he shall pardon find;
Nearchus' sin is his, — and yet the grace
He shall not win, thy Polyeucte may embrace!
My duty — to a father's love betrayed
Hath of thy sire a fond accomplice made;
A healing balm I bring for all thy fears,
I look for thanks, and lo — thou giv'st me tears!

PAUL.
I give no thanks — no cause for thanks I find;
I know the Christian temper — know their mind,
They can blaspheme, but ah, they cannot lie!
They know not how to yield — but they can die!

FELIX
As bird in hand, he holds his pardon still.

PAUL.
The bird escapes, when 'tis the owner's will.

FELIX
He death escapes — if so he do elect.

PAUL.
He death embraces — as doth all his sect.
Is't thus a father pleads for his own son?

FELIX
Who wills his death is by himself undone.

PAUL.
He cannot see!

FELIX
Because he chooses night.
Who loves the darkness hateth still the light.

PAUL.
O, by the Gods —

FELIX
Nay, daughter, save thy breath;
Spurned — outraged — 'tis the Gods demand his death.

PAUL.
They hear our prayers —

FELIX
Nay, then let Polyeucte pray!

PAUL.
Since Decius gives thee power, — that word unsay!

FELIX
He gives me power, Pauline, to do his will
Against his foes — 'gainst all who work him ill.

PAUL.
Is Polyeucte his foe?

FELIX
All Christians rebels are.

PAUL.
Thy son shall plead more loud than policy or war.
For mine is thine; O father, save thine own —

FELIX
The son who is a traitor I disown!
For treason is a crime without redress,
'Gainst which all else sinks into nothingness.

PAUL.
Too great thy rigour!

FELIX
Yet more great his guilt.

PAUL.
Too true my dream! Must his dear blood be spilt?
With Polyeucte, I too — thy child — shall fall!

FELIX
The Gods — the Emperor — rule over all.

PAUL.
O hear our dying supplication — hear!

FELIX

Not Jove alone, but Decius I fear: —
But why anticipate a doom so sad?
Shall this — his blindness — make thy Polyeucte mad?
Fresh Christian zeal remains not always new,
The sight of death compels a saner view.

PAUL.
O, if thou lov'st him still, all hope forsake!
In one day can he two conversions make?
Not this the Christians' mould: they never change;
His heart is fixed — past power of man to estrange.
This is no poison quaffed all unawares,
What martyrs do and dare — that Polyeucte dares;
He saw the lure by which he was enticed,
He thinks the universe well lost for Christ.
I know the breed; I know their courage high,
They love the cross, — so, for the cross, they die.
We see two stakes of wood, the felon's shame,
They see a halo round one matchless Name.
To powers of earth, and hell, and torture blind,
In death, for Him they love, they rapture find.
They joy in agony, — our gain their loss,
To die for Christ they count the world but dross:
Our rack their crown, our pain their highest pleasure,
And in the world's contempt they find their treasure.
Their cherished heritage is — martyrdom!

FELIX
Let then this heir into his kingdom come! No more! —

PAUL.
O father!

(Enter ALBIN)

FELIX

Albin, is it done?

ALBIN
It is, — Nearchus' frantic race is run!

FELIX
And with what eye saw Polyeucte the sight?

ALBIN
With envious eye, — as one who sees a light
That lures him, moth-like, to devouring flame.
His heart is fixed, his mind is still the same.

PAUL.
'Tis as I said — oh, father, yet once more
If thou hast ever loved me, — I implore!
Let filial duty and obedience plead
For his dear life! To my last prayer give heed!

FELIX
Too much thou lovest an unworthy lord!

PAUL.
Thou gavest him my hand, 'twas at thy word
I gave both love and duty; what I give
I take not back; oh, Polyeucte must live!
For his dear sake I quenched another flame
Most pure. Is he my lord alone in name?
O, by my blind and swift obedience paid
To thy command — be thy hard words unsaid!
I gave thee all a daughter had to give,
Grant, father, this one prayer — Let Polyeucte live!
By thy stern power, which now I only fear,
Make thou that power benignant, honoured, dear!
Thou gav'st that gift unsought, — that gift restore!
I claim it at the giver's hand once more!

FELIX

Importunate! Although my heart is soft,
It is not wax, — and these entreaties oft
Repeated waste thy breath, and vex mine ear,
For man is deaf to what he will not hear.
I am the master! This let all men know,
And if thou force that note thou'lt find 'tis so.
Prepare to see thy cursed Christian fool,
Do thou caress when I have scourged the mule, —
Go! vex no more a loving father's ear,
From Polyeucte's self win what thou hold'st so dear.

PAUL.

In pity! — —

FELIX

Leave me, leave me here alone! —
Say more — my goaded heart will turn to stone;
Vex me no more — I will not be denied!
Go, save thy madman from his suicide!

(Exit Pauline.)

How met Nearchus death?

ALBIN

The fiend abhorred
He hailed, — embraced: 'For Christ!' his latest word;
No sigh, no tear, — he passed without amaze
Adown the narrow vale with upward gaze.

FELIX

And he — his friend?

ALBIN
Is, as I said, unmoved
He looks on death but as a friend beloved,
He clasped the scaffold as a guide most sure,
And, in his prison, he can still endure.

FELIX
Oh, wretched that I am!

ALBIN
All pity thee.

FELIX
With reason greater than they know. Ah, me!
Thought surges upon thought, and has its will,
Care, gnawing upon care, my soul must kill;
Love — hate — fear — pain: I am of each the prey,
I grope for light, but never find the day!
Oh, what I suffer thou canst not conceive,
Each passion rages, but can ne'er relieve;
For I have noble thoughts that die still-born,
And I have thoughts so base my soul I scorn.
I love the foolish wretch who is my son,
I hate the folly which hath all undone;
I mourn his death, — yet, if I Polyeucte save,
I see of all my hopes the cruel grave!
'Gainst Gods and Emperor too sore the strife,
For my renown I fear, — fear for my life.
I must myself undo to save my son,
For, should I spare him, then am I undone!

ALBIN
Decius a father is, and must excuse
A father's love — oh, he will not refuse!

FELIX

His edict is most clear: — 'All Christians are my foes.'
The higher be their rank the more the evil grows.
If birth and state be high, their crime shows more notorious,
If he who shield be great, his fall the more inglorious;
And if I give Nearchus to the flame
Yet stoop to shield my own — thrice damned my name!

ALBIN

If by thy fiat he cannot escape the grave,
Implore of Decius' grace the life thou canst not save.

FELIX

So would Severus work my ruin quite —
I fear his power, his wrath, — for might is right —
If crime with punishment I do not mate.
How high soe'er, worth what it may, I fear his hate,
For he is man, and feels as man, and I
Once spurned his suit with base indignity.
Yes, he at Decius' ear would work may woe,
He loves Pauline, thus Polyeucte is his foe:
All weapons possible to love and war,
And those who let them rust but laggards are.
I fear — and fear doth give our vision scope —
E'en now he cherisheth a tender hope;
He sees his rival prostrate in the dust,
So, as a man he hopes — because he must.
Can dark despair to love and hope give place
To save the guilty from deserved disgrace?
And were his worth so matchless, so divine,
As to forbear all ill to me and mine
Still I must own the base, the coward hope,
'Gainst which my strength is all too weak to cope,
That hope whose phoenix ashes yet enthrall
The wretch who rises but once more to fall;
Ambition is my master, iron Fate,

I feel, obey, adore thee, while I hate!
Polyeucte was once my guard, my pride, my shield,
Yet can I, by Severus, weapons wield,
Should he my daughter wed, more tried, more true:
What wills Severus — that will Decius do.
Upheld by him, e'en Fortune I defy
And yet I shrink! — for them, thrice base were I!

ALBIN
Perish the word! It ne'er was made for thee,
But wilt thou deal just meed to treachery?

FELIX
I go to Polyeucte's cell, — though my poor breath
Should there be spent in vain to avert his death;
Then, then my fated child her strength shall try.

ALBIN
What wilt thou do if both he still defy?

FELIX
O, press me not in agony so great!
To thee alone I turn — resistless Fate!

ACT IV — POLYEUCTE. FABIAN. THREE OTHER GUARDS

POLY.
What is thy will?

FABIAN.
Pauline would see my lord.

POLY.
Ah, how my heart quails at that single word!
Thee, Felix, I o'ercame within my cell,
Laughed at thy threats if death and torture fell;
Yet hast thou still one arm to rouse my fears,
The rest I scorn, but dread thy daughter's tears!
One only talisman remains; great God, 'tis mine,
Sufficient for my every need His strength divine!
O thou, dear saint, thy scars all healed, white-robed, in
glory crowned,
Plead that I too may victory win, thou who hast victory found!
Nearchus, who hast clasped in Heaven that dear, that pierced
hand,
Plead that thy friend, who wrestles here, may safely by thee stand!
Ye Guards, one last kind service, I would ask,
Well may ye grant it, 'tis an easy task:
I do not seek deliverance from these thralls,
(Looks at his chains.)
I do not care to scale my prison walls,
But, since three warriors armed can surely guard
One fettered man in safest watch and ward,
Go one, and beg of great Severus' grace
That he would deign to meet me face to face;
To him would I a secret now impart,
Which much concerns his joy and peace of heart.

FABIAN.
On willing foot, my lord, do I obey.

POLY.
Severus must this kindly service pay;
Ah, lose no time, time now has fleetest wings.

FABIAN.
Full soon to thee thy prayer Severus brings.

(Exit FABIAN. Guardsmen retire to background.)

POLY.
The fount is pure, yet bitter waters flow,
Sin taints — men poison what was made all fair.
They will not choose immortal streams: they go
To seek for pleasure — but find only care:
Their pleasure wed to strife — ah, death the gate of life, —
Christ's servants, none but they His crown shall wear!
So pain
Is gain:
Count not the cost!
The world well lost,
His Heaven to share!
O Pleasure, think not that I sigh for thee,
Thy charms, that once enslaved, no more delight;
In Christ's dear name I bid the tempter flee,
His foes are mine, — unlovely in my sight.
The mighty from their seat He hurls beneath His feet,
His fan is in His hand, His vengeful sword is bright.
Their crown
Cast down.
All hopes most dear
They cherish here
Shall end in night.
O Decius! Tiger! Pitiless! Athirst

With quenchless rage, for blood of Christ's redeemed —
Armenia shall arise, by thee accursed,
On her at last has Light of Asia beamed,
And our Deliverer from the holy east
Shall dash the cup from thy Belshazzar feast!
Secure,
And pure,
Christ's saints shall reign,
And, purged by pain,
For aye endure!
Let Felix sacrifice me to thine ire,
Yea, let my rival captivate the soul
Of her who now with Decius doth conspire
To chain immortal hope to earthly goal;
Let earth-bound men pursue the world's desire,
Sense charms not him who doth to Heaven aspire!
Hail pain!
Disdain
All Earthly love,
To seek above
A holier fire!
Oh, Love that passeth knowledge be my stay,
And fire my heart to beat alone for thee!
Sun of my soul? — oh, flash one purest ray
In that last hour supreme — to comfort me,
So life's brief night shall merge in endless day!
Come, Death!
Last breath
Shall praise thy name,
The same, the same,
For aye! For aye!
O heavenly fire, most pure, embracing all,
Come, shield me from Pauline, else must I fall!
I see her, but no more as once I saw —
I am encased in armour without flaw:
To eyes that gaze alone on heavenly light,

Naught else is pure, or dear, or fair, or bright!

(Enter Pauline)

With what intent, Pauline, hast thou come here?
Have I a friend to aid, or foe to fear?
Is it Christ's soldier that thou com'st to greet?
Or wouldst thou sink my triumph in defeat?
If thou wouldst bid me spurn the debt I owe,
Not Decius, but Pauline, my deadliest foe!

PAUL.
All, save thyself, to thee, my love, are friends:
Love but thyself, love me, — thy torment ends.
Alone thou seal'st thy doom, alone wouldst shed
That blood by all Armenia honoured.
Yes, thou art saved, if thou for mercy plead;
Demand thy death, and thou are lost indeed.
Think of the worth of this self-hated life,
And think in pity of Pauline, — thy wife!
Think of the people that their prince adores,
Think of the honours Felix on thee pours!
Oh, I am nothing, nothing unto thee,
But, husband, think how dear thou art to me!
Think how the path of glory on thee opes,
Thou dearest lodestar of a nation's hopes!
Shall blood of kings be but the headsman's sport?
Is life a toy wherewith thy death to court?

POLY.
I think of more than this; I know what thou wouldst say.
Our life is ours to use, and we that debt must pay.
What life is this men love? An idle, empty dream,
Where nothing can endure, — where all things only seem.
Death ends their every joy which fickle Fortune leaves,
They gain a royal throne to learn how pomp deceives;

They gather wealth that men may envy their estate,
They clear a path by blood, so envy turns to hate.
Such vast ambition mine as Caesar never knew,
Death bounds it not, for death is but its servant true.
Peace that the world ne'er gave, and cannot take away,
That peace, Pauline, is mine, mine wholly, mine for aye!
Nor time, nor fate, nor chance, nor cruel war,
Can touch this peace, or this my kingdom mar.
Is this poor life — the creature of a day
For endless peace too great a price to pay?

PAUL.
'Out on these Christian dreams!' my reason cries;
Whene'er they speak of truth, they utter lies.
Thou say'st: 'To win such prize my life is naught!'
But is thy life thine own? How was it bought?
Our life an heirloom to our country due;
What gave thee birth, demands thy service too?
Pay, then thy debt to her who has the right!

POLY.
Ah, for my country I would gladly fight!
I know the glory of a hero's name,
I feel the thrill, — I recognize the claim.
My life I owe to whom I owe my sword —
But most to Him who gave it — to the Lord!
Oh, if to die for fatherland be sweet,
To die for Him — my God — what word is meet?

PAUL.
Which God?

POLY.
Hush! hush! Pauline; the God who hears
And answers prayers, — gives hopes, assuages fears.
Thy gods are deaf and senseless, maimed and weak,

Tongues, mouths they have, and yet they cannot speak.
The Christians' God alone is mine, — is thine,
Jehovah only rules — supreme — divine!

PAUL.
Adore Him in thy heart, but say no word!

POLY.
What! Can I call Jove and Jehovah — Lord?

PAUL.
One moment feign. Ah, let Severus go!
Let but my father all his kindness show!

POLY.
Another Father mine! His love most dear
Removes me from a world begirt with fear.
For life's stern race too weak, too frail am I,
So, by kind death, He gives me Victory.
Pure from the holy font — (His mercies never fail!)
He brings His barque to port, when it hath scarce set sail.
Couldst thou but understand how poor this earth,
Couldst thou but grasp how great this second birth!
And yet, why speak of treasure rare concealed
From one to whom light is yet unrevealed?

PAUL.
O cruel! I can strangle pain no more!
Is this the fruit of all thy heavenly lore?
They say thy Christ His enemies did bless,
Thou addest insult to my deep distress.
How is my soul so dark — which was so fair? —
Thou call'dst me 'lovely' — 'dear' — 'beyond compare!' —
Of my bereavement have I said no word,
I stilled my grief that I might soothe my lord!
They say that love has wings, and all they say is true,

For all thy love has flown; yet can I ne'er undo
The vows I made, the troth I plighted binds me still!
Thou fain wouldst quit thy wife, and thou shalt have thy will.
Oh, but to leave my side with rapture, ecstasy,
No jealous Christ can will: why grudge me one poor sigh?
This joy, this transport fierce, endeavour to conceal.
I do not share thy creed, but I, at least, can feel!
Why gloat o'er heavenly gain, crowns, palms, I know not what —
Where Polyeucte is blest, but where Pauline is not?
Soul, body, spirit, I am thy true wife, to own
That I am but a bar to happiness unknown!

POLY.
Alas!

PAUL.
O! that 'Alas!' — so faint, so tame!
Yet, if repentant from thy heart it came,
'Twould waken hope, still brief, and banish fears:
I wait the birth of thy reluctant tears.

POLY.
These tears I shed! O, might the Spirit pour
Through them the light, the light that I adore —
Then were my only grief all swept away,
For thou wouldst join me in the realms of day!
Else Heaven itself would have its bitterness,
Should I look down to witness thy distress!
O God, who lov'st the dust on which Thy breath
Hath stamped Thine image true — save her from death!
The only death that kills, and let my love
From Heaven woo her to the realms above!
Lord, hear my call! My inmost heart now see,
Who lives a Christian life must Christian be!
Her nature god-like, stamped from print divine;
She must be sealed Thine own, yes, only Thine!

Say, must she burn, condemned to depths of hell? —
Thy Will be done — Who doest all things well!

PAUL.
O wretch, what words are these? Thou dost desire — —

POLY.
To snatch thee from a never-ending fire.

PAUL.
Or else?

POLY.
O God, I trust to Thy control,
Who when we think not, canst illume the soul!
The when — the how — is His — here am I dumb, —
I wait — I wait — That blessed hour will come!

PAUL.
Oh, leave illusions! Love me!

POLY.
Thee I love
Far more than self, but less than God above!

PAUL.
For love's dear sake, ah, listen to my prayer!

POLY.
For love's dear sake — await the answer *there!*

PAUL.
To leave me here is naught! Thou wouldst seduce my soul!

POLY.
Heaven is scarce Heaven for me, if thou reach not the goal.

PAUL.
O fancy-fooled!

POLY.
Nay, led by heavenly light!

PAUL.
Thy faith is blindness!

POLY.
Faith is more than sight!

PAUL.
Ah, death, strange rival to a wife's pure love!

POLY.
This world our rival with the joys above!

PAUL.
Go, monster! woo thy death! Thou lov'dst me never!

POLY.
Go, seek the world! and yet I love thee ever!

PAUL.
Yes, I will go — if absence bring relief —

(Enter Severus, Fabian and Guards)

Who comes to invade, ah, not to cure my grief?
Severus! Who could guess that thou wouldst show
Revenge unworthy o'er a prostrate foe?

POLY.
Unworthy thee the thought, Pauline, for I

Severus called, and he hath heard my cry.
My importunity he will excuse,
My prayer I know that he will not refuse.
Severus — this — the treasure that was mine
To thy most tender care I now resign:
To thee, as noblest man that I have known; —
Since earthly ties and joys I must disown.
The gift is worthy thee, — I know thy worth
Is great, but she no equal hath on earth.
My life, the bar, — my death the link shall be, —
Oh, grudge me not my dear brief ecstasy!
Oh, ease the heart that once was hers, — and guide
Her doubting footsteps to the Crucified!
This my last benison! All else is poor!
Await the promised light! Believe! Endure!
But words are vain!

(Polyeucte signs to Guards to conduct him back to prison.
Exeunt
Polyeucte and Guards.)

SEV.
Most vain! No word have I
Such blindness must amaze! must stupefy!
Nay, this is frenzy! I cannot conceive
A mind so strange! Mine ears cannot believe
That one who loved thee — yet, who would not love
A face that must the great immortals move? —
Blessed by thy heart! — Thy sweetest lips to taste! —
Then leave, refuse, spurn — yield with clamorous haste,
To yield a girl so dear — so pure — so fair!
And of that gift to make thy rival heir —
This beggars madness! Or the Christian bliss
Beyond man's soul to grasp! To spurn thy kiss! —
We treasure barter for a just exchange,
But to buy pain for thee! Pauline, 'tis strange!

Not thus, ye Gods! Severus had been blind
To perfect bliss — had Fortune been more kind
The only heaven for me is in thine eyes,
These are my kings, these my divinities!
To me — for thee — were death with torture dear;
But to renounce thee!

PAUL.
Nay, I must not hear!
Thy words bring back the dear, the bygone days,
When I, a maid, might listen to thy praise:
Severus, thou must know my inmost heart;
I hear the knell bids Polyeucte depart.
He dies, — the victim of thine Emperor's laws,
And thou, though innocent, art yet the cause.
Oh, if thy soul, to thy desires a slave,
See hope emerging from my husband's grave
Then will I wed with pain — despair embrace, —
But wed Severus? Never! 'Twere disgrace!
To light fresh torch from that pale, flickering fire —
Oh, bliss too monstrous! Thrice abhorred desire!
Back, hope! Back, happiness! The mate for me
When Polyeucte leaves my side — is Constancy!
Were this my will, were this, ye Gods, my fate —
To shame would memory turn, as love must yield to hate!
But generous art thou — most generous be!
His pardon will my father grant to thee.
He fears thee: more, if Polyeucte's life he take,
For thee he slays him — yes, 'tis for thy sake.
Christ died for man — let pagan virtue dim
His fame: plead for thy foe! so rival him!
No easy boon I ask, there needs a soul most rare;
But when the fight is fierce — then is the victory fair.
To help a man to be what thou wouldst be
Is triumph that belongs alone to thee!
Let this suffice thee: she, whom thou hast loved,

She, who by thy great love was not unmoved,
Of thee, and of no other dares to crave
That thou, Severus, shouldst my husband save!
Farewell! of this thy labour gauge the scope:
If thou art less than I yet dare to hope,
Then tell me not! all else Pauline can bear!

(Exit Pauline.)

SEV.
Where am I, Fabian? Has the crack of doom
Turned heaven to hell? made life a living tomb?
Nearer and dearer ever — but to go!
The prize within my grasp must I o'erthrow?
This — Fortune's brimming cup, with poison filled,
She bids me drain; — so new-born hope is killed.
Before I proffer aught, I am refused;
Thus sad, amazed, ashamed, in doubt, abused,
I see the ghost I laid, to life revive,
The more seductive still the more I strive.
Ah! must a woman, sunk in deep despair,
Teach me that shame is base, and honour fair?
And while I madly shriek, 'O love, be kind!'
Pauline, death-stricken, keeps an equal mind!
O generous, but stern! Must these dear eyes,
Because I love them, o'er love tyrannise?
'Tis not enough to lose thee, I must give
My aid — to make my faithless rival live!
'Tis not enough: his death I would not plan,
But I must save him! bless where I would ban!

FABIAN
Ah, let the whole crew light one funeral pyre;
Yes, let the daughter perish with her sire!
This curs'd Armenian is one hornet's nest —
Crush all, then sail for Rome, ah! this were best!

She loves thee not. What canst thou hope to gain?

SEV.

A glory that shall triumph over pain;
'Tis hers, and, by the Gods, it shall be mine!
Nor God nor fiend can sully such a shrine!

FABIAN

Speak low, for Jove has bolts, and Hell has ears!
The dangers of this course arouse my fears.
What? Decius implore a Nazarene to save!
'Tis death that hath thy heart; thou woo'st a grave.
His rage against the sect thou knowest well,
His power unbridled — his revenge is fell.
To plead for Christians is a task too great,
For man or God: thou rushest on thy fate.

SEV.

Yes, such advice, I know, is much approved,
Yet not thus can Severus' soul be moved.
To Fate unequal — equal to myself —
In duty's path I go. For power and pelf
I never swerve where honour leads the way;
Come weal, come woe, her call I must obey.
Let fate depress an all unequal scale,
Let Clothe hold her distaff — I'll not fail!
Yet one more word — this to thy private ear —
The fables that thou dost of Christians hear
Are fables only, coined, I know not why,
Distorted are they seen in Decius' eye.
They practice the black art, — so all men say.
I sought to learn the laws that they obey,
And to discover what the secret guilt
The which to expiate their blood is spilt.
Yet priests of Cybele dark rites pursue
At Rome — untrammelled — this is nothing new:

To thousand gods men build, unchecked, their fanes,
The Christians' God alone our state disdains.
Each foul Egyptian beast his temple rears,
Caligula a god to Roman ears —
Tiberius is enshrined — a Nero deified —
To Christ — to Christ alone — a temple is denied!
Such metamorphoses confuse the mind
As gods in cats, and saints in fiends we find;
As Ruler absolute Jehovah stands,
Alone o'er heaven and earth and hell commands,
While pagan gods each 'gainst the other strive,
And ne'er one queen is found o'er all the hive,
Now — (strike me dead, Jove's tarrying thunderbolt!)
So many masters must provoke revolt.
And ah! where Christians live — there life is pure,
Vice dies untended, virtues all endure.
We give these men to rack, and cord, and flame,
While they forgive us — in their Pardoner's name.
They no sedition raise, they ne'er rebel,
Rome makes them soldiers, and they serve her well.
They rage in battle, faithful ward they keep,
They fight like lions, but they die like sheep.
They serve the State: Rome's servant must defend
Those who to might of Rome such succour lend.
Pauline, I will obey, whate'er befall;
The man who loseth honour loseth all.

ACT V — FELIX ALBIN FABIAN

FELIX
Caught in Severus' net thy Felix see!
He hates and holds me — oh, the misery!

ALBIN
I see a generous man, who cries, 'Forgive,
Let Pauline smile once more — let Polyeucte live!'

FELIX
His soul thou canst not read — tho' noble heart he feigns.
The father he abhors, — the daughter he disdains!
What Polyeucte won he sought: his suit denied,
Severus sues no more, — I know his pride.
His words, his prayers, his threats for Polyeucte plead,
His *tongue* says, 'Listen, or be lost indeed!'
Unskilled the fowler who his snare reveals:
If at the bait I snatch — my doom is sealed:
Too plain, too coarse, this web for any fly —
Shall I this spider hail in my fatuity?
His wrath is wrath arranged, his generous fire is nursed,
That I, at Decius' hand, may meet the doom accurst,
If I should pardon grant — that grace my crime would be,
For he the spoil would reap of my credulity.
No simpleton am I, each promise to believe,
Words — oaths — are but the tools wherewith all men deceive;
Too oft escaped am I to be so lightly caught;
I know that words are wind. I know that wind is naught.
The trapper shall be trapped, — the biter shall be bit,
Unravelled is the web that he, poor fool, hath knit!

ALBIN
Jove! What a plague to thee is this mistrust!

FELIX
Nay, those at court must fence; their weapons never rust,
If once thou yield the clue to thread the maze,
The sequence is most plain — the man betrayed betrays;
Severus, and his gifts, alike I fear!
If Polyeucte still to reason close his ear,
Severus' love is hate — his peace is strife —
First law of nature this, 'Preserve thy life!'

ALBIN
Ah, let Pauline at least thy grace obtain!

FELIX
If Decius grace withhold, my pardon vain!
And — far from saving this rebellious son —
Behold us all alike entrapped, undone!

ALBIN
Severus' promise — —

FELIX
He can never keep!
For Decius' rage and hatred never sleep:
If for that sect abhorred Severus plead,
He trebles loss — so are we lost indeed!
One only way is ours, — that way I try:
(To Guards)
Bring Polyeucte and if he still defy,
Self-doomed, insensate, this my proffered grace,
He shall the death he wooes forthwith embrace!

ALBIN
Ah, this is stern!

FELIX
'Tis stern, 'tis just — as fate;

When justice drags a halting foot, too late,
She is not justice — for the vengeful mob
(Whose hearts for Polyeucte ne'er cease to throb),
Usurps her place, and, spurning curb and rein,
The felon crowns, and all our work is vain.
My sceptre trembles, and all insecure
Totters my crown, — a prey for every boor.
Then, swift, Severus hears the welcome news,
The jaundiced mind of Decius to abuse.
Shall I, the rabble's lord, obey the rabble's will?

ALBIN
Who ill in all around foresees, — but doubles ill.
Each prop thou hast is but a sword to pierce;
If Polyeucte hold their heart, the people fierce
Will gather fiercer courage from despair.

FELIX
Death settles all; they'll find no helper there,
And if — without a head — the body should rebel,
Convulsive throes I mock, and nerveless fury quell.
Whate'er ensues the Emperor must approve,
I shall have done my part, and win his love.
Here comes the man

(Enter Polyeucte and Soldiers)

I still must try to save;
If he repent — 'tis well! If not — the grave!
(To Polyeucte)
Is life still hateful? Doth death still allure?
Is earth still naught? Do heavenly joys endure?
Doth Christ still counsel thee to hate thy wife; —
To sheathe thy sword, — to cast away thy life?

POLY.

I never hated life, or wooed a grave,
To life I am a servant — not a slave.
Here service free I give upon this earth below, —
For higher service changed when to His Home I go.
Eternal life is this: to tread the path He trod;
To Him your body yield! Then trust your soul to God!

FELIX
Yes, trust to an abyss of depth unknown!

POLY.
No, trust to Holy Cross! That Cross my own!

FELIX
The steep ascent, my son, I too would climb,
Yes, I would Christian be, — but — give me time, —
By Jove! I'll tread thy path! This my desire.
Else at thy hand the judge may me require!

POLY.
Nay, laugh not, Felix! He thy Judge will be,
No refuge there for impious blasphemy!
Nor kings nor clowns can 'scape His righteous ire,
His slaughtered Saints of thee will He require!

FELIX
I'll slay no more; — by Hercules I swear!
So I a Christian crown perchance may wear;
I will protect the flock!

POLY.
Nay, rather be
A goad, a scourge, for their felicity!
Let suffering purify each Christian soul,
Cross, rack, and flame but lead them to their goal;
What here they lose — in Heaven an hundredfold they find.

Be cruel, — persecute! — and so alone be kind!
My words thou canst not read; thine eyes are blinded here,
Wait the unveiling *There!* Then understand and fear!

FELIX
Nay, nay, in truth I would a Christian be!

POLY.
In thy hard heart alone a bar I see.

FELIX (whispering).
This Roman knight — —

POLY (aloud).
Severus, thou wouldst say.

FELIX
Once let him sail, I will no more delay,
For this I anger feign; — let him depart!

POLY.
'Tis thus thou wouldst reveal a Christian heart?
To idols dumb — to Pagans blind, thy sugared poison bear,
Christ's servants quaff another cup, sure refuge from despair.

FELIX
What is this deadly draught that thou wouldst drain?
I'll drink thy wine. — Till then, from death refrain!

POLY.
To swine no more my holy pearls I cast,
Faith, — *faith* — not reason, shall see light at last;
Soon — when I see my God — yes, face to face,
I will implore that Felix may find grace.

FELIX

O dearest son, thy loss were death to me!

POLY.
This loss can be repaired — the remedy
Find in Severus; he will take my place;
By Decius honoured he will not disgrace
Thy house: my death will an advantage win
For thee, for her, for me. — The work begin!

FELIX
Such my reward! Yes, insult is the child
Of injury. The grace I grant, reviled,
Shall turn to swift revenge. The gods defied
May do their will and speed the suicide!

POLY.
I thought the gods were dead, but they revive
With human passion; Felix, do not strive
Against thy nature; lay aside thy ruth;
Who loves a lie can never follow truth.

FELIX
I humoured madness, but the mood is o'er,
I am myself again; I did implore, —
'Twas vain; the dark abyss that yawns for thee
May hold thee now, tomb to thy constancy.
The hope I cherished — fondled — now is flown
Severus will be king, and I o'erthrown; —
Shall I the gods by incense pacify?
Or by thy death? for thou, at last, must die!

POLY.
Incense might but incense; I cannot tell:

(Enter Pauline)

Pauline!

PAUL.
That word broke from thee like a knell;
Who seeks my doom to-day? Thou — or my sire?
Who fires the brand? Who lights the funeral pyre?
My father should, by nature, be my friend,
And lover's heart to love an ear should lend.
Who here is mine ally, and who my foe?
Who has a heart to feel? — this would I know.

FELIX
Nay, to thy lord appeal.

(Pauline turns to Polyeucte)

POLY.
Severus wed!

PAUL.
Ah, this is outrage! Rather strike me dead!

POLY.
Oh, dearer than myself to me thy weal!
My love would never wound, it seeks to heal.
I see thee wrestle with thy deep distress
Alone — unless Severus bring redress;
His merit, that once gained thy maiden heart,
Hath still that worth when I from thee must part,
Once loved — and loving still — his honour grows.

PAUL.
Thy wife's true heart another treatment owes:
O base reproach! For this I crushed for thee
My former love: that I disdained might be?
This my reward for dearest victory won, —

I did that love undo — to be myself undone!
Resolve, faith, abnegation, all were vain,
For thy return is outrage heaped on pain.
Oh, sunk in tomb of shame, most vile, most mean,
Come back to life — to honour — to Pauline!
(Holds out her arms.)
To learn from her that loyalty and faith
Religion are: — and all beside but death!
Once more Alcestis wrestles with the tomb,
Arise, arise from thy enthralling doom!
And if my invocation feeble be,
Regard the tears — the sighs, — shed — breathed for thee!
Love is too weak a word — I thee adore!

POLY.
Once have I said — yet now I say once more —
'Live with Severus, or — with Polyeucte die!'
Thy tears are mine, and thy pure constancy
I share: But — I am soldier of the Cross!
Take up thine own, and count all gain but loss!
Pauline — no more!
(To FELIX)
Thy slumbering wrath rewake!
Thy fates and furies wait! Their vengeance slake!

PAUL.
His life is saved! These fetters all undo! —
For justice never yet a madman slew;
And he is mad, — but, father, thou art sane,
And thou, his father, must his friend remain.
A father cannot less than father be,
Oh, be to him what thou hast been to me!
But cast upon thy child a kinder eye, —
Slay him? — Then know that I am doomed to die!
But even if justly done to death were he,
The sentence wrong that, with him, slayeth me.

For double death would double wrong present,
And slay the guilty with the innocent.
'Twas thou didst link us closely hand in hand,
'To live in bliss together' thy command.
Oh, shall the will that both our lives did bless
Doom both these lives to death — to nothingness?
When lips are sealed to lips, and heart to heart,
'Tis tyranny, not law, such love to part.
Oh, not a tyrant, but a father be,
Forgive, — give back — restore my love to me!

FELIX
Dear child, thy father is thy father still,
Nothing hath parted us, and nothing will.
My heart is tender, and it beats for thee:
Against this madman let us joined be.
O wretched man, hast thou no eyes to see, no heart to feel?
Thy guilt, thy crime, I would efface, thy pardon I would seal,
For thee my daughter cannot die — say, must she die *with* thee?
A victim to the only sin which ne'er can pardoned be.
O sight most strange! Here at thy knees as suppliant I sue!
(Felix kneels.)
The evil that thyself hast wrought — that ill thyself undo!

POLY.
Arise, old man, from knees unused to bend,
Or to another ear petition send!
This artifice befits nor me nor thee,
To beg of one twice threatened! — Mockery!
First, by thy hand Nearchus felt the flame,
Then love, forsooth, thy plea — (profaned name!)
The path of Christian neophyte hast thou trod,
And, in God's name, hast mocked Almighty God!
Earth, heaven, and hell in turn have been thy tool,
And him thou hast traduced thou wouldst befool!
Go, — bully-flatterer — liar! — Every part

Thou playest, while delay doth break my heart!
Enough of dallying! While thou dost dissolve
Thy feeble soul in doubt, hear my resolve:
The God who made me — Him will I adore;
He holds my plighted faith, — and evermore
He works salvation for his ransomed race —
Who gave His Son to death that we might life embrace;
And this — Christ's sacrifice — continued day by day,
The Christ reveals and pleads — The Life — The Truth — The
Way!
No more His mysteries to self-stopped ears
Will I disclose — (he heedeth not nor hears.)
(Pointing to FELIX)
Pray then to these thy gods of wood and stone,
To gods who every deed of crime enthrone,
Who boast their malice, and their foul incest,
Vaunt theft and murder — all that we detest.
This, their example, — Pagan — follow thou!
To Pluto bend, to Aphrodite bow!
For this I broke their altars, rased their shrine, —
Yea, for those crimes that thou dost call divine!
And what I did, that would I do once more
Before Severus — Decius, — nay, before
The eyes of all men; — so would I proclaim
One God alone adored, — one Holiest Name!

FELIX
At last my bounties yield to wrath most stern, most just.
Die! or the gods adore!

POLY.
A Christian I!

FELIX
Thou must
Adore the gods I say! Adore, or die!

POLY.
I am a Christian.

FELIX
This is thy reply?
Ye Guards, do my behest — prepare the knife!

PAUL.
Where goes he?

FELIX
To his death!

POLY.
Ah, no to life!
(To Pauline.)
Remember me! Farewell, Pauline, farewell!

PAUL.
Nay, I will follow thee — to heaven or hell!

FELIX
Begone! For all our ills this one redress!

(Exeunt Pauline, Polyeucte and Guards)
(Enter Albin)

O task ungrateful to my gentle mind!
Well did he say, 'Be cruel to be kind!'
The people I defy, ah, let them rage!
Severus may in war of words engage.
Yes, I have saved myself — I mean *the State*,
To wilful man there comes relentless fate;
My conscience pure of all reproach, — for I
Have lied and stormed to shake his constancy.

To give his hot young blood due time to cool
I played the coward — nay, I played the fool!
Why did he thus assail the gods and me
With insult, and with horrid blasphemy?
But interest helped me, and resentment too.
Else had I found my duty hard to do!

ALBIN
Soon mayst thou this thy dear-bought victory rue,
For thou hast done what thou canst ne'er undo!
Unworthy deed for Roman knight! ah, me!
(Aside.)
I would that I could add, 'unworthy *thee!*'

FELIX
Manlius and Brutus both a son have slain,
And neither did thereby his glory stain;
The part that is diseased — that part we bleed,
So is the State from knaves and caitiffs freed.

ALBIN
Revenge and pressing peril thee unman,
Else — couldst thou bless a deed all men must ban?
When she, thy widowed daughter, comes — the air
Of heaven will echo to her deep despair!

FELIX
Thou dost remind me she with Polyeucte went —
I know not with what mind, with what intent:
But her despair awakes my fond alarm,
Go, Albin, go, and guard my child from harm!
She might the execution of the law
Impede: I would not that his death she saw.
Try to console her — Go! what dost thou fear?

(Enter Pauline)

ALBIN
I need not go, for ah — Pauline is here!

PAUL.
Tyrant, why leave thy butchery half done?
Come, slay thy daughter, thou hast slain thy son!
For, hear! — His villainy — or worth — is mine!
Why stay thy hand while I my neck incline?
Thy sword in me shall find a kindred food,
I too am new baptized, baptized in blood!
These drops that fell from off the murderous knife,
Have made the martyr's widow a true wife.
I see! — I feel! — I know! My darkest night
Is o'er — to break in purest heavenly light.
I too, at last, am Christ's: that word says all,
Those hands were pierced for me — I hear His call:
Death — lovely death — thy beckoning hand I hail!
Oh, help my passage, or thy schemes may fail!
Dread Decius! Fear Severus! Fear thy fall!
Oh, speed me to my lord — my love — my all!
My husband calls me to his happier land —
See! — there Nearchus at his side doth stand!
Lead me to these — the gods by thee confest,
Some shrines spared Polyeucte, I will break the rest!
There, there the gods thou fearest I will brave,
Oh, bare thy knife! — no other gift I crave.
Thou hast my master been: another Lord
Claims my obedience now; yes, raise thy sword!
Revolt is holy when for Christ we fight, —
My day has dawned, the day that knows no night!
Once more I cry — 'Christ only has my heart!'
Thy bliss and mine secure! Let me depart!
Keep thou thy kingdom! Safe its treasure hold!
My kingdom there — with Christ — within the fold!

(Enter Severus)

SEV.
Unnatural sire, whose craft leads to the grave,
The slaves of fear themselves alone enslave.
Yes, Polyeucte is slain, and slain by thee, —
A sacrifice to greed and treachery.
I offered rescue from the opening tomb,
Base doubts enthralled thee, didst seal his doom;
I prayed, I threatened, thou wouldst not believe,
Deceiver thou, so must all men deceive.
Thou thoughtst me coward, liar — thou shalt see
All oaths Severus swears fulfilled shall be.
Poor moth! I might have saved thee — nay, I planned to save,
Thy perfidy the torch that marks thee for the grave.
Drench earth in blood, — for Jove pour forth malignant zeal,
The strokes that thou hast dealt redoubled shalt thou feel!
I go: the storm shall break o'er this devoted land,
From Jove the bolt? — maybe — but I direct his hand.

FELIX
Why lags that hand? A willing victim I,
I choose to suffer for my perfidy;
My doubts, my fears unworthy, all I own,
I have offended — let my death atone.
Take thou my honours, their poor lustre thine,
I kneel before another, nobler shrine.
The Power that moved me, groping through the night
Of wrong and darkness, wafts me to The Light!
I slew thee, Polyeucte, but thy pardoning hand
Shall guide thy murderer to the better land!
He prays for me, and by his sacrifice,
New-born upon his ashes I arise.
(To Pauline.)
Raised by his death from out the grave of sin,
Thou tread'st the path thy father shall begin;

By me his martyr-crown, as all my bliss
By him. His Christ is mine, and I am his;
O, blessed Christian vengeance! All my loss
Is turned to gain by the redeeming Cross!
Now, Pauline, am I thine, a Christian I,
That Death gives life by which alike we die!
(To Severus.)
Then slay us both! Behold a willing prey!

PAUL.
(To FELIX)
Yes, mine for ever now! Hail, glorious day,
That sees earth's loss transformed to endless gain!

FELIX
The gain, the glory, Christ's! By Him we reign.

SEV.
Now am I dumb, some miracle is here;
Their courage and their faith must I revere;
We slay them; yet, like Cadmus' seed, new-born
They sprout afresh, and laugh our scythe to scorn.
We give them cord and flame, they torture hail;
Friends fail them, but themselves they never fail.
We mow them down, fresh nurslings to unbare,
What moves the seed lies hid, but *it is there*.
They bless the world, though by the world accurst,
Their shield am I — let Decius do his worst.
I yet may own their power, though now my will
That each to his own gods be faithful still,
Let each still search for truth, and truth adore.
(To Felix).
A Christian thou? Then fear my wrath no more,
Thy sect I cherish; this their awful cult
Severus will protect, but ne'er insult.
Keep thou thy power from Roman sword secure,

So long as loyalty with faith endure;
I swear it: ay, the Emperor shall learn
The guiltless from the traitor to discern;
His persecution baseless as his fear.

FELIX
Severus — thou who hast the hearing ear, —
Freeman of Rome — God's Spirit grant thee grace
To be Christ's Freeman, and behold His face:
To these — Christ's martyrs — earth's last rites be given,
Earth, guard their ashes as a trust for Heaven!
Earth hides their dust. When envious time is o'er,
That dust shall wake to life for evermore!

Phaedra
JEAN BAPTISTE RACINE

CHARACTERS

THESEUS, son of Aegeus and King of Athens
PHAEDRA, wife of Theseus and Daughter of Minos and
Pasiphae
HIPPOLYTUS, son of Theseus and Antiope, Queen of the
Amazons
ARICIA, Princess of the Blood Royal of Athens
OENONE, nurse of Phaedra
THERAMENES, tutor of Hippolytus
ISMENE, bosom friend of Aricia
PANOPE, waiting-woman of Phaedra
GUARDS

The scene is laid at Troezen, a town of the Peloponnesus.

ACT I

SCENE I

HIPPOLYTUS, THERAMENES

HIPPOLYTUS
My mind is settled, dear Theramenes,
And I can stay no more in lovely Troezen.
In doubt that racks my soul with mortal anguish,
I grow ashamed of such long idleness.
Six months and more my father has been gone,
And what may have befallen one so dear
I know not, nor what corner of the earth
Hides him.

THERAMENES
And where, prince, will you look for him?
Already, to content your just alarm,
Have I not cross'd the seas on either side
Of Corinth, ask'd if aught were known of Theseus
Where Acheron is lost among the Shades,
Visited Elis, doubled Toenarus,
And sail'd into the sea that saw the fall
Of Icarus? Inspired with what new hope,
Under what favour'd skies think you to trace
His footsteps? Who knows if the King, your father,
Wishes the secret of his absence known?
Perchance, while we are trembling for his life,
The hero calmly plots some fresh intrigue,
And only waits till the deluded fair —

HIPPOLYTUS
Cease, dear Theramenes, respect the name
Of Theseus. Youthful errors have been left

Behind, and no unworthy obstacle
Detains him. Phaedra long has fix'd a heart
Inconstant once, nor need she fear a rival.
In seeking him I shall but do my duty,
And leave a place I dare no longer see.

THERAMENES
Indeed! When, prince, did you begin to dread
These peaceful haunts, so dear to happy childhood,
Where I have seen you oft prefer to stay,
Rather than meet the tumult and the pomp
Of Athens and the court? What danger shun you,
Or shall I say what grief?

HIPPOLYTUS
That happy time
Is gone, and all is changed, since to these shores
The gods sent Phaedra.

THERAMENES
I perceive the cause
Of your distress. It is the queen whose sight
Offends you. With a step-dame's spite she schemed
Your exile soon as she set eyes on you.
But if her hatred is not wholly vanish'd,
It has at least taken a milder aspect.
Besides, what danger can a dying woman,
One too who longs for death, bring on your head?
Can Phaedra, sick'ning of a dire disease
Of which she will not speak, weary of life
And of herself, form any plots against you?

HIPPOLYTUS
It is not her vain enmity I fear,
Another foe alarms Hippolytus.
I fly, it must be own'd, from young Aricia,

The sole survivor of an impious race.

THERAMENES
What! You become her persecutor too!
The gentle sister of the cruel sons
Of Pallas shared not in their perfidy;
Why should you hate such charming innocence?

HIPPOLYTUS
I should not need to fly, if it were hatred.

THERAMENES
May I, then, learn the meaning of your flight?
Is this the proud Hippolytus I see,
Than whom there breathed no fiercer foe to love
And to that yoke which Theseus has so oft
Endured? And can it be that Venus, scorn'd
So long, will justify your sire at last?
Has she, then, setting you with other mortals,
Forced e'en Hippolytus to offer incense
Before her? Can you love?

HIPPOLYTUS
Friend, ask me not.
You, who have known my heart from infancy
And all its feelings of disdainful pride,
Spare me the shame of disavowing all
That I profess'd. Born of an Amazon,
The wildness that you wonder at I suck'd
With mother's milk. When come to riper age,
Reason approved what Nature had implanted.
Sincerely bound to me by zealous service,
You told me then the story of my sire,
And know how oft, attentive to your voice,
I kindled when I heard his noble acts,
As you described him bringing consolation

To mortals for the absence of Alcides,
The highways clear'd of monsters and of robbers,
Procrustes, Cercyon, Sciro, Sinnis slain,
The Epidaurian giant's bones dispersed,
Crete reeking with the blood of Minotaur.
But when you told me of less glorious deeds,
Troth plighted here and there and everywhere,
Young Helen stolen from her home at Sparta,
And Periboea's tears in Salamis,
With many another trusting heart deceived
Whose very names have 'scaped his memory,
Forsaken Ariadne to the rocks
Complaining, last this Phaedra, bound to him
By better ties, — you know with what regret
I heard and urged you to cut short the tale,
Happy had I been able to erase
From my remembrance that unworthy part
Of such a splendid record. I, in turn,
Am I too made the slave of love, and brought
To stoop so low? The more contemptible
That no renown is mine such as exalts
The name of Theseus, that no monsters quell'd
Have given me a right to share his weakness.
And if my pride of heart must needs be humbled,
Aricia should have been the last to tame it.
Was I beside myself to have forgotten
Eternal barriers of separation
Between us? By my father's stern command
Her brethren's blood must ne'er be reinforced
By sons of hers; he dreads a single shoot
From stock so guilty, and would fain with her
Bury their name, that, even to the tomb
Content to be his ward, for her no torch
Of Hymen may be lit. Shall I espouse
Her rights against my sire, rashly provoke
His wrath, and launch upon a mad career —

THERAMENES
The gods, dear prince, if once your hour is come,
Care little for the reasons that should guide us.
Wishing to shut your eyes, Theseus unseals them;
His hatred, stirring a rebellious flame
Within you, lends his enemy new charms.
And, after all, why should a guiltless passion
Alarm you? Dare you not essay its sweetness,
But follow rather a fastidious scruple?
Fear you to stray where Hercules has wander'd?
What heart so stout that Venus has not vanquish'd?
Where would you be yourself, so long her foe,
Had your own mother, constant in her scorn
Of love, ne'er glowed with tenderness for Theseus?
What boots it to affect a pride you feel not?
Confess it, all is changed; for some time past
You have been seldom seen with wild delight
Urging the rapid car along the strand,
Or, skilful in the art that Neptune taught,
Making th' unbroken steed obey the bit;
Less often have the woods return'd our shouts;
A secret burden on your spirits cast
Has dimm'd your eye. How can I doubt you love?
Vainly would you conceal the fatal wound.
Has not the fair Aricia touch'd your heart?

HIPPOLYTUS
Theramenes, I go to find my father.

THERAMENES
Will you not see the queen before you start,
My prince?

HIPPOLYTUS
That is my purpose: you can tell her.

Yes, I will see her; duty bids me do it.
But what new ill vexes her dear Oenone?

SCENE II

HIPPOLYTUS, OENONE, THERAMENES

OENONE
Alas, my lord, what grief was e'er like mine?
The queen has almost touch'd the gates of death.
Vainly close watch I keep by day and night,
E'en in my arms a secret malady
Slays her, and all her senses are disorder'd.
Weary yet restless from her couch she rises,
Pants for the outer air, but bids me see
That no one on her misery intrudes.
She comes.

HIPPOLYTUS
Enough. She shall not be disturb'd,
Nor be confronted with a face she hates.

SCENE III

PHAEDRA, OENONE

PHAEDRA
We have gone far enough. Stay, dear Oenone;
Strength fails me, and I needs must rest awhile.
My eyes are dazzled with this glaring light

So long unseen, my trembling knees refuse
Support. Ah me!

OENONE
Would Heaven that our tears
Might bring relief!

PHAEDRA
Ah, how these cumbrous gauds,
These veils oppress me! What officious hand
Has tied these knots, and gather'd o'er my brow
These clustering coils? How all conspires to add
To my distress!

OENONE
What is one moment wish'd,
The next, is irksome. Did you not just now,
Sick of inaction, bid us deck you out,
And, with your former energy recall'd,
Desire to go abroad, and see the light
Of day once more? You see it, and would fain
Be hidden from the sunshine that you sought.

PHAEDRA
Thou glorious author of a hapless race,
Whose daughter 'twas my mother's boast to be,
Who well may'st blush to see me in such plight,
For the last time I come to look on thee,
O Sun!

OENONE
What! Still are you in love with death?
Shall I ne'er see you, reconciled to life,
Forego these cruel accents of despair?

PHAEDRA
Would I were seated in the forest's shade!
When may I follow with delighted eye,
Thro' glorious dust flying in full career,
A chariot —

OENONE
Madam?

PHAEDRA
Have I lost my senses?
What said I? and where am I? Whither stray
Vain wishes? Ah! The gods have made me mad.
I blush, Oenone, and confusion covers
My face, for I have let you see too clearly
The shame of grief that, in my own despite,
O'erflows these eyes of mine.

OENONE
If you must blush,
Blush at a silence that inflames your woes.
Resisting all my care, deaf to my voice,
Will you have no compassion on yourself,
But let your life be ended in mid course?
What evil spell has drain'd its fountain dry?
Thrice have the shades of night obscured the heav'ns
Since sleep has enter'd thro' your eyes, and thrice
The dawn has chased the darkness thence, since food
Pass'd your wan lips, and you are faint and languid.
To what dread purpose is your heart inclined?
How dare you make attempts upon your life,
And so offend the gods who gave it you,
Prove false to Theseus and your marriage vows,
Ay, and betray your most unhappy children,
Bending their necks yourself beneath the yoke?
That day, be sure, which robs them of their mother,

Will give high hopes back to the stranger's son,
To that proud enemy of you and yours,
To whom an Amazon gave birth, I mean
Hippolytus —

PHAEDRA
Ye gods!

OENONE
Ah, this reproach
Moves you!

PHAEDRA
Unhappy woman, to what name
Gave your mouth utterance?

OENONE
Your wrath is just.
'Tis well that that ill-omen'd name can rouse
Such rage. Then live. Let love and duty urge
Their claims. Live, suffer not this son of Scythia,
Crushing your children 'neath his odious sway,
To rule the noble offspring of the gods,
The purest blood of Greece. Make no delay;
Each moment threatens death; quickly restore
Your shatter'd strength, while yet the torch of life
Holds out, and can be fann'd into a flame.

PHAEDRA
Too long have I endured its guilt and shame!

OENONE
Why? What remorse gnaws at your heart? What crime
Can have disturb'd you thus? Your hands are not
Polluted with the blood of innocence?

PHAEDRA
Thanks be to Heav'n, my hands are free from stain.
Would that my soul were innocent as they!

OENONE
What awful project have you then conceived,
Whereat your conscience should be still alarm'd?

PHAEDRA
Have I not said enough? Spare me the rest.
I die to save myself a full confession.

OENONE
Die then, and keep a silence so inhuman;
But seek some other hand to close your eyes.
Tho' but a spark of life remains within you,
My soul shall go before you to the Shades.
A thousand roads are always open thither;
Pain'd at your want of confidence, I'll choose
The shortest. Cruel one, when has my faith
Deceived you! Think how in my arms you lay
New born. For you, my country and my children
I have forsaken. Do you thus repay
My faithful service?

PHAEDRA
What do you expect
From words so bitter? Were I to break silence
Horror would freeze your blood.

OENONE
What can you say
To horrify me more than to behold
You die before my eyes?

PHAEDRA
When you shall know
My crime, my death will follow none the less,
But with the added stain of guilt.

OENONE
Dear Madam,
By all the tears that I have shed for you,
By these weak knees I clasp, relieve my mind
From torturing doubt.

PHAEDRA
It is your wish. Then rise.

OENONE
I hear you. Speak.

PHAEDRA
Heav'ns! How shall I begin?

OENONE
Dismiss vain fears, you wound me with distrust.

PHAEDRA
O fatal animosity of Venus!
Into what wild distractions did she cast
My mother!

OENONE
Be they blotted from remembrance,
And for all time to come buried in silence.

PHAEDRA
My sister Ariadne, by what love
Were you betray'd to death, on lonely shores
Forsaken!

OENONE
Madam, what deep-seated pain
Prompts these reproaches against all your kin?

PHAEDRA
It is the will of Venus, and I perish,
Last, most unhappy of a family
Where all were wretched.

OENONE
Do you love?

PHAEDRA
I feel
All its mad fever.

OENONE
Ah! For whom?

PHAEDRA
Hear now
The crowning horror. Yes, I love — my lips
Tremble to say his name.

OENONE
Whom?

PHAEDRA
Know you him,
Son of the Amazon, whom I've oppress'd
So long?

OENONE
Hippolytus? Great gods!

PHAEDRA
'Tis you
Have named him.

OENONE
All my blood within my veins
Seems frozen. O despair! O cursed race!
Ill-omen'd journey! Land of misery!
Why did we ever reach thy dangerous shores?

PHAEDRA
My wound is not so recent. Scarcely had I
Been bound to Theseus by the marriage yoke,
And happiness and peace seem'd well secured,
When Athens show'd me my proud enemy.
I look'd, alternately turn'd pale and blush'd
To see him, and my soul grew all distraught;
A mist obscured my vision, and my voice
Falter'd, my blood ran cold, then burn'd like fire;
Venus I felt in all my fever'd frame,
Whose fury had so many of my race
Pursued. With fervent vows I sought to shun
Her torments, built and deck'd for her a shrine,
And there, 'mid countless victims did I seek
The reason I had lost; but all for naught,
No remedy could cure the wounds of love!
In vain I offer'd incense on her altars;
When I invoked her name my heart adored
Hippolytus, before me constantly;
And when I made her altars smoke with victims,
'Twas for a god whose name I dared not utter.
I fled his presence everywhere, but found him —
O crowning horror! — in his father's features.
Against myself, at last, I raised revolt,
And stirr'd my courage up to persecute
The enemy I loved. To banish him

I wore a step — dame's harsh and jealous carriage,
With ceaseless cries I clamour'd for his exile,
Till I had torn him from his father's arms.
I breathed once more, Oenone; in his absence
My days flow'd on less troubled than before,
And innocent. Submissive to my husband,
I hid my grief, and of our fatal marriage
Cherish'd the fruits. Vain caution! Cruel Fate!
Brought hither by my spouse himself, I saw
Again the enemy whom I had banish'd,
And the old wound too quickly bled afresh.
No longer is it love hid in my heart,
But Venus in her might seizing her prey.
I have conceived just terror for my crime;
I hate my life, and hold my love in horror.
Dying I wish'd to keep my fame unsullied,
And bury in the grave a guilty passion;
But I have been unable to withstand
Tears and entreaties, I have told you all;
Content, if only, as my end draws near,
You do not vex me with unjust reproaches,
Nor with vain efforts seek to snatch from death
The last faint lingering sparks of vital breath.

SCENE IV

PHAEDRA, OENONE, PANOPE

PANOPE
Fain would I hide from you tidings so sad,
But 'tis my duty, Madam, to reveal them.
The hand of death has seized your peerless husband,
And you are last to hear of this disaster.

OENONE
What say you, Panope?

PANOPE
The queen, deceived
By a vain trust in Heav'n, begs safe return
For Theseus, while Hippolytus his son
Learns of his death from vessels that are now
In port.

PHAEDRA
Ye gods!

PANOPE
Divided counsels sway
The choice of Athens; some would have the prince,
Your child, for master; others, disregarding
The laws, dare to support the stranger's son.
'Tis even said that a presumptuous faction
Would crown Aricia and the house of Pallas.
I deem'd it right to warn you of this danger.
Hippolytus already is prepared
To start, and should he show himself at Athens,
'Tis to be fear'd the fickle crowd will all
Follow his lead.

OENONE
Enough. The queen, who hears you,
By no means will neglect this timely warning.

SCENE V

PHAEDRA, OENONE

OENONE
Dear lady, I had almost ceased to urge
The wish that you should live, thinking to follow
My mistress to the tomb, from which my voice
Had fail'd to turn you; but this new misfortune
Alters the aspect of affairs, and prompts
Fresh measures. Madam, Theseus is no more,
You must supply his place. He leaves a son,
A slave, if you should die, but, if you live,
A King. On whom has he to lean but you?
No hand but yours will dry his tears. Then live
For him, or else the tears of innocence
Will move the gods, his ancestors, to wrath
Against his mother. Live, your guilt is gone,
No blame attaches to your passion now.
The King's decease has freed you from the bonds
That made the crime and horror of your love.
Hippolytus no longer need be dreaded,
Him you may see henceforth without reproach.
It may be, that, convinced of your aversion,
He means to head the rebels. Undeceive him,
Soften his callous heart, and bend his pride.
King of this fertile land, in Troezen here
His portion lies; but as he knows, the laws
Give to your son the ramparts that Minerva
Built and protects. A common enemy
Threatens you both, unite them to oppose
Aricia.

PHAEDRA
To your counsel I consent.

Yes, I will live, if life can be restored,
If my affection for a son has pow'r
To rouse my sinking heart at such a dangerous hour.

ACT II

SCENE I

ARICIA, ISMENE

ARICIA
Hippolytus request to see me here!
Hippolytus desire to bid farewell!
Is't true, Ismene? Are you not deceived?

ISMENE
This is the first result of Theseus' death.
Prepare yourself to see from every side.
Hearts turn towards you that were kept away
By Theseus. Mistress of her lot at last,
Aricia soon shall find all Greece fall low,
To do her homage.

ARICIA
'Tis not then, Ismene,
An idle tale? Am I no more a slave?
Have I no enemies?

ISMENE
The gods oppose
Your peace no longer, and the soul of Theseus
Is with your brothers.

ARICIA
Does the voice of fame
Tell how he died?

ISMENE
Rumours incredible

Are spread. Some say that, seizing a new bride,
The faithless husband by the waves was swallow'd.
Others affirm, and this report prevails,
That with Pirithous to the world below
He went, and saw the shores of dark Cocytus,
Showing himself alive to the pale ghosts;
But that he could not leave those gloomy realms,
Which whoso enters there abides for ever.

ARICIA
Shall I believe that ere his destined hour
A mortal may descend into the gulf
Of Hades? What attraction could o'ercome
Its terrors?

ISMENE
He is dead, and you alone
Doubt it. The men of Athens mourn his loss.
Troezen already hails Hippolytus
As King. And Phaedra, fearing for her son,
Asks counsel of the friends who share her trouble,
Here in this palace.

ARICIA
Will Hippolytus,
Think you, prove kinder than his sire, make light
My chains, and pity my misfortunes?

ISMENE
Yes,
I think so, Madam.

ARICIA
Ah, you know him not
Or you would never deem so hard a heart
Can pity feel, or me alone except

From the contempt in which he holds our sex.
Has he not long avoided every spot
Where we resort?

ISMENE
I know what tales are told
Of proud Hippolytus, but I have seen
Him near you, and have watch'd with curious eye
How one esteem'd so cold would bear himself.
Little did his behavior correspond
With what I look'd for; in his face confusion
Appear'd at your first glance, he could not turn
His languid eyes away, but gazed on you.
Love is a word that may offend his pride,
But what the tongue disowns, looks can betray.

ARICIA
How eagerly my heart hears what you say,
Tho' it may be delusion, dear Ismene!
Did it seem possible to you, who know me,
That I, sad sport of a relentless Fate,
Fed upon bitter tears by night and day,
Could ever taste the maddening draught of love?
The last frail offspring of a royal race,
Children of Earth, I only have survived
War's fury. Cut off in the flow'r of youth,
Mown by the sword, six brothers have I lost,
The hope of an illustrious house, whose blood
Earth drank with sorrow, near akin to his
Whom she herself produced. Since then, you know
How thro' all Greece no heart has been allow'd
To sigh for me, lest by a sister's flame
The brothers' ashes be perchance rekindled.
You know, besides, with what disdain I view'd
My conqueror's suspicions and precautions,
And how, oppos'd as I have ever been

To love, I often thank'd the King's injustice
Which happily confirm'd my inclination.
But then I never had beheld his son.
Not that, attracted merely by the eye, I
love him for his beauty and his grace,
Endowments which he owes to Nature's bounty,
Charms which he seems to know not or to scorn.
I love and prize in him riches more rare,
The virtues of his sire, without his faults.
I love, as I must own, that generous pride
Which ne'er has stoop'd beneath the amorous yoke.
Phaedra reaps little glory from a lover
So lavish of his sighs; I am too proud
To share devotion with a thousand others,
Or enter where the door is always open.
But to make one who ne'er has stoop'd before
Bend his proud neck, to pierce a heart of stone,
To bind a captive whom his chains astonish,
Who vainly 'gainst a pleasing yoke rebels, —
That piques my ardour, and I long for that.
'Twas easier to disarm the god of strength
Than this Hippolytus, for Hercules
Yielded so often to the eyes of beauty,
As to make triumph cheap. But, dear Ismene,
I take too little heed of opposition
Beyond my pow'r to quell, and you may hear me,
Humbled by sore defeat, upbraid the pride
I now admire. What! Can he love? and I
Have had the happiness to bend —

ISMENE
He comes
Yourself shall hear him.

SCENE II

HIPPOLYTUS, ARICIA, ISMENE

HIPPOLYTUS
Lady, ere I go
My duty bids me tell you of your change
Of fortune. My worst fears are realized;
My sire is dead. Yes, his protracted absence
Was caused as I foreboded. Death alone,
Ending his toils, could keep him from the world
Conceal'd so long. The gods at last have doom'd
Alcides' friend, companion, and successor.
I think your hatred, tender to his virtues,
Can hear such terms of praise without resentment,
Knowing them due. One hope have I that soothes
My sorrow: I can free you from restraint.
Lo, I revoke the laws whose rigour moved
My pity; you are at your own disposal,
Both heart and hand; here, in my heritage,
In Troezen, where my grandsire Pittheus reign'd
Of yore and I am now acknowledged King,
I leave you free, free as myself, — and more.

ARICIA
Your kindness is too great, 'tis overwhelming.
Such generosity, that pays disgrace
With honour, lends more force than you can think
To those harsh laws from which you would release me.

HIPPOLYTUS
Athens, uncertain how to fill the throne
Of Theseus, speaks of you, anon of me,
And then of Phaedra's son.

ARICIA
Of me, my lord?

HIPPOLYTUS
I know myself excluded by strict law:
Greece turns to my reproach a foreign mother.
But if my brother were my only rival,
My rights prevail o'er his clearly enough
To make me careless of the law's caprice.
My forwardness is check'd by juster claims:
To you I yield my place, or, rather, own
That it is yours by right, and yours the sceptre,
As handed down from Earth's great son, Erechtheus.
Adoption placed it in the hands of Aegeus:
Athens, by him protected and increased,
Welcomed a king so generous as my sire,
And left your hapless brothers in oblivion.
Now she invites you back within her walls;
Protracted strife has cost her groans enough,
Her fields are glutted with your kinsmen's blood
Fatt'ning the furrows out of which it sprung
At first. I rule this Troezen; while the son
Of Phaedra has in Crete a rich domain.
Athens is yours. I will do all I can
To join for you the votes divided now
Between us.

ARICIA
Stunn'd at all I hear, my lord,
I fear, I almost fear a dream deceives me.
Am I indeed awake? Can I believe
Such generosity? What god has put it
Into your heart? Well is the fame deserved
That you enjoy! That fame falls short of truth!
Would you for me prove traitor to yourself?
Was it not boon enough never to hate me,

So long to have abstain'd from harbouring
The enmity —

HIPPOLYTUS
To hate you? I, to hate you?
However darkly my fierce pride was painted,
Do you suppose a monster gave me birth?
What savage temper, what envenom'd hatred
Would not be mollified at sight of you?
Could I resist the soul-bewitching charm —

ARICIA
Why, what is this, Sir?

HIPPOLYTUS
I have said too much
Not to say more. Prudence in vain resists
The violence of passion. I have broken
Silence at last, and I must tell you now
The secret that my heart can hold no longer.
You see before you an unhappy instance
Of hasty pride, a prince who claims compassion
I, who, so long the enemy of Love,
Mock'd at his fetters and despised his captives,
Who, pitying poor mortals that were shipwreck'd,
In seeming safety view'd the storms from land,
Now find myself to the same fate exposed,
Toss'd to and fro upon a sea of troubles!
My boldness has been vanquish'd in a moment,
And humbled is the pride wherein I boasted.
For nearly six months past, ashamed, despairing,
Bearing where'er I go the shaft that rends
My heart, I struggle vainly to be free
From you and from myself; I shun you, present;
Absent, I find you near; I see your form
In the dark forest depths; the shades of night,

Nor less broad daylight, bring back to my view
The charms that I avoid; all things conspire
To make Hippolytus your slave. For fruit
Of all my bootless sighs, I fail to find
My former self. My bow and javelins
Please me no more, my chariot is forgotten,
With all the Sea God's lessons; and the woods
Echo my groans instead of joyous shouts
Urging my fiery steeds.

Hearing this tale
Of passion so uncouth, you blush perchance
At your own handiwork. With what wild words
I offer you my heart, strange captive held
By silken jess! But dearer in your eyes
Should be the offering, that this language comes
Strange to my lips; reject not vows express'd
So ill, which but for you had ne'er been form'd.

SCENE III

HIPPOLYTUS, ARICIA, THERAMENES, ISMENE

THERAMENES
Prince, the Queen comes. I herald her approach.
'Tis you she seeks.

HIPPOLYTUS
Me?

THERAMENES
What her thought may be
I know not. But I speak on her behalf.

She would converse with you ere you go hence.

HIPPOLYTUS
What shall I say to her? Can she expect —

ARICIA
You cannot, noble Prince, refuse to hear her,
Howe'er convinced she is your enemy,
Some shade of pity to her tears is due.

HIPPOLYTUS
Shall we part thus? and will you let me go,
Not knowing if my boldness has offended
The goddess I adore? Whether this heart,
Left in your hands —

ARICIA
Go, Prince, pursue the schemes
Your generous soul dictates, make Athens own
My sceptre. All the gifts you offer me
Will I accept, but this high throne of empire
Is not the one most precious in my sight.

SCENE IV

HIPPOLYTUS, THERAMENES

HIPPOLYTUS
Friend, is all ready?
But the Queen approaches.
Go, see the vessel in fit trim to sail.
Haste, bid the crew aboard, and hoist the signal:
Then soon return, and so deliver me

From interview most irksome.

SCENE V

PHAEDRA, HIPPOLYTUS, OENONE

PHAEDRA (to OENONE)
There I see him!
My blood forgets to flow, my tongue to speak
What I am come to say.

OENONE
Think of your son,
How all his hopes depend on you.

PHAEDRA
I hear
You leave us, and in haste. I come to add
My tears to your distress, and for a son
Plead my alarm. No more has he a father,
And at no distant day my son must witness
My death. Already do a thousand foes
Threaten his youth. You only can defend him
But in my secret heart remorse awakes,
And fear lest I have shut your ears against
His cries. I tremble lest your righteous anger
Visit on him ere long the hatred earn'd
By me, his mother.

HIPPOLYTUS
No such base resentment,
Madam, is mine.

PHAEDRA
I could not blame you, Prince,
If you should hate me. I have injured you:
So much you know, but could not read my heart.
T' incur your enmity has been mine aim.
The self-same borders could not hold us both;
In public and in private I declared
Myself your foe, and found no peace till seas
Parted us from each other. I forbade
Your very name to be pronounced before me.
And yet if punishment should be proportion'd
To the offence, if only hatred draws
Your hatred, never woman merited
More pity, less deserved your enmity.

HIPPOLYTUS
A mother jealous of her children's rights
Seldom forgives the offspring of a wife
Who reign'd before her. Harassing suspicions
Are common sequels of a second marriage.
Of me would any other have been jealous
No less than you, perhaps more violent.

PHAEDRA
Ah, Prince, how Heav'n has from the general law
Made me exempt, be that same Heav'n my witness!
Far different is the trouble that devours me!

HIPPOLYTUS
This is no time for self-reproaches, Madam.
It may be that your husband still beholds
The light, and Heav'n may grant him safe return,
In answer to our prayers. His guardian god
Is Neptune, ne'er by him invoked in vain.

PHAEDRA

He who has seen the mansions of the dead
Returns not thence. Since to those gloomy shores
Theseus is gone, 'tis vain to hope that Heav'n
May send him back. Prince, there is no release
From Acheron's greedy maw. And yet, methinks,
He lives, and breathes in you. I see him still
Before me, and to him I seem to speak;
My heart —
Oh! I am mad; do what I will,
I cannot hide my passion.

HIPPOLYTUS

Yes, I see
The strange effects of love. Theseus, tho' dead,
Seems present to your eyes, for in your soul
There burns a constant flame.

PHAEDRA

Ah, yes for Theseus
I languish and I long, not as the Shades
Have seen him, of a thousand different forms
The fickle lover, and of Pluto's bride
The would-be ravisher, but faithful, proud
E'en to a slight disdain, with youthful charms
Attracting every heart, as gods are painted,
Or like yourself. He had your mien, your eyes,
Spoke and could blush like you, when to the isle
Of Crete, my childhood's home, he cross'd the waves,
Worthy to win the love of Minos' daughters.
What were you doing then? Why did he gather
The flow'r of Greece, and leave Hippolytus?
Oh, why were you too young to have embark'd
On board the ship that brought thy sire to Crete?
At your hands would the monster then have perish'd,
Despite the windings of his vast retreat.

To guide your doubtful steps within the maze
My sister would have arm'd you with the clue.
But no, therein would Phaedra have forestall'd her,
Love would have first inspired me with the thought;
And I it would have been whose timely aid
Had taught you all the labyrinth's crooked ways.
What anxious care a life so dear had cost me!
No thread had satisfied your lover's fears:
I would myself have wish'd to lead the way,
And share the peril you were bound to face;
Phaedra with you would have explored the maze,
With you emerged in safety, or have perish'd.

HIPPOLYTUS
Gods! What is this I hear? Have you forgotten
That Theseus is my father and your husband?

PHAEDRA
Why should you fancy I have lost remembrance
Thereof, and am regardless of mine honour?

HIPPOLYTUS
Forgive me, Madam. With a blush I own
That I misconstrued words of innocence.
For very shame I cannot bear your sight
Longer. I go —

PHAEDRA
Ah! cruel Prince, too well
You understood me. I have said enough
To save you from mistake. I love. But think not
That at the moment when I love you most
I do not feel my guilt; no weak compliance
Has fed the poison that infects my brain.
The ill-starr'd object of celestial vengeance,
I am not so detestable to you

As to myself. The gods will bear me witness,
Who have within my veins kindled this fire,
The gods, who take a barbarous delight
In leading a poor mortal's heart astray.
Do you yourself recall to mind the past:
'Twas not enough for me to fly, I chased you
Out of the country, wishing to appear
Inhuman, odious; to resist you better,
I sought to make you hate me. All in vain!
Hating me more I loved you none the less:
New charms were lent to you by your misfortunes.
I have been drown'd in tears, and scorch'd by fire;
Your own eyes might convince you of the truth,
If for one moment you could look at me.
What is't I say? Think you this vile confession
That I have made is what I meant to utter?
Not daring to betray a son for whom
I trembled, 'twas to beg you not to hate him
I came. Weak purpose of a heart too full
Of love for you to speak of aught besides!
Take your revenge, punish my odious passion;
Prove yourself worthy of your valiant sire,
And rid the world of an offensive monster!
Does Theseus' widow dare to love his son?
The frightful monster! Let her not escape you!
Here is my heart. This is the place to strike.
Already prompt to expiate its guilt,
I feel it leap impatiently to meet
Your arm. Strike home. Or, if it would disgrace you
To steep your hand in such polluted blood,
If that were punishment too mild to slake
Your hatred, lend me then your sword, if not
Your arm. Quick, give't.

OENONE
What, Madam, will you do?

Just gods! But someone comes. Go, fly from shame,
You cannot 'scape if seen by any thus.

SCENE VI

HIPPOLYTUS, THERAMENES

THERAMENES
Is that the form of Phaedra that I see
Hurried away? What mean these signs of sorrow?
Where is your sword? Why are you pale, confused?

HIPPOLYTUS
Friend, let us fly. I am, indeed, confounded
With horror and astonishment extreme.
Phaedra — but no; gods, let this dreadful secret
Remain for ever buried in oblivion.

THERAMENES
The ship is ready if you wish to sail.
But Athens has already giv'n her vote;
Their leaders have consulted all her tribes;
Your brother is elected, Phaedra wins.

HIPPOLYTUS
Phaedra?

THERAMENES
A herald, charged with a commission
From Athens, has arrived to place the reins
Of power in her hands. Her son is King.

HIPPOLYTUS

Ye gods, who know her, do ye thus reward
Her virtue?

THERAMENES
A faint rumour meanwhile whispers
That Theseus is not dead, but in Epirus
Has shown himself. But, after all my search,
I know too well —

HIPPOLYTUS
Let nothing be neglected.
This rumour must be traced back to its source.
If it be found unworthy of belief,
Let us set sail, and cost whate'er it may,
To hands deserving trust the sceptre's sway.

ACT III

SCENE I

PHAEDRA, OENONE

PHAEDRA

Ah! Let them take elsewhere the worthless honours
They bring me. Why so urgent I should see them?
What flattering balm can soothe my wounded heart?
Far rather hide me: I have said too much.
My madness has burst forth like streams in flood,
And I have utter'd what should ne'er have reach'd
His ear. Gods! How he heard me! How reluctant
To catch my meaning, dull and cold as marble,
And eager only for a quick retreat!
How oft his blushes made my shame the deeper!
Why did you turn me from the death I sought?
Ah! When his sword was pointed to my bosom,
Did he grow pale, or try to snatch it from me?
That I had touch'd it was enough for him
To render it for ever horrible,
Leaving defilement on the hand that holds it.

OENONE

Thus brooding on your bitter disappointment,
You only fan a fire that must be stifled.
Would it not be more worthy of the blood
Of Minos to find peace in nobler cares,
And, in defiance of a wretch who flies
From what he hates, reign, mount the proffer'd throne?

PHAEDRA

I reign! Shall I the rod of empire sway,
When reason reigns no longer o'er myself?

When I have lost control of all my senses?
When 'neath a shameful yoke I scarce can breathe?
When I am dying?

OENONE
Fly.

PHAEDRA
I cannot leave him.

OENONE
Dare you not fly from him you dared to banish?

PHAEDRA
The time for that is past. He knows my frenzy.
I have o'erstepp'd the bounds of modesty,
And blazon'd forth my shame before his eyes.
Hope stole into my heart against my will.
Did you not rally my declining pow'rs?
Was it not you yourself recall'd my soul
When fluttering on my lips, and with your counsel,
Lent me fresh life, and told me I might love him?

OENONE
Blame me or blame me not for your misfortunes,
Of what was I incapable, to save you?
But if your indignation e'er was roused
By insult, can you pardon his contempt?
How cruelly his eyes, severely fix'd,
Survey'd you almost prostrate at his feet!
How hateful then appear'd his savage pride!
Why did not Phaedra see him then as I
Beheld him?

PHAEDRA
This proud mood that you resent

May yield to time. The rudeness of the forests
Where he was bred, inured to rigorous laws,
Clings to him still; love is a word he ne'er
Had heard before. It may be his surprise
Stunn'd him, and too much vehemence was shown
In all I said.

OENONE
Remember that his mother
Was a barbarian.

PHAEDRA
Scythian tho' she was,
She learned to love.

OENONE
He has for all the sex
Hatred intense.

PHAEDRA
Then in his heart no rival
Shall ever reign. Your counsel comes too late
Oenone, serve my madness, not my reason.
His heart is inaccessible to love.
Let us attack him where he has more feeling.
The charms of sovereignty appear'd to touch him;
He could not hide that he was drawn to Athens;
His vessels' prows were thither turn'd already,
All sail was set to scud before the breeze.
Go you on my behalf, to his ambition
Appeal, and let the prospect of the crown
Dazzle his eyes. The sacred diadem
Shall deck his brow, no higher honour mine
Than there to bind it. His shall be the pow'r
I cannot keep; and he shall teach my son
How to rule men. It may be he will deign

To be to him a father. Son and mother
He shall control. Try ev'ry means to move him;
Your words will find more favour than can mine.
Urge him with groans and tears; show Phaedra dying.
Nor blush to use the voice of supplication.
In you is my last hope; I'll sanction all
You say; and on the issue hangs my fate.

SCENE II

PHAEDRA (alone)
Venus implacable, who seest me shamed
And sore confounded, have I not enough
Been humbled? How can cruelty be stretch'd
Farther? Thy shafts have all gone home, and thou
Hast triumph'd. Would'st thou win a new renown?
Attack an enemy more contumacious:
Hippolytus neglects thee, braves thy wrath,
Nor ever at thine altars bow'd the knee.
Thy name offends his proud, disdainful ears.
Our interests are alike: avenge thyself,
Force him to love —
But what is this? Oenone
Return'd already? He detests me then,
And will not hear you.

SCENE III

PHAEDRA, OENONE

OENONE
Madam, you must stifle
A fruitless love. Recall your former virtue:
The king who was thought dead will soon appear
Before your eyes, Theseus has just arrived,
Theseus is here. The people flock to see him
With eager haste. I went by your command
To find the prince, when with a thousand shouts
The air was rent —

PHAEDRA
My husband is alive,
That is enough, Oenone. I have own'd
A passion that dishonours him. He lives:
I ask to know no more.

OENONE
What?

PHAEDRA
I foretold it,
But you refused to hear. Your tears prevail'd
Over my just remorse. Dying this morn,
I had deserved compassion; your advice
I took, and die dishonour'd.

OENONE
Die?

PHAEDRA
Just Heav'ns!
What have I done to-day? My husband comes,
With him his son: and I shall see the witness
Of my adulterous flame watch with what face
I greet his father, while my heart is big
With sighs he scorn'd, and tears that could not move him

Moisten mine eyes. Think you that his respect
For Theseus will induce him to conceal
My madness, nor disgrace his sire and king?
Will he be able to keep back the horror
He has for me? His silence would be vain.
I know my treason, and I lack the boldness
Of those abandon'd women who can taste
Tranquillity in crime, and show a forehead
All unabash'd. I recognize my madness,
Recall it all. These vaulted roofs, methinks,
These walls can speak, and, ready to accuse me,
Wait but my husband's presence to reveal
My perfidy. Death only can remove
This weight of horror. Is it such misfortune
To cease to live? Death causes no alarm
To misery. I only fear the name
That I shall leave behind me. For my sons
How sad a heritage! The blood of Jove
Might justly swell the pride that boasts descent
From Heav'n, but heavy weighs a mother's guilt
Upon her offspring. Yes, I dread the scorn
That will be cast on them, with too much truth,
For my disgrace. I tremble when I think
That, crush'd beneath that curse, they'll never dare
To raise their eyes.

OENONE
Doubt not I pity both;
Never was fear more just than yours. Why, then,
Expose them to this ignominy? Why
Will you accuse yourself? You thus destroy
The only hope that's left; it will be said
That Phaedra, conscious of her perfidy,
Fled from her husband's sight. Hippolytus
Will be rejoiced that, dying, you should lend
His charge support. What can I answer him?

He'll find it easy to confute my tale,
And I shall hear him with an air of triumph
To every open ear repeat your shame.
Sooner than that may fire from heav'n consume me!
Deceive me not. Say, do you love him still?
How look you now on this contemptuous prince?

PHAEDRA
As on a monster frightful to mine eyes.

OENONE
Why yield him, then, an easy victory?
You fear him? Venture to accuse him first,
As guilty of the charge which he may bring
This day against you. Who can say 'tis false?
All tells against him: in your hands his sword
Happily left behind, your present trouble,
Your past distress, your warnings to his father,
His exile which your earnest pray'rs obtain'd.

PHAEDRA
What! Would you have me slander innocence?

OENONE
My zeal has need of naught from you but silence.
Like you I tremble, and am loath to do it;
More willingly I'd face a thousand deaths,
But since without this bitter remedy
I lose you, and to me your life outweighs
All else, I'll speak. Theseus, howe'er enraged
Will do no worse than banish him again.
A father, when he punishes, remains
A father, and his ire is satisfied
With a light sentence. But if guiltless blood
Should flow, is not your honour of more moment?
A treasure far too precious to be risk'd?

You must submit, whatever it dictates;
For, when our reputation is at stake,
All must be sacrificed, conscience itself.
But someone comes. 'Tis Theseus.

PHAEDRA
And I see
Hippolytus, my ruin plainly written
In his stern eyes. Do what you will; I trust
My fate to you. I cannot help myself.

SCENE IV

THESEUS, HIPPOLYTUS, PHAEDRA, OENONE,
THERAMENES

THESEUS
Fortune no longer fights against my wishes,
Madam, and to your arms restores —

PHAEDRA
Stay, Theseus!
Do not profane endearments that were once
So sweet, but which I am unworthy now
To taste. You have been wrong'd. Fortune has proved
Spiteful, nor in your absence spared your wife.
I am unfit to meet your fond caress,
How I may bear my shame my only care
Henceforth.

SCENE V

THESEUS, HIPPOLYTUS, THERAMENES

THESEUS
Strange welcome for your father, this!
What does it mean, my son?

HIPPOLYTUS
Phaedra alone
Can solve this mystery. But if my wish
Can move you, let me never see her more;
Suffer Hippolytus to disappear
For ever from the home that holds your wife.

THESEUS
You, my son! Leave me?

HIPPOLYTUS
'Twas not I who sought her:
'Twas you who led her footsteps to these shores.
At your departure you thought meet, my lord,
To trust Aricia and the Queen to this
Troezenian land, and I myself was charged
With their protection. But what cares henceforth
Need keep me here? My youth of idleness
Has shown its skill enough o'er paltry foes
That range the woods. May I not quit a life
Of such inglorious ease, and dip my spear
In nobler blood? Ere you had reach'd my age
More than one tyrant, monster more than one
Had felt the weight of your stout arm. Already,
Successful in attacking insolence,
You had removed all dangers that infested
Our coasts to east and west. The traveller fear'd

Outrage no longer. Hearing of your deeds,
Already Hercules relied on you,
And rested from his toils. While I, unknown
Son of so brave a sire, am far behind
Even my mother's footsteps. Let my courage
Have scope to act, and if some monster yet
Has 'scaped you, let me lay the glorious spoils
Down at your feet; or let the memory
Of death faced nobly keep my name alive,
And prove to all the world I was your son.

THESEUS
Why, what is this? What terror has possess'd
My family to make them fly before me?
If I return to find myself so fear'd,
So little welcome, why did Heav'n release me
From prison? My sole friend, misled by passion,
Was bent on robbing of his wife the tyrant
Who ruled Epirus. With regret I lent
The lover aid, but Fate had made us blind,
Myself as well as him. The tyrant seized me
Defenceless and unarm'd. Pirithous
I saw with tears cast forth to be devour'd
By savage beasts that lapp'd the blood of men.
Myself in gloomy caverns he inclosed,
Deep in the bowels of the earth, and nigh
To Pluto's realms. Six months I lay ere Heav'n
Had pity, and I 'scaped the watchful eyes
That guarded me. Then did I purge the world
Of a foul foe, and he himself has fed
His monsters. But when with expectant joy
To all that is most precious I draw near
Of what the gods have left me, when my soul
Looks for full satisfaction in a sight
So dear, my only welcome is a shudder,
Embrace rejected, and a hasty flight.

Inspiring, as I clearly do, such terror,
Would I were still a prisoner in Epirus!
Phaedra complains that I have suffer'd outrage.
Who has betray'd me? Speak. Why was I not
Avenged? Has Greece, to whom mine arm so oft
Brought useful aid, shelter'd the criminal?
You make no answer. Is my son, mine own
Dear son, confederate with mine enemies?
I'll enter. This suspense is overwhelming.
I'll learn at once the culprit and the crime,
And Phaedra must explain her troubled state.

SCENE VI

HIPPOLYTUS, THERAMENES

HIPPOLYTUS
What do these words portend, which seem'd to freeze
My very blood? Will Phaedra, in her frenzy
Accuse herself, and seal her own destruction?
What will the King say? Gods! What fatal poison
Has love spread over all his house! Myself,
Full of a fire his hatred disapproves,
How changed he finds me from the son he knew!
With dark forebodings in my mind alarm'd,
But innocence has surely naught to fear.
Come, let us go, and in some other place
Consider how I best may move my sire
To tenderness, and tell him of a flame
Vex'd but not vanquish'd by a father's blame.

ACT IV

SCENE I

THESEUS, OENONE

THESEUS
Ah! What is this I hear? Presumptuous traitor!
And would he have disgraced his father's honour?
With what relentless footsteps Fate pursues me!
Whither I go I know not, nor where know
I am. O kind affection ill repaid!
Audacious scheme! Abominable thought!
To reach the object of his foul desire
The wretch disdain'd not to use violence.
I know this sword that served him in his fury,
The sword I gave him for a nobler use.
Could not the sacred ties of blood restrain him?
And Phaedra, — was she loath to have him punish'd?
She held her tongue. Was that to spare the culprit?

OENONE
Nay, but to spare a most unhappy father.
O'erwhelm'd with shame that her eyes should have kindled
So infamous a flame and prompted him
To crime so heinous, Phaedra would have died.
I saw her raise her arm, and ran to save her.
To me alone you owe it that she lives;
And, in my pity both for her and you,
Have I against my will interpreted
Her tears.

THESEUS
The traitor! He might well turn pale.

'Twas fear that made him tremble when he saw me.
I was astonish'd that he show'd no pleasure;
His frigid greeting chill'd my tenderness.
But was this guilty passion that devours him
Declared already ere I banish'd him
From Athens?

OENONE
Sire, remember how the Queen
Urged you. Illicit love caused all her hatred.

THESEUS
And then this fire broke out again at Troezen?

OENONE
Sire, I have told you all. Too long the Queen
Has been allow'd to bear her grief alone
Let me now leave you and attend to her.

SCENE II

THESEUS, HIPPOLYTUS

THESEUS
Ah! There he is. Great gods! That noble mien
Might well deceive an eye less fond than mine!
Why should the sacred stamp of virtue gleam
Upon the forehead of an impious wretch?
Ought not the blackness of a traitor's heart
To show itself by sure and certain signs?

HIPPOLYTUS
My father, may I ask what fatal cloud

Has troubled your majestic countenance?
Dare you not trust this secret to your son?

THESEUS
Traitor, how dare you show yourself before me?
Monster, whom Heaven's bolts have spared too long!
Survivor of that robber crew whereof
I cleansed the earth. After your brutal lust
Scorn'd even to respect my marriage bed,
You venture — you, my hated foe — to come
Into my presence, here, where all is full
Of your foul infamy, instead of seeking
Some unknown land that never heard my name.
Fly, traitor, fly! Stay not to tempt the wrath
That I can scarce restrain, nor brave my hatred.
Disgrace enough have I incurr'd for ever
In being father of so vile a son,
Without your death staining indelibly
The glorious record of my noble deeds.
Fly, and unless you wish quick punishment
To add you to the criminals cut off
By me, take heed this sun that lights us now
Ne'er sees you more set foot upon this soil.
I tell you once again, — fly, haste, return not,
Rid all my realms of your atrocious presence.
To thee, to thee, great Neptune, I appeal
If erst I clear'd thy shores of foul assassins
Recall thy promise to reward those efforts,
Crown'd with success, by granting my first pray'r.
Confined for long in close captivity,
I have not yet call'd on thy pow'rful aid,
Sparing to use the valued privilege
Till at mine utmost need. The time is come
I ask thee now. Avenge a wretched father!
I leave this traitor to thy wrath; in blood
Quench his outrageous fires, and by thy fury

Theseus will estimate thy favour tow'rds him.

HIPPOLYTUS
Phaedra accuses me of lawless passion!
This crowning horror all my soul confounds;
Such unexpected blows, falling at once,
O'erwhelm me, choke my utterance, strike me dumb.

THESEUS
Traitor, you reckon'd that in timid silence
Phaedra would bury your brutality.
You should not have abandon'd in your flight
The sword that in her hands helps to condemn you;
Or rather, to complete your perfidy,
You should have robb'd her both of speech and life.

HIPPOLYTUS
Justly indignant at a lie so black
I might be pardon'd if I told the truth;
But it concerns your honour to conceal it.
Approve the reverence that shuts my mouth;
And, without wishing to increase your woes,
Examine closely what my life has been.
Great crimes are never single, they are link'd
To former faults. He who has once transgress'd
May violate at last all that men hold
Most sacred; vice, like virtue, has degrees
Of progress; innocence was never seen
To sink at once into the lowest depths
Of guilt. No virtuous man can in a day
Turn traitor, murderer, an incestuous wretch.
The nursling of a chaste, heroic mother,
I have not proved unworthy of my birth.
Pittheus, whose wisdom is by all esteem'd,
Deign'd to instruct me when I left her hands.
It is no wish of mine to vaunt my merits,

But, if I may lay claim to any virtue,
I think beyond all else I have display'd
Abhorrence of those sins with which I'm charged.
For this Hippolytus is known in Greece,
So continent that he is deem'd austere.
All know my abstinence inflexible:
The daylight is not purer than my heart.
How, then, could I, burning with fire profane —

THESEUS
Yes, dastard, 'tis that very pride condemns you.
I see the odious reason of your coldness
Phaedra alone bewitch'd your shameless eyes;
Your soul, to others' charms indifferent,
Disdain'd the blameless fires of lawful love.

HIPPOLYTUS
No, father, I have hidden it too long,
This heart has not disdain'd a sacred flame.
Here at your feet I own my real offence:
I love, and love in truth where you forbid me;
Bound to Aricia by my heart's devotion,
The child of Pallas has subdued your son.
A rebel to your laws, her I adore,
And breathe forth ardent sighs for her alone.

THESEUS
You love her? Heav'ns!
But no, I see the trick.
You feign a crime to justify yourself.

HIPPOLYTUS
Sir, I have shunn'd her for six months, and still
Love her. To you yourself I came to tell it,
Trembling the while. Can nothing clear your mind
Of your mistake? What oath can reassure you?

By heav'n and earth and all the pow'rs of nature —

THESEUS
The wicked never shrink from perjury.
Cease, cease, and spare me irksome protestations,
If your false virtue has no other aid.

HIPPOLYTUS
Tho' it to you seem false and insincere,
Phaedra has secret cause to know it true.

THESEUS
Ah! how your shamelessness excites my wrath!

HIPPOLYTUS
What is my term and place of banishment?

THESEUS
Were you beyond the Pillars of Alcides,
Your perjured presence were too near me yet.

HIPPOLYTUS
What friends will pity me, when you forsake
And think me guilty of a crime so vile?

THESEUS
Go, look you out for friends who hold in honour
Adultery and clap their hands at incest,
Low, lawless traitors, steep'd in infamy,
The fit protectors of a knave like you.

HIPPOLYTUS
Are incest and adultery the words
You cast at me? I hold my tongue. Yet think
What mother Phaedra had; too well you know
Her blood, not mine, is tainted with those horrors.

THESEUS
What! Does your rage before my eyes lose all
Restraint? For the last time, — out of my sight!
Hence, traitor! Wait not till a father's wrath
Force thee away 'mid general execration.

SCENE III

THESEUS (alone)
Wretch! Thou must meet inevitable ruin.
Neptune has sworn by Styx — to gods themselves
A dreadful oath, — and he will execute
His promise. Thou canst not escape his vengeance.
I loved thee; and, in spite of thine offence,
My heart is troubled by anticipation
For thee. But thou hast earn'd thy doom too well.
Had father ever greater cause for rage?
Just gods, who see the grief that overwhelms me,
Why was I cursed with such a wicked son?

SCENE IV

PHAEDRA, THESEUS

PHAEDRA
My lord, I come to you, fill'd with just dread.
Your voice raised high in anger reach'd mine ears,
And much I fear that deeds have follow'd threats.
Oh, if there yet is time, spare your own offspring.
Respect your race and blood, I do beseech you.
Let me not hear that blood cry from the ground;
Save me the horror and perpetual pain

Of having caused his father's hand to shed it.

THESEUS
No, Madam, from that stain my hand is free.
But, for all that, the wretch has not escaped me.
The hand of an Immortal now is charged
With his destruction. 'Tis a debt that Neptune
Owes me, and you shall be avenged.

PHAEDRA
A debt
Owed you? Pray'rs made in anger —

THESEUS
Never fear
That they will fail. Rather join yours to mine
In all their blackness paint for me his crimes,
And fan my tardy passion to white heat.
But yet you know not all his infamy;
His rage against you overflows in slanders;
Your mouth, he says, is full of all deceit,
He says Aricia has his heart and soul,
That her alone he loves.

PHAEDRA
Aricia?

THESEUS
Aye,
He said it to my face! an idle pretext!
A trick that gulls me not! Let us hope Neptune
Will do him speedy justice. To his altars
I go, to urge performance of his oaths.

SCENE V

PHAEDRA (alone)
Ah, he is gone! What tidings struck mine ears?
What fire, half smother'd, in my heart revives?
What fatal stroke falls like a thunderbolt?
Stung by remorse that would not let me rest,
I tore myself out of Oenone's arms,
And flew to help Hippolytus with all
My soul and strength. Who knows if that repentance
Might not have moved me to accuse myself?
And, if my voice had not been choked with shame,
Perhaps I had confess'd the frightful truth.
Hippolytus can feel, but not for me!
Aricia has his heart, his plighted troth.
Ye gods, when, deaf to all my sighs and tears,
He arm'd his eye with scorn, his brow with threats,
I deem'd his heart, impregnable to love,
Was fortified 'gainst all my sex alike.
And yet another has prevail'd to tame
His pride, another has secured his favour.
Perhaps he has a heart easily melted;
I am the only one he cannot bear!
And shall I charge myself with his defence?

SCENE VI

PHAEDRA, OENONE

PHAEDRA
Know you, dear Nurse, what I have learn'd just now?

OENONE
No; but I come in truth with trembling limbs.

I dreaded with what purpose you went forth,
The fear of fatal madness made me pale.

PHAEDRA
Who would have thought it, Nurse? I had a rival.

OENONE
A rival?

PHAEDRA
Yes, he loves. I cannot doubt it.
This wild untamable Hippolytus,
Who scorn'd to be admired, whom lovers' sighs
Wearied, this tiger, whom I fear'd to rouse,
Fawns on a hand that has subdued his pride:
Aricia has found entrance to his heart.

OENONE
Aricia?

PHAEDRA
Ah! anguish as yet untried!
For what new tortures am I still reserved?
All I have undergone, transports of passion,
Longings and fears, the horrors of remorse,
The shame of being spurn'd with contumely,
Were feeble foretastes of my present torments.
They love each other! By what secret charm
Have they deceived me? Where, and when, and how
Met they? You knew it all. Why was I cozen'd?
You never told me of those stolen hours
Of amorous converse. Have they oft been seen
Talking together? Did they seek the shades
Of thickest woods? Alas! full freedom had they
To see each other. Heav'n approved their sighs;
They loved without the consciousness of guilt;

And every morning's sun for them shone clear,
While I, an outcast from the face of Nature,
Shunn'd the bright day, and sought to hide myself.
Death was the only god whose aid I dared
To ask: I waited for the grave's release.
Water'd with tears, nourish'd with gall, my woe
Was all too closely watch'd; I did not dare
To weep without restraint. In mortal dread
Tasting this dangerous solace, I disguised
My terror 'neath a tranquil countenance,
And oft had I to check my tears, and smile.

OENONE
What fruit will they enjoy of their vain love?
They will not see each other more.

PHAEDRA
That love
Will last for ever. Even while I speak,
Ah, fatal thought, they laugh to scorn the madness
Of my distracted heart. In spite of exile
That soon must part them, with a thousand oaths
They seal yet closer union. Can I suffer
A happiness, Oenone, which insults me?
I crave your pity. She must be destroy'd.
My husband's wrath against a hateful stock
Shall be revived, nor must the punishment
Be light: the sister's guilt passes the brothers'.
I will entreat him in my jealous rage.
What am I saying? Have I lost my senses?
Is Phaedra jealous, and will she implore
Theseus for help? My husband lives, and yet
I burn. For whom? Whose heart is this I claim
As mine? At every word I say, my hair
Stands up with horror. Guilt henceforth has pass'd
All bounds. Hypocrisy and incest breathe

At once thro' all. My murderous hands are ready
To spill the blood of guileless innocence.
Do I yet live, wretch that I am, and dare
To face this holy Sun from whom I spring?
My father's sire was king of all the gods;
My ancestors fill all the universe.
Where can I hide? In the dark realms of Pluto?
But there my father holds the fatal urn;
His hand awards th' irrevocable doom:
Minos is judge of all the ghosts in hell.
Ah! how his awful shade will start and shudder
When he shall see his daughter brought before him,
Forced to confess sins of such varied dye,
Crimes it may be unknown to hell itself!
What wilt thou say, my father, at a sight
So dire? I think I see thee drop the urn,
And, seeking some unheard-of punishment,
Thyself become my executioner.
Spare me! A cruel goddess has destroy'd
Thy race; and in my madness recognize
Her wrath. Alas! My aching heart has reap'd
No fruit of pleasure from the frightful crime
The shame of which pursues me to the grave,
And ends in torment life-long misery.

OENONE
Ah, Madam, pray dismiss a groundless dread:
Look less severely on a venial error.
You love. We cannot conquer destiny.
You were drawn on as by a fatal charm.
Is that a marvel without precedent
Among us? Has love triumph'd over you,
And o'er none else? Weakness is natural
To man. A mortal, to a mortal's lot
Submit. You chafe against a yoke that others
Have long since borne. The dwellers in Olympus,

The gods themselves, who terrify with threats
The sins of men, have burn'd with lawless fires.

PHAEDRA
What words are these I hear? What counsel this
You dare to give me? Will you to the end
Pour poison in mine ears? You have destroy'd me.
You brought me back when I should else have quitted
The light of day, made me forget my duty
And see Hippolytus, till then avoided.
What hast thou done? Why did your wicked mouth
With blackest lies slander his blameless life?
Perhaps you've slain him, and the impious pray'r
Of an unfeeling father has been answer'd.
No, not another word! Go, hateful monster;
Away, and leave me to my piteous fate.
May Heav'n with justice pay you your deserts!
And may your punishment for ever be
A terror to all those who would, like you,
Nourish with artful wiles the weaknesses
Of princes, push them to the brink of ruin
To which their heart inclines, and smooth the path
Of guilt. Such flatterers doth the wrath of Heav'n
Bestow on kings as its most fatal gift.

OENONE (alone)
O gods! to serve her what have I not done?
This is the due reward that I have won.

ACT V

SCENE I

HIPPOLYTUS, ARICIA

ARICIA
Can you keep silent in this mortal peril?
Your father loves you. Will you leave him thus
Deceived? If in your cruel heart you scorn
My tears, content to see me nevermore,
Go, part from poor Aricia; but at least,
Going, secure the safety of your life.
Defend your honor from a shameful stain,
And force your father to recall his pray'rs.
There yet is time. Why out of mere caprice
Leave the field free to Phaedra's calumnies?
Let Theseus know the truth.

HIPPOLYTUS
Could I say more,
Without exposing him to dire disgrace?
How should I venture, by revealing all,
To make a father's brow grow red with shame?
The odious mystery to you alone
Is known. My heart has been outpour'd to none
Save you and Heav'n. I could not hide from you
(Judge if I love you), all I fain would hide
E'en from myself. But think under what seal
I spoke. Forget my words, if that may be;
And never let so pure a mouth disclose
This dreadful secret. Let us trust to Heav'n
My vindication, for the gods are just;
For their own honour will they clear the guiltless;
Sooner or later punish'd for her crime,
Phaedra will not escape the shame she merits.

I ask no other favour than your silence;
In all besides I give my wrath free scope.
Make your escape from this captivity,
Be bold to bear me company in flight;
Linger not here on this accursed soil,
Where virtue breathes a pestilential air.
To cover your departure take advantage
Of this confusion, caused by my disgrace.
The means of flight are ready, be assured;
You have as yet no other guards than mine.
Pow'rful defenders will maintain our quarrel;
Argos spreads open arms, and Sparta calls us.
Let us appeal for justice to our friends,
Nor suffer Phaedra, in a common ruin
Joining us both, to hunt us from the throne,
And aggrandize her son by robbing us.
Embrace this happy opportunity:
What fear restrains? You seem to hesitate.
Your interest alone prompts me to urge
Boldness. When I am all on fire, how comes it
That you are ice? Fear you to follow then
A banish'd man?

ARICIA
Ah, dear to me would be
Such exile! With what joy, my fate to yours
United, could I live, by all the world
Forgotten! but not yet has that sweet tie
Bound us together. How then can I steal
Away with you? I know the strictest honour
Forbids me not out of your father's hands
To free myself; this is no parent's home,
And flight is lawful when one flies from tyrants.
But you, Sir, love me; and my virtue shrinks —

HIPPOLYTUS

No, no, your reputation is to me
As dear as to yourself. A nobler purpose
Brings me to you. Fly from your foes, and follow
A husband. Heav'n, that sends us these misfortunes,
Sets free from human instruments the pledge
Between us. Torches do not always light
The face of Hymen.
At the gates of Troezen,
'Mid ancient tombs where princes of my race
Lie buried, stands a temple, ne'er approach'd
By perjurers, where mortals dare not make
False oaths, for instant punishment befalls
The guilty. Falsehood knows no stronger check
Than what is present there — the fear of death
That cannot be avoided. Thither then
We'll go, if you consent, and swear to love
For ever, take the guardian god to witness
Our solemn vows, and his paternal care
Entreat. I will invoke the name of all
The holiest Pow'rs; chaste Dian, and the Queen
Of Heav'n, yea all the gods who know my heart
Will guarantee my sacred promises.

ARICIA

The King draws near. Depart, — make no delay.
To mask my flight, I linger yet one moment.
Go you; and leave with me some trusty guide,
To lead my timid footsteps to your side.

SCENE II

THESEUS, ARICIA, ISMENE

THESEUS
Ye gods, throw light upon my troubled mind,
Show me the truth which I am seeking here.

ARICIA (aside to ISMENE)
Get ready, dear Ismene, for our flight.

SCENE III

THESEUS, ARICIA

THESEUS
Your colour comes and goes, you seem confused,
Madame! What business had my son with you?

ARICIA
Sire, he was bidding me farewell for ever.

THESEUS
Your eyes, it seems, can tame that stubborn pride;
And the first sighs he breathes are paid to you.

ARICIA
I can't deny the truth; he has not, Sire,
Inherited your hatred and injustice;
He did not treat me like a criminal.

THESEUS
That is to say, he swore eternal love.
Do not rely on that inconstant heart;
To others has he sworn as much before.

ARICIA
He, Sire?

THESEUS
You ought to check his roving taste.
How could you bear a partnership so vile?

ARICIA
And how can you endure that vilest slanders
Should make a life so pure as black as pitch?
Have you so little knowledge of his heart?
Do you so ill distinguish between guilt
And innocence? What mist before your eyes
Blinds them to virtue so conspicuous?
Ah! 'tis too much to let false tongues defame him.
Repent; call back your murderous wishes, Sire;
Fear, fear lest Heav'n in its severity
Hate you enough to hear and grant your pray'rs.
Oft in their wrath the gods accept our victims,
And oftentimes chastise us with their gifts.

THESEUS
No, vainly would you cover up his guilt.
Your love is blind to his depravity.
But I have witness irreproachable:
Tears have I seen, true tears, that may be trusted.

ARICIA
Take heed, my lord. Your hands invincible
Have rid the world of monsters numberless;
But all are not destroy'd, one you have left
Alive — Your son forbids me to say more.
Knowing with what respect he still regards you,
I should too much distress him if I dared
Complete my sentence. I will imitate
His reverence, and, to keep silence, leave you.

SCENE IV

THESEUS (alone)
What is there in her mind? What meaning lurks
In speech begun but to be broken short?
Would both deceive me with a vain pretence?
Have they conspired to put me to the torture?
And yet, despite my stern severity,
What plaintive voice cries deep within my heart?
A secret pity troubles and alarms me.
Oenone shall be questioned once again,
I must have clearer light upon this crime.
Guards, bid Oenone come, and come alone.

SCENE V

THESEUS, PANOPE

PANOPE
I know not what the Queen intends to do,
But from her agitation dread the worst.
Fatal despair is painted on her features;
Death's pallor is already in her face.
Oenoné, shamed and driven from her sight,
Has cast herself into the ocean depths.
None knows what prompted her to deed so rash;
And now the waves hide her from us for ever.

THESEUS
What say you?

PANOPE
Her sad fate seems to have added
Fresh trouble to the Queen's tempestuous soul.
Sometimes, to soothe her secret pain, she clasps
Her children close, and bathes them with her tears;
Then suddenly, the mother's love forgotten,
She thrusts them from her with a look of horror,
She wanders to and fro with doubtful steps;
Her vacant eye no longer knows us. Thrice
She wrote, and thrice did she, changing her mind,
Destroy the letter ere 'twas well begun.
Vouchsafe to see her, Sire: vouchsafe to help her.

THESEUS
Heav'ns! Is Oenone dead, and Phaedra bent
On dying too? Oh, call me back my son!
Let him defend himself, and I am ready
To hear him. Be not hasty to bestow
Thy fatal bounty, Neptune; let my pray'rs
Rather remain ever unheard. Too soon
I lifted cruel hands, believing lips
That may have lied! Ah! What despair may follow!

SCENE VI

THESEUS, THERAMENES

THESEUS
Theramenes, is't thou? Where is my son?
I gave him to thy charge from tenderest childhood.
But whence these tears that overflow thine eyes?

How is it with my son?

THERAMENES
Concern too late!
Affection vain! Hippolytus is dead.

THESEUS
Gods!

THERAMENES
I have seen the flow'r of all mankind
Cut off, and I am bold to say that none
Deserved it less.

THESEUS
What! My son dead! When I
Was stretching out my arms to him, has Heav'n
Hasten'd his end? What was this sudden stroke?

THERAMENES
Scarce had we pass'd out of the gates of Troezen,
He silent in his chariot, and his guards
Downcast and silent too, around him ranged;
To the Mycenian road he turn'd his steeds,
Then, lost in thought, allow'd the reins to lie
Loose on their backs. His noble chargers, erst
So full of ardour to obey his voice,
With head depress'd and melancholy eye
Seem'd now to mark his sadness and to share it.
A frightful cry, that issues from the deep,
With sudden discord rends the troubled air;
And from the bosom of the earth a groan
Is heard in answer to that voice of terror.
Our blood is frozen at our very hearts;
With bristling manes the list'ning steeds stand still.
Meanwhile upon the watery plain there rises

A mountain billow with a mighty crest
Of foam, that shoreward rolls, and, as it breaks
Before our eyes vomits a furious monster.
With formidable horns its brow is arm'd,
And all its body clothed with yellow scales,
In front a savage bull, behind a dragon
Turning and twisting in impatient rage.
Its long continued bellowings make the shore
Tremble; the sky seems horror-struck to see it;
The earth with terror quakes; its poisonous breath
Infects the air. The wave that brought it ebbs
In fear. All fly, forgetful of the courage
That cannot aid, and in a neighbouring temple
Take refuge — all save bold Hippolytus.
A hero's worthy son, he stays his steeds,
Seizes his darts, and, rushing forward, hurls
A missile with sure aim that wounds the monster
Deep in the flank. With rage and pain it springs
E'en to the horses' feet, and, roaring, falls,
Writhes in the dust, and shows a fiery throat
That covers them with flames, and blood, and smoke.
Fear lends them wings; deaf to his voice for once,
And heedless of the curb, they onward fly.
Their master wastes his strength in efforts vain;
With foam and blood each courser's bit is red.
Some say a god, amid this wild disorder,
Was seen with goads pricking their dusty flanks.
O'er jagged rocks they rush urged on by terror;
Crash! goes the axle-tree. Th' intrepid youth
Sees his car broken up, flying to pieces;
He falls himself entangled in the reins.
Pardon my grief. That cruel spectacle
Will be for me a source of endless tears.
I saw thy hapless son, I saw him, Sire,
Drag'd by the horses that his hands had fed,
Pow'rless to check their fierce career, his voice

But adding to their fright, his body soon
One mass of wounds. Our cries of anguish fill
The plain. At last they slacken their swift pace,
Then stop, not far from those old tombs that mark
Where lie the ashes of his royal sires.
Panting I thither run, and after me
His guard, along the track stain'd with fresh blood
That reddens all the rocks; caught in the briers
Locks of his hair hang dripping, gory spoils!
I come, I call him. Stretching forth his hand,
He opens his dying eyes, soon closed again.
"The gods have robb'd me of a guiltless life,"
I hear him say: "Take care of sad Aricia
When I am dead. Dear friend, if e'er my father
Mourn, undeceived, his son's unhappy fate
Falsely accused; to give my spirit peace,
Tell him to treat his captive tenderly,
And to restore — " With that the hero's breath
Fails, and a mangled corpse lies in my arms,
A piteous object, trophy of the wrath
Of Heav'n — so changed, his father would not know him.

THESEUS
Alas, my son! Dear hope for ever lost!
The ruthless gods have served me but too well.
For what a life of anguish and remorse
Am I reserved!

THERAMENES
Aricia at that instant,
Flying from you, comes timidly, to take him
For husband, there, in presence of the gods.
Thus drawing nigh, she sees the grass all red
And reeking, sees (sad sight for lover's eye!)
Hippolytus stretch'd there, pale and disfigured.
But, for a time doubtful of her misfortune,

Unrecognized the hero she adores,
She looks, and asks — "Where is Hippolytus?"
Only too sure at last that he lies there
Before her, with sad eyes that silently
Reproach the gods, she shudders, groans, and falls
Swooning and all but lifeless, at his feet.
Ismene, all in tears, kneels down beside her,
And calls her back to life — life that is naught
But sense of pain. And I, to whom this light
Is darkness now, come to discharge the duty
The hero has imposed on me, to tell thee
His last request — a melancholy task.
But hither comes his mortal enemy.

SCENE VII

THESEUS, PHAEDRA, THERAMENES, PANOPE,
GUARDS

THESEUS
Madame, you've triumph'd, and my son is kill'd!
Ah, but what room have I for fear! How justly
Suspicion racks me that in blaming him
I err'd! But he is dead; accept your victim;
Rightly or wrongly slain, let your heart leap
For joy. My eyes shall be for ever blind:
Since you accuse him, I'll believe him guilty.
His death affords me cause enough for tears,
Without a foolish search for further light
Which, pow'rless to restore him to my grief,
Might only serve to make me more unhappy,
Far from this shore and far from you I'll fly,
For here the image of my mangled son
Would haunt my memory and drive me mad.

From the whole world I fain would banish me,
For all the world seems to rise up in judgment
Against me; and my very glory weights
My punishment; for, were my name less known
'Twere easier to hide me. All the favours
The gods have granted me I mourn and hate,
Nor will I importune them with vain pray'rs
Henceforth for ever. Give me what they may,
What they have taken will all else outweigh.

PHAEDRA
Theseus, I cannot hear you and keep silence:
I must repair the wrong that he has suffer'd —
Your son was innocent.

THESEUS
Unhappy father!
And it was on your word that I condemn'd him!
Think you such cruelty can be excused —

PHAEDRA
Moments to me are precious; hear me, Theseus.
'Twas I who cast an eye of lawless passion
On chaste and dutiful Hippolytus.
Heav'n in my bosom kindled baleful fire,
And vile Oenone's cunning did the rest.
She fear'd Hippolytus, knowing my madness,
Would make that passion known which he regarded
With horror; so advantage of my weakness
She took, and hasten'd to accuse him first.
For that she has been punish'd, tho' too mildly;
Seeking to shun my wrath she cast herself
Beneath the waves. The sword ere now had cut
My thread of life, but slander'd innocence
Made its cry heard, and I resolved to die
In a more lingering way, confessing first

My penitence to you. A poison, brought
To Athens by Medea, runs thro' my veins.
Already in my heart the venom works,
Infusing there a strange and fatal chill;
Already as thro' thickening mists I see
The spouse to whom my presence is an outrage;
Death, from mine eyes veiling the light of heav'n,
Restores its purity that they defiled.

PANOPE
She dies my lord!

THESEUS
Would that the memory
Of her disgraceful deed could perish with her!
Ah, disabused too late! Come, let us go,
And with the blood of mine unhappy son
Mingle our tears, clasping his dear remains,
In deep repentance for a pray'r detested.
Let him be honour'd as he well deserves;
And, to appease his sore offended ghost,
Be her near kinsmen's guilt whate'er it may,
Aricia shall be held my daughter from to-day.

Tartuffe, or the Hypocrite
JEAN BAPTISTE POQUELIN MOLIÈRE

CHARACTERS

MADAME PERNELLE, mother of Orgon
ORGON, husband of Elmire
ELMIRE, wife of Orgon
DAMIS, son of Orgon
MARIANE, daughter of Orgon, in love with Valere
CLEANTE, brother-in-law of Orgon
TARTUFFE, a hypocrite
DORINE, Mariane's maid
M. LOYAL, a bailiff
A Police Officer
FLIPOTTE, Madame Pernelle's servant

The Scene is at Paris

ACT I

SCENE I

MADAME PERNELLE and FLIPOTTE, her servant;
ELMIRE, MARIANE, CLEANTE,
DAMIS, DORINE

MADAME PERNELLE
Come, come, Flipotte, and let me get away.

ELMIRE
You hurry so, I hardly can attend you.

MADAME PERNELLE
Then don't, my daughter-in law. Stay where you are.
I can dispense with your polite attentions.

ELMIRE
We're only paying what is due you, mother.
Why must you go away in such a hurry?

MADAME PERNELLE
Because I can't endure your carryings-on,
And no one takes the slightest pains to please me.
I leave your house, I tell you, quite disgusted;
You do the opposite of my instructions;
You've no respect for anything; each one
Must have his say; it's perfect pandemonium.

DORINE
If . . .

MADAME PERNELLE
You're a servant wench, my girl, and much

Too full of gab, and too impertinent
And free with your advice on all occasions.

DAMIS
But . . .

MADAME PERNELLE
You're a fool, my boy — f, o, o, l
Just spells your name. Let grandma tell you that
I've said a hundred times to my poor son,
Your father, that you'd never come to good
Or give him anything but plague and torment.

MARIANE
I think . . .

MADAME PERNELLE
O dearie me, his little sister!
You're all demureness, butter wouldn't melt
In your mouth, one would think to look at you.
Still waters, though, they say . . . you know the proverb;
And I don't like your doings on the sly.

ELMIRE
But, mother . . .

MADAME PERNELLE
Daughter, by your leave, your conduct
In everything is altogether wrong;
You ought to set a good example for 'em;
Their dear departed mother did much better.
You are extravagant; and it offends me,
To see you always decked out like a princess.
A woman who would please her husband's eyes
Alone, wants no such wealth of fineries.

CLEANTE
But, madam, after all . . .

MADAME PERNELLE
Sir, as for you,
The lady's brother, I esteem you highly,
Love and respect you. But, sir, all the same,
If I were in my son's, her husband's, place,
I'd urgently entreat you not to come
Within our doors. You preach a way of living
That decent people cannot tolerate.
I'm rather frank with you; but that's my way —
I don't mince matters, when I mean a thing.

DAMIS
Mr. Tartuffe, your friend, is mighty lucky . . .

MADAME PERNELLE
He is a holy man, and must be heeded;
I can't endure, with any show of patience,
To hear a scatterbrains like you attack him.

DAMIS
What! Shall I let a bigot criticaster
Come and usurp a tyrant's power here?
And shall we never dare amuse ourselves
Till this fine gentleman deigns to consent?

DORINE
If we must hark to him, and heed his maxims,
There's not a thing we do but what's a crime;
He censures everything, this zealous carper.

MADAME PERNELLE
And all he censures is well censured, too.
He wants to guide you on the way to heaven;

My son should train you all to love him well.

DAMIS
No, madam, look you, nothing — not my father
Nor anything — can make me tolerate him.
I should belie my feelings not to say so.
His actions rouse my wrath at every turn;
And I foresee that there must come of it
An open rupture with this sneaking scoundrel.

DORINE
Besides, 'tis downright scandalous to see
This unknown upstart master of the house —
This vagabond, who hadn't, when he came,
Shoes to his feet, or clothing worth six farthings,
And who so far forgets his place, as now
To censure everything, and rule the roost!

MADAME PERNELLE
Eh! Mercy sakes alive! Things would go better
If all were governed by his pious orders.

DORINE
He passes for a saint in your opinion.
In fact, he's nothing but a hypocrite.

MADAME PERNELLE
Just listen to her tongue!

DORINE
I wouldn't trust him,
Nor yet his Lawrence, without bonds and surety.

MADAME PERNELLE
I don't know what the servant's character
May be; but I can guarantee the master

A holy man. You hate him and reject him
Because he tells home truths to all of you.
'Tis sin alone that moves his heart to anger,
And heaven's interest is his only motive.

DORINE
Of course. But why, especially of late,
Can he let nobody come near the house?
Is heaven offended at a civil call
That he should make so great a fuss about it?
I'll tell you, if you like, just what I think;
(Pointing to Elmire)
Upon my word, he's jealous of our mistress.

MADAME PERNELLE
You hold your tongue, and think what you are saying.
He's not alone in censuring these visits;
The turmoil that attends your sort of people,
Their carriages forever at the door,
And all their noisy footmen, flocked together,
Annoy the neighbourhood, and raise a scandal.
I'd gladly think there's nothing really wrong;
But it makes talk; and that's not as it should be.

CLEANTE
Eh! madam, can you hope to keep folk's tongues
From wagging? It would be a grievous thing
If, for the fear of idle talk about us,
We had to sacrifice our friends. No, no;
Even if we could bring ourselves to do it,
Think you that everyone would then be silenced?
Against backbiting there is no defence
So let us try to live in innocence,
To silly tattle pay no heed at all,
And leave the gossips free to vent their gall.

DORINE

Our neighbour Daphne, and her little husband,
Must be the ones who slander us, I'm thinking.
Those whose own conduct's most ridiculous,
Are always quickest to speak ill of others;
They never fail to seize at once upon
The slightest hint of any love affair,
And spread the news of it with glee, and give it
The character they'd have the world believe in.
By others' actions, painted in their colours,
They hope to justify their own; they think,
In the false hope of some resemblance, either
To make their own intrigues seem innocent,
Or else to make their neighbours share the blame
Which they are loaded with by everybody.

MADAME PERNELLE

These arguments are nothing to the purpose.
Orante, we all know, lives a perfect life;
Her thoughts are all of heaven; and I have heard
That she condemns the company you keep.

DORINE

O admirable pattern! Virtuous dame!
She lives the model of austerity;
But age has brought this piety upon her,
And she's a prude, now she can't help herself.
As long as she could capture men's attentions
She made the most of her advantages;
But, now she sees her beauty vanishing,
She wants to leave the world, that's leaving her,
And in the specious veil of haughty virtue
She'd hide the weakness of her worn-out charms.
That is the way with all your old coquettes;
They find it hard to see their lovers leave 'em;
And thus abandoned, their forlorn estate

Can find no occupation but a prude's.
These pious dames, in their austerity,
Must carp at everything, and pardon nothing.
They loudly blame their neighbours' way of living,
Not for religion's sake, but out of envy,
Because they can't endure to see another
Enjoy the pleasures age has weaned them from.

MADAME PERNELLE (to Elmire)
There! That's the kind of rigmarole to please you,
Daughter-in-law. One never has a chance
To get a word in edgewise, at your house,
Because this lady holds the floor all day;
But none the less, I mean to have my say, too.
I tell you that my son did nothing wiser
In all his life, than take this godly man
Into his household; heaven sent him here,
In your great need, to make you all repent;
For your salvation, you must hearken to him;
He censures nothing but deserves his censure.
These visits, these assemblies, and these balls,
Are all inventions of the evil spirit.
You never hear a word of godliness
At them — but idle cackle, nonsense, flimflam.
Our neighbour often comes in for a share,
The talk flies fast, and scandal fills the air;
It makes a sober person's head go round,
At these assemblies, just to hear the sound
Of so much gab, with not a word to say;
And as a learned man remarked one day
Most aptly, 'tis the Tower of Babylon,
Where all, beyond all limit, babble on.
And just to tell you how this point came in . . .

(To Cleante)
So! Now the gentlemen must snicker, must he?

Go find fools like yourself to make you laugh
And don't . . .

(To Elmire)
Daughter, good-bye; not one word more.
As for this house, I leave the half unsaid;
But I shan't soon set foot in it again,

(Cuffing Flipotte)
Come, you! What makes you dream and stand agape,
Hussy! I'll warm your ears in proper shape!
March, trollop, march!

SCENE II

CLEANTE, DORINE

CLEANTE
I won't escort her down,
For fear she might fall foul of me again;
The good old lady . . .

DORINE
Bless us! What a pity
She shouldn't hear the way you speak of her!
She'd surely tell you you're too "good" by half,
And that she's not so "old" as all that, neither!

CLEANTE
How she got angry with us all for nothing!
And how she seems possessed with her Tartuffe!

DORINE
Her case is nothing, though, beside her son's!

To see him, you would say he's ten times worse!
His conduct in our late unpleasantness [1]
Had won him much esteem, and proved his courage
In service of his king; but now he's like
A man besotted, since he's been so taken
With this Tartuffe. He calls him brother, loves him
A hundred times as much as mother, son,
Daughter, and wife. He tells him all his secrets
And lets him guide his acts, and rule his conscience.
He fondles and embraces him; a sweetheart
Could not, I think, be loved more tenderly;
At table he must have the seat of honour,
While with delight our master sees him eat
As much as six men could; we must give up
The choicest tidbits to him; if he belches,
('tis a servant speaking) [2]
Master exclaims: "God bless you!" — Oh, he dotes
Upon him! he's his universe, his hero;
He's lost in constant admiration, quotes him
On all occasions, takes his trifling acts
For wonders, and his words for oracles.
The fellow knows his dupe, and makes the most on't,
He fools him with a hundred masks of virtue,
Gets money from him all the time by canting,
And takes upon himself to carp at us.
Even his silly coxcomb of a lackey
Makes it his business to instruct us too;
He comes with rolling eyes to preach at us,
And throws away our ribbons, rouge, and patches.
The wretch, the other day, tore up a kerchief
That he had found, pressed in the /Golden Legend/,
Calling it a horrid crime for us to mingle
The devil's finery with holy things.

[Footnote 1: Referring to the rebellion called La Fronde, during
the

minority of Louis XIV.]

[Footnote 2: Moliere's note, inserted in the text of all the old editions. It is a curious illustration of the desire for uniformity and dignity of style in dramatic verse of the seventeenth century, that Moliere feels called on to apologize for a touch of realism like
this. Indeed, these lines were even omitted when the play was given.]

SCENE III

ELMIRE, MARIANE, DAMIS, CLEANTE, DORINE

ELMIRE (to Cleante)
You're very lucky to have missed the speech
She gave us at the door. I see my husband
Is home again. He hasn't seen me yet,
So I'll go up and wait till he comes in.

CLEANTE
And I, to save time, will await him here;
I'll merely say good-morning, and be gone.

SCENE IV

CLEANTE, DAMIS, DORINE

DAMIS
I wish you'd say a word to him about
My sister's marriage; I suspect Tartuffe
Opposes it, and puts my father up

To all these wretched shifts. You know, besides,
How nearly I'm concerned in it myself;
If love unites my sister and Valere,
I love his sister too; and if this marriage
Were to . . .

DORINE
He's coming.

SCENE V

ORGON, CLEANTE, DORINE

ORGON
Ah! Good morning, brother.

CLEANTE
I was just going, but am glad to greet you.
Things are not far advanced yet, in the country?

ORGON
Dorine . . .

(To Cleante)
Just wait a bit, please, brother-in-law.
Let me allay my first anxiety
By asking news about the family.

(To Dorine)
Has everything gone well these last two days?
What's happening? And how is everybody?

DORINE
Madam had fever, and a splitting headache

Day before yesterday, all day and evening.

ORGON
And how about Tartuffe?

DORINE
Tartuffe? He's well;
He's mighty well; stout, fat, fair, rosy-lipped.

ORGON
Poor man!

DORINE
At evening she had nausea
And could't touch a single thing for supper,
Her headache still was so severe.

ORGON
And how
About Tartuffe?

DORINE
He supped alone, before her,
And unctuously ate up two partridges,
As well as half a leg o' mutton, deviled.

ORGON
Poor man!

DORINE
All night she couldn't get a wink
Of sleep, the fever racked her so; and we
Had to sit up with her till daylight.

ORGON
How

About Tartuffe?

DORINE
Gently inclined to slumber,
He left the table, went into his room,
Got himself straight into a good warm bed,
And slept quite undisturbed until next morning.

ORGON
Poor man!

DORINE
At last she let us all persuade her,
And got up courage to be bled; and then
She was relieved at once.

ORGON
And how about
Tartuffe?

DORINE
He plucked up courage properly,
Bravely entrenched his soul against all evils,
And to replace the blood that she had lost,
He drank at breakfast four huge draughts of wine.

ORGON
Poor man!

DORINE
So now they both are doing well;
And I'll go straightway and inform my mistress
How pleased you are at her recovery.

SCENE VI

ORGON, CLEANTE

CLEANTE
Brother, she ridicules you to your face;
And I, though I don't want to make you angry,
Must tell you candidly that she's quite right.
Was such infatuation ever heard of?
And can a man to-day have charms to make you
Forget all else, relieve his poverty,
Give him a home, and then . . . ?

ORGON
Stop there, good brother,
You do not know the man you're speaking of.

CLEANTE
Since you will have it so, I do not know him;
But after all, to tell what sort of man
He is . . .

ORGON
Dear brother, you'd be charmed to know him;
Your raptures over him would have no end.
He is a man . . . who . . . ah! . . . in fact . . .a man
Whoever does his will, knows perfect peace,
And counts the whole world else, as so much dung.
His converse has transformed me quite; he weans
My heart from every friendship, teaches me
To have no love for anything on earth;
And I could see my brother, children, mother,
And wife, all die, and never care — a snap.

CLEANTE
Your feelings are humane, I must say, brother!

ORGON

Ah! If you'd seen him, as I saw him first,
You would have loved him just as much as I.
He came to church each day, with contrite mien,
Kneeled, on both knees, right opposite my place,
And drew the eyes of all the congregation,
To watch the fervour of his prayers to heaven;
With deep-drawn sighs and great ejaculations,
He humbly kissed the earth at every moment;
And when I left the church, he ran before me
To give me holy water at the door.
I learned his poverty, and who he was,
By questioning his servant, who is like him,
And gave him gifts; but in his modesty
He always wanted to return a part.
"It is too much," he'd say, "too much by half;
I am not worthy of your pity." Then,
When I refused to take it back, he'd go,
Before my eyes, and give it to the poor.
At length heaven bade me take him to my home,
And since that day, all seems to prosper here.
He censures everything, and for my sake
He even takes great interest in my wife;
He lets me know who ogles her, and seems
Six times as jealous as I am myself.
You'd not believe how far his zeal can go:
He calls himself a sinner just for trifles;
The merest nothing is enough to shock him;
So much so, that the other day I heard him
Accuse himself for having, while at prayer,
In too much anger caught and killed a flea.

CLEANTE

Zounds, brother, you are mad, I think! Or else
You're making sport of me, with such a speech.

What are you driving at with all this nonsense . . . ?

ORGON
Brother, your language smacks of atheism;
And I suspect your soul's a little tainted
Therewith. I've preached to you a score of times
That you'll draw down some judgment on your head.

CLEANTE
That is the usual strain of all your kind;
They must have every one as blind as they.
They call you atheist if you have good eyes;
And if you don't adore their vain grimaces,
You've neither faith nor care for sacred things.
No, no; such talk can't frighten me; I know
What I am saying; heaven sees my heart.
We're not the dupes of all your canting mummers;
There are false heroes — and false devotees;
And as true heroes never are the ones
Who make much noise about their deeds of honour,
Just so true devotees, whom we should follow,
Are not the ones who make so much vain show.
What! Will you find no difference between
Hypocrisy and genuine devoutness?
And will you treat them both alike, and pay
The self-same honour both to masks and faces
Set artifice beside sincerity,
Confuse the semblance with reality,
Esteem a phantom like a living person,
And counterfeit as good as honest coin?
Men, for the most part, are strange creatures, truly!
You never find them keep the golden mean;
The limits of good sense, too narrow for them,
Must always be passed by, in each direction;
They often spoil the noblest things, because
They go too far, and push them to extremes.

I merely say this by the way, good brother.

ORGON
You are the sole expounder of the doctrine;
Wisdom shall die with you, no doubt, good brother,
You are the only wise, the sole enlightened,
The oracle, the Cato, of our age.
All men, compared to you, are downright fools.

CLEANTE
I'm not the sole expounder of the doctrine,
And wisdom shall not die with me, good brother.
But this I know, though it be all my knowledge,
That there's a difference 'twixt false and true.
And as I find no kind of hero more
To be admired than men of true religion,
Nothing more noble or more beautiful
Than is the holy zeal of true devoutness;
Just so I think there's naught more odious
Than whited sepulchres of outward unction,
Those barefaced charlatans, those hireling zealots,
Whose sacrilegious, treacherous pretence
Deceives at will, and with impunity
Makes mockery of all that men hold sacred;
Men who, enslaved to selfish interests,
Make trade and merchandise of godliness,
And try to purchase influence and office
With false eye-rollings and affected raptures;
Those men, I say, who with uncommon zeal
Seek their own fortunes on the road to heaven;
Who, skilled in prayer, have always much to ask,
And live at court to preach retirement;
Who reconcile religion with their vices,
Are quick to anger, vengeful, faithless, tricky,
And, to destroy a man, will have the boldness
To call their private grudge the cause of heaven;

All the more dangerous, since in their anger
They use against us weapons men revere,
And since they make the world applaud their passion,
And seek to stab us with a sacred sword.
There are too many of this canting kind.
Still, the sincere are easy to distinguish;
And many splendid patterns may be found,
In our own time, before our very eyes
Look at Ariston, Periandre, Oronte,
Alcidamas, Clitandre, and Polydore;
No one denies their claim to true religion;
Yet they're no braggadocios of virtue,
They do not make insufferable display,
And their religion's human, tractable;
They are not always judging all our actions,
They'd think such judgment savoured of presumption;
And, leaving pride of words to other men,
'Tis by their deeds alone they censure ours.
Evil appearances find little credit
With them; they even incline to think the best
Of others. No caballers, no intriguers,
They mind the business of their own right living.
They don't attack a sinner tooth and nail,
For sin's the only object of their hatred;
Nor are they over-zealous to attempt
Far more in heaven's behalf than heaven would have 'em.
That is my kind of man, that is true living,
That is the pattern we should set ourselves.
Your fellow was not fashioned on this model;
You're quite sincere in boasting of his zeal;
But you're deceived, I think, by false pretences.

ORGON
My dear good brother-in-law, have you quite done?

CLEANTE
Yes.

ORGON
I'm your humble servant.

(Starts to go.)

CLEANTE
Just a word.
We'll drop that other subject. But you know
Valere has had the promise of your daughter.

ORGON
Yes.

CLEANTE
You had named the happy day.

ORGON
'Tis true.

CLEANTE
Then why put off the celebration of it?

ORGON
I can't say.

CLEANTE
Can you have some other plan
In mind?

ORGON
Perhaps.

CLEANTE

You mean to break your word?

ORGON
I don't say that.

CLEANTE
I hope no obstacle
Can keep you from performing what you've promised.

ORGON
Well, that depends.

CLEANTE
Why must you beat about?
Valere has sent me here to settle matters.

ORGON
Heaven be praised!

CLEANTE
What answer shall I take him?

ORGON
Why, anything you please.

CLEANTE
But we must know
Your plans. What are they?

ORGON
I shall do the will
Of Heaven.

CLEANTE
Come, be serious. You've given
Your promise to Valere. Now will you keep it?

ORGON
Good-bye.

CLEANTE (alone)
His love, methinks, has much to fear;
I must go let him know what's happening here.

ACT II

SCENE I

ORGON, MARIANE

ORGON
Now, Mariane.

MARIANE
Yes, father?

ORGON
Come; I'll tell you
A secret.

MARIANE
Yes . . . What are you looking for?

ORGON (looking into a small closet-room)
To see there's no one there to spy upon us;
That little closet's mighty fit to hide in.
There! We're all right now. Mariane, in you
I've always found a daughter dutiful
And gentle. So I've always love you dearly.

MARIANE
I'm grateful for your fatherly affection.

ORGON
Well spoken, daughter. Now, prove you deserve it
By doing as I wish in all respects.

MARIANE
To do so is the height of my ambition.

ORGON
Excellent well. What say you of — Tartuffe?

MARIANE
Who? I?

ORGON
Yes, you. Look to it how you answer.

MARIANE
Why! I'll say of him — anything you please.

SCENE II

ORGON, MARIANE, DORINE (coming in quietly and standing behind
Orgon, so that he does not see her)

ORGON
Well spoken. A good girl. Say then, my daughter,
That all his person shines with noble merit,
That he has won your heart, and you would like
To have him, by my choice, become your husband.
Eh?

MARIANE
Eh?

ORGON
What say you?

MARIANE
Please, what did you say?

ORGON
What?

MARIANE
Surely I mistook you, sir?

ORGON
How now?

MARIANE
Who is it, father, you would have me say
Has won my heart, and I would like to have
Become my husband, by your choice?

ORGON
Tartuffe.

MARIANE
But, father, I protest it isn't true!
Why should you make me tell this dreadful lie?

ORGON
Because I mean to have it be the truth.
Let this suffice for you: I've settled it.

MARIANE
What, father, you would . . . ?

ORGON
Yes, child, I'm resolved
To graft Tartuffe into my family.
So he must be your husband. That I've settled.
And since your duty . .

(Seeing Dorine)
What are you doing there?

Your curiosity is keen, my girl,
To make you come eavesdropping on us so.

DORINE
Upon my word, I don't know how the rumour
Got started — if 'twas guess-work or mere chance
But I had heard already of this match,
And treated it as utter stuff and nonsense.

ORGON
What! Is the thing incredible?

DORINE
So much so
I don't believe it even from yourself, sir.

ORGON
I know a way to make you credit it.

DORINE
No, no, you're telling us a fairly tale!

ORGON
I'm telling you just what will happen shortly.

DORINE
Stuff!

ORGON
Daughter, what I say is in good earnest.

DORINE
There, there, don't take your father seriously;
He's fooling.

ORGON
But I tell you . . .

DORINE
No. No use.
They won't believe you.

ORGON
If I let my anger . . .

DORINE
Well, then, we do believe you; and the worse
For you it is. What! Can a grown-up man
With that expanse of beard across his face
Be mad enough to want . . .?

ORGON
You hark me:
You've taken on yourself here in this house
A sort of free familiarity
That I don't like, I tell you frankly, girl.

DORINE
There, there, let's not get angry, sir, I beg you.
But are you making game of everybody?
Your daughter's not cut out for bigot's meat;
And he has more important things to think of.
Besides, what can you gain by such a match?
How can a man of wealth, like you, go choose
A wretched vagabond for son-in-law?

ORGON
You hold your tongue. And know, the less he has,
The better cause have we to honour him.
His poverty is honest poverty;
It should exalt him more than worldly grandeur,

For he has let himself be robbed of all,
Through careless disregard of temporal things
And fixed attachment to the things eternal.
My help may set him on his feet again,
Win back his property — a fair estate
He has at home, so I'm informed — and prove him
For what he is, a true-born gentleman.

DORINE
Yes, so he says himself. Such vanity
But ill accords with pious living, sir.
The man who cares for holiness alone
Should not so loudly boast his name and birth;
The humble ways of genuine devoutness
Brook not so much display of earthly pride.
Why should he be so vain? . . . But I offend you:
Let's leave his rank, then, — take the man himself:
Can you without compunction give a man
Like him possession of a girl like her?
Think what a scandal's sure to come of it!
Virtue is at the mercy of the fates,
When a girl's married to a man she hates;
The best intent to live an honest woman
Depends upon the husband's being human,
And men whose brows are pointed at afar
May thank themselves their wives are what they are.
For to be true is more than woman can,
With husbands built upon a certain plan;
And he who weds his child against her will
Owes heaven account for it, if she do ill.
Think then what perils wait on your design.

ORGON (to Mariane)
So! I must learn what's what from her, you see!

DORINE
You might do worse than follow my advice.

ORGON
Daughter, we can't waste time upon this nonsense;
I know what's good for you, and I'm your father.
True, I had promised you to young Valere;
But, first, they tell me he's inclined to gamble,
And then, I fear his faith is not quite sound.
I haven't noticed that he's regular
At church.

DORINE
You'd have him run there just when you do.
Like those who go on purpose to be seen?

ORGON
I don't ask your opinion on the matter.
In short, the other is in Heaven's best graces,
And that is riches quite beyond compare.
This match will bring you every joy you long for;
'Twill be all steeped in sweetness and delight.
You'll live together, in your faithful loves,
Like two sweet children, like two turtle-doves;
You'll never fail to quarrel, scold, or tease,
And you may do with him whate'er you please.

DORINE
With him? Do naught but give him horns, I'll warrant.

ORGON
Out on thee, wench!

DORINE
I tell you he's cut out for't;
However great your daughter's virtue, sir,

His destiny is sure to prove the stronger.

ORGON
Have done with interrupting. Hold your tongue.
Don't poke your nose in other people's business.

DORINE (She keeps interrupting him, just as he turns and starts
to speak to his daughter).
If I make bold, sir, 'tis for your own good.

ORGON
You're too officious; pray you, hold your tongue.

DORINE
'Tis love of you . . .

ORGON
I want none of your love.

DORINE
Then I will love you in your own despite.

ORGON
You will, eh?

DORINE
Yes, your honour's dear to me;
I can't endure to see you made the butt
Of all men's ridicule.

ORGON
Won't you be still?

DORINE
'Twould be a sin to let you make this match.

ORGON
Won't you be still, I say, you impudent viper!

DORINE
What! you are pious, and you lose your temper?

ORGON
I'm all wrought up, with your confounded nonsense;
Now, once for all, I tell you hold your tongue.

DORINE
Then mum's the word; I'll take it out in thinking.

ORGON
Think all you please; but not a syllable
To me about it, or . . . you understand!

(Turning to his daughter.)
As a wise father, I've considered all
With due deliberation.

DORINE
I'll go mad
If I can't speak.
(She stops the instant he turns his head.)

ORGON
Though he's no lady's man,
Tartuffe is well enough . . .

DORINE
A pretty phiz!

ORGON
So that, although you may not care at all
For his best qualities . . .

DORINE
A handsome dowry!

(Orgon turns and stands in front of her, with arms folded, eyeing her.)
Were I in her place, any man should rue it
Who married me by force, that's mighty certain;
I'd let him know, and that within a week,
A woman's vengeance isn't far to seek.

ORGON (to Dorine)
So — nothing that I say has any weight?

DORINE
Eh? What's wrong now? I didn't speak to you.

ORGON
What were you doing?

DORINE
Talking to myself.

ORGON
Oh! Very well. (Aside.) Her monstrous impudence
Must be chastised with one good slap in the face.

(He stands ready to strike her, and, each time he speaks to his daughter, he glances toward her; but she stands still and says not a word.) [3]

[Footnote 3: As given at the Comedie francaise, the action is as follows: While Orgon says, "You must approve of my design," Dorine is
making signs to Mariane to resist his orders; Orgon turns around

suddenly; but Dorine quickly changes her gesture and with the hand
which she had lifted calmly arranges her hair and her cap. Orgon goes
on, "Think of the husband . . ." and stops before the middle of his
sentence to turn and catch the beginning of Dorine's gesture; but he
is too quick this time, and Dorine stands looking at his furious
countenance with a sweet and gentle expression. He turns and goes on,
and the obstinate Dorine again lifts her hand behind his shoulder to
urge Mariane to resistance: this time he catches her; but just as he
swings his shoulder to give her the promised blow, she stops him by
changing the intent of her gesture, and carefully picking from the top
of his sleeve a bit of fluff which she holds carefully between her
fingers, then blows into the air, and watches intently as it floats
away. Orgon is paralysed by her innocence of expression, and compelled
to hide his rage. — Regnier, /Le Tartuffe des Comediens/.]

ORGON
Daughter, you must approve of my design. . . .
Think of this husband . . . I have chosen for you. . .

(To Dorine)
Why don't you talk to yourself?

DORINE
Nothing to say.

ORGON
One little word more.

DORINE
Oh, no, thanks. Not now.

ORGON
Sure, I'd have caught you.

DORINE
Faith, I'm no such fool.

ORGON
So, daughter, now obedience is the word;
You must accept my choice with reverence.

DORINE (running away)
You'd never catch me marrying such a creature.

ORGON (swinging his hand at her and missing her)
Daughter, you've such a pestilent hussy there
I can't live with her longer, without sin.
I can't discuss things in the state I'm in.
My mind's so flustered by her insolent talk,
To calm myself, I must go take a walk.

SCENE III

MARIANE, DORINE

DORINE
Say, have you lost the tongue from out your head?
And must I speak your role from A to Zed?
You let them broach a project that's absurd,
And don't oppose it with a single word!

MARIANE
What can I do? My father is the master.

DORINE
Do? Everything, to ward off such disaster.

MARIANE
But what?

DORINE
Tell him one doesn't love by proxy;
Tell him you'll marry for yourself, not him;
Since you're the one for whom the thing is done,
You are the one, not he, the man must please;
If his Tartuffe has charmed him so, why let him
Just marry him himself — no one will hinder.

MARIANE
A father's rights are such, it seems to me,
That I could never dare to say a word.

DORINE
Came, talk it out. Valere has asked your hand:
Now do you love him, pray, or do you not?

MARIANE
Dorine! How can you wrong my love so much,
And ask me such a question? Have I not
A hundred times laid bare my heart to you?
Do you know how ardently I love him?

DORINE
How do I know if heart and words agree,
And if in honest truth you really love him?

MARIANE
Dorine, you wrong me greatly if you doubt it;
I've shown my inmost feelings, all too plainly.

DORINE
So then, you love him?

MARIANE
Yes, devotedly.

DORINE
And he returns your love, apparently?

MARIANE
I think so.

DORINE
And you both alike are eager
To be well married to each other?

MARIANE
Surely.

DORINE
Then what's your plan about this other match?

MARIANE
To kill myself, if it is forced upon me.

DORINE
Good! That's a remedy I hadn't thought of.
Just die, and everything will be all right.
This medicine is marvellous, indeed!
It drives me mad to hear folk talk such nonsense.

MARIANE
Oh dear, Dorine you get in such a temper!
You have no sympathy for people's troubles.

DORINE
I have no sympathy when folk talk nonsense,
And flatten out as you do, at a pinch.

MARIANE
But what can you expect? — if one is timid? —

DORINE
But what is love worth, if it has no courage?

MARIANE
Am I not constant in my love for him?
Is't not his place to win me from my father?

DORINE
But if your father is a crazy fool,
And quite bewitched with his Tartuffe? And breaks
His bounden word? Is that your lover's fault?

MARIANE
But shall I publicly refuse and scorn
This match, and make it plain that I'm in love?
Shall I cast off for him, whate'er he be,
Womanly modesty and filial duty?
You ask me to display my love in public . . . ?

DORINE
No, no, I ask you nothing. You shall be
Mister Tartuffe's; why, now I think of it,
I should be wrong to turn you from this marriage.
What cause can I have to oppose your wishes?
So fine a match! An excellent good match!

Mister Tartuffe! Oh ho! No mean proposal!
Mister Tartuffe, sure, take it all in all,
Is not a man to sneeze at — oh, by no means!
'Tis no small luck to be his happy spouse.
The whole world joins to sing his praise already;
He's noble — in his parish; handsome too;
Red ears and high complexion — oh, my lud!
You'll be too happy, sure, with him for husband.

MARIANE
Oh dear! . . .

DORINE
What joy and pride will fill your heart
To be the bride of such a handsome fellow!

MARIANE
Oh, stop, I beg you; try to find some way
To help break off the match. I quite give in,
I'm ready to do anything you say.

DORINE
No, no, a daughter must obey her father,
Though he should want to make her wed a monkey.
Besides, your fate is fine. What could be better!
You'll take the stage-coach to his little village,
And find it full of uncles and of cousins,
Whose conversation will delight you. Then
You'll be presented in their best society.
You'll even go to call, by way of welcome,
On Mrs. Bailiff, Mrs. Tax-Collector,
Who'll patronize you with a folding-stool.
There, once a year, at carnival, you'll have
Perhaps — a ball; with orchestra — two bag-pipes;
And sometimes a trained ape, and Punch and Judy;
Though if your husband . . .

MARIANE
Oh, you'll kill me. Please
Contrive to help me out with your advice.

DORINE
I thank you kindly.

MARIANE
Oh! Dorine, I beg you . . .

DORINE
To serve you right, this marriage must go through.

MARIANE
Dear girl!

DORINE
No.

MARIANE
If I say I love Valere . . .

DORINE
No, no. Tartuffe's your man, and you shall taste him.

MARIANE
You know I've always trusted you; now help me . . .

DORINE
No, you shall be, my faith! Tartuffified.

MARIANE
Well, then, since you've no pity for my fate
Let me take counsel only of despair;
It will advise and help and give me courage;

There's one sure cure, I know, for all my troubles.

(She starts to go.)

DORINE
There, there! Come back. I can't be angry long.
I must take pity on you, after all.

MARIANE
Oh, don't you see, Dorine, if I must bear
This martyrdom, I certainly shall die.

DORINE
Now don't you fret. We'll surely find some way.
To hinder this . . . But here's Valere, your lover.

SCENE IV

VALERE, MARIANE, DORINE

VALERE
Madam, a piece of news — quite new to me —
Has just come out, and very fine it is.

MARIANE
What piece of news?

VALERE
Your marriage with Tartuffe.

MARIANE
'Tis true my father has this plan in mind.

VALERE

Your father, madam . . .

MARIANE
Yes, he's changed his plans,
And did but now propose it to me.

VALERE
What!
Seriously?

MARIANE
Yes, he was serious,
And openly insisted on the match.

VALERE
And what's your resolution in the matter,
Madam?

MARIANE
I don't know.

VALERE
That's a pretty answer.
You don't know?

MARIANE
No.

VALERE
No?

MARIANE
What do you advise?

VALERE
I? My advice is, marry him, by all means.

MARIANE
That's your advice?

VALERE
Yes.

MARIANE
Do you mean it?

VALERE
Surely.
A splendid choice, and worthy of your acceptance.

MARIANE
Oh, very well, sir! I shall take your counsel.

VALERE
You'll find no trouble taking it, I warrant.

MARIANE
No more than you did giving it, be sure.

VALERE
I gave it, truly, to oblige you, madam.

MARIANE
And I shall take it to oblige you, sir.

Dorine (withdrawing to the back of the stage)
Let's see what this affair will come to.

VALERE
So,
That is your love? And it was all deceit
When you . . .

MARIANE
I beg you, say no more of that.
You told me, squarely, sir, I should accept
The husband that is offered me; and I
Will tell you squarely that I mean to do so,
Since you have given me this good advice.

VALERE
Don't shield yourself with talk of my advice.
You had your mind made up, that's evident;
And now you're snatching at a trifling pretext
To justify the breaking of your word.

MARIANE
Exactly so.

VALERE
Of course it is; your heart
Has never known true love for me.

MARIANE
Alas!
You're free to think so, if you please.

VALERE
Yes, yes,
I'm free to think so; and my outraged love
May yet forestall you in your perfidy,
And offer elsewhere both my heart and hand.

MARIANE
No doubt of it; the love your high deserts
May win . . .

VALERE

Good Lord, have done with my deserts!
I know I have but few, and you have proved it.
But I may find more kindness in another;
I know of someone, who'll not be ashamed
To take your leavings, and make up my loss.

MARIANE
The loss is not so great; you'll easily
Console yourself completely for this change.

VALERE
I'll try my best, that you may well believe.
When we're forgotten by a woman's heart,
Our pride is challenged; we, too, must forget;
Or if we cannot, must at least pretend to.
No other way can man such baseness prove,
As be a lover scorned, and still in love.

MARIANE
In faith, a high and noble sentiment.

VALERE
Yes; and it's one that all men must approve.
What! Would you have me keep my love alive,
And see you fly into another's arms
Before my very eyes; and never offer
To someone else the heart that you had scorned?

MARIANE
Oh, no, indeed! For my part, I could wish
That it were done already.

VALERE
What! You wish it?

MARIANE
Yes.

VALERE
This is insult heaped on injury;
I'll go at once and do as you desire.

(He takes a step or two as if to go away.)

MARIANE
Oh, very well then.

VALERE (turning back)
But remember this.
'Twas you that drove me to this desperate pass.

MARIANE
Of course.

VALERE (turning back again)
And in the plan that I have formed
I only follow your example.

MARIANE
Yes.

VALERE (at the door)
Enough; you shall be punctually obeyed.

MARIANE
So much the better.

VALERE (coming back again)
This is once for all.

MARIANE
So be it, then.

VALERE (He goes toward the door, but just as he reaches it, turns
around)
Eh?

MARIANE
What?

VALERE
You didn't call me?

MARIANE
I? You are dreaming.

VALERE
Very well, I'm gone. Madam, farewell.

(He walks slowly away.)

MARIANE
Farewell, sir.

DORINE
I must say
You've lost your senses and both gone clean daft!
I've let you fight it out to the end o' the chapter
To see how far the thing could go. Oho, there,
Mister Valere!

(She goes and seizes him by the arm, to stop him. He makes a great
show of resistance.)

VALERE
What do you want, Dorine?

DORINE
Come here.

VALERE
No, no, I'm quite beside myself.
Don't hinder me from doing as she wishes.

DORINE
Stop!

VALERE
No. You see, I'm fixed, resolved, determined.

DORINE
So!

MARIANE (aside)
Since my presence pains him, makes him go,
I'd better go myself, and leave him free.

DORINE (leaving Valere, and running after Mariane)
Now t'other! Where are you going?

MARIANE
Let me be.

DORINE.
Come back.

MARIANE
No, no, it isn't any use.

VALERE (aside)
'Tis clear the sight of me is torture to her;
No doubt, t'were better I should free her from it.

DORINE (leaving Mariane and running after Valere)
Same thing again! Deuce take you both, I say.
Now stop your fooling; come here, you; and you.

(She pulls first one, then the other, toward the middle of the
stage.)

VALERE (to Dorine)
What's your idea?

MARIANE (to Dorine)
What can you mean to do?

DORINE
Set you to rights, and pull you out o' the scrape.

(To Valere)
Are you quite mad, to quarrel with her now?

VALERE
Didn't you hear the things she said to me?

DORINE (to Mariane)
Are you quite mad, to get in such a passion?

MARIANE
Didn't you see the way he treated me?

DORINE
Fools, both of you.

(To Valere)

She thinks of nothing else
But to keep faith with you, I vouch for it.

(To Mariane)
And he loves none but you, and longs for nothing
But just to marry you, I stake my life on't.

MARIANE (to Valere)
Why did you give me such advice then, pray?

VALERE (to Mariane)
Why ask for my advice on such a matter?

DORINE
You both are daft, I tell you. Here, your hands.

(To Valere)
Come, yours.

VALERE (giving Dorine his hand)
What for?

DORINE (to Mariane)
Now, yours.

MARIANE (giving Dorine her hand)
But what's the use?

DORINE
Oh, quick now, come along. There, both of you —
You love each other better than you think.

(Valere and Mariane hold each other's hands some time without looking
at each other.)

VALERE (at last turning toward Mariane)
Come, don't be so ungracious now about it;
Look at a man as if you didn't hate him.

(Mariane looks sideways toward Valere, with just a bit of a
smile.)

DORINE
My faith and troth, what fools these lovers be!

VALERE (to Mariane)
But come now, have I not a just complaint?
And truly, are you not a wicked creature
To take delight in saying what would pain me?

MARIANE
And are you not yourself the most ungrateful . . . ?

DORINE
Leave this discussion till another time;
Now, think how you'll stave off this plaguy marriage.

MARIANE
Then tell us how to go about it.

DORINE
Well,
We'll try all sorts of ways.

(To Mariane)
Your father's daft;

(To Valere)
This plan is nonsense.

(To Mariane)

You had better humour
His notions by a semblance of consent,
So that in case of danger, you can still
Find means to block the marriage by delay.
If you gain time, the rest is easy, trust me.
One day you'll fool them with a sudden illness,
Causing delay; another day, ill omens:
You've met a funeral, or broke a mirror,
Or dreamed of muddy water. Best of all,
They cannot marry you to anyone
Without your saying yes. But now, methinks,
They mustn't find you chattering together.

(To Valere)
You, go at once and set your friends at work
To make him keep his word to you; while we
Will bring the brother's influence to bear,
And get the step-mother on our side, too.
Good-bye.

VALERE (to Mariane)
Whatever efforts we may make,
My greatest hope, be sure, must rest on you.

MARIANE (to Valere)
I cannot answer for my father's whims;
But no one save Valere shall ever have me.

VALERE
You thrill me through with joy! Whatever comes . . .

DORINE
Oho! These lovers! Never done with prattling!
Now go.

VALERE (starting to go, and coming back again)

One last word . . .

DORINE
What a gabble and pother!
Be off! By this door, you. And you, by t'other.

(She pushes them off, by the shoulders, in opposite directions.)

ACT III

SCENE I

DAMIS, DORINE

DAMIS
May lightning strike me dead this very instant,
May I be everywhere proclaimed a scoundrel,
If any reverence or power shall stop me,
And if I don't do straightway something desperate!

DORINE
I beg you, moderate this towering passion;
Your father did but merely mention it.
Not all things that are talked of turn to facts;
The road is long, sometimes, from plans to acts.

DAMIS
No, I must end this paltry fellow's plots,
And he shall hear from me a truth or two.

DORINE
So ho! Go slow now. Just you leave the fellow —
Your father too — in your step-mother's hands.
She has some influence with this Tartuffe,
He makes a point of heeding all she says,
And I suspect that he is fond of her.
Would God 'twere true! — 'Twould be the height of humour
Now, she has sent for him, in your behalf,
To sound him on this marriage, to find out
What his ideas are, and to show him plainly
What troubles he may cause, if he persists
In giving countenance to this design.
His man says, he's at prayers, I mustn't see him,

But likewise says, he'll presently be down.
So off with you, and let me wait for him.

DAMIS
I may be present at this interview.

DORINE
No, no! They must be left alone.

DAMIS
I won't
So much as speak to him.

DORINE
Go on! We know you
And your high tantrums. Just the way to spoil things!
Be off.

DAMIS
No, I must see — I'll keep my temper.

DORINE
Out on you, what a plague! He's coming. Hide!

(Damis goes and hides in the closet at the back of the stage.)

SCENE II

TARTUFFE, DORINE

TARTUFFE (speaking to his valet, off the stage, as soon as he sees
Dorine is there)
Lawrence, put up my hair-cloth shirt and scourge,

And pray that Heaven may shed its light upon you.
If any come to see me, say I'm gone
To share my alms among the prisoners.

DORINE (aside)
What affectation and what showing off!

TARTUFFE
What do you want with me?

DORINE
To tell you . . .

TARTUFFE (taking a handkerchief from his pocket)
Ah!
Before you speak, pray take this handkerchief.

DORINE
What?

TARTUFFE
Cover up that bosom, which I can't
Endure to look on. Things like that offend
Our souls, and fill our minds with sinful thoughts.

DORINE
Are you so tender to temptation, then,
And has the flesh such power upon your senses?
I don't know how you get in such a heat;
For my part, I am not so prone to lust,
And I could see you stripped from head to foot,
And all your hide not tempt me in the least.

TARTUFFE
Show in your speech some little modesty,
Or I must instantly take leave of you.

DORINE
No, no, I'll leave you to yourself; I've only
One thing to say: Madam will soon be down,
And begs the favour of a word with you.

TARTUFFE
Ah! Willingly.

DORINE (aside)
How gentle all at once!
My faith, I still believe I've hit upon it.

TARTUFFE
Will she come soon?

DORINE
I think I hear her now.
Yes, here she is herself; I'll leave you with her.

SCENE III

ELMIRE, TARTUFFE

TARTUFFE
May Heaven's overflowing kindness ever
Give you good health of body and of soul,
And bless your days according to the wishes
And prayers of its most humble votary!

ELMIRE
I'm very grateful for your pious wishes.
But let's sit down, so we may talk at ease.

TARTUFFE (after sitting down)
And how are you recovered from your illness?

ELMIRE (sitting down also)
Quite well; the fever soon let go its hold.

TARTUFFE
My prayers, I fear, have not sufficient merit
To have drawn down this favour from on high;
But each entreaty that I made to Heaven
Had for its object your recovery.

ELMIRE
You're too solicitous on my behalf.

TARTUFFE
We could not cherish your dear health too much;
I would have given mine, to help restore it.

ELMIRE
That's pushing Christian charity too far;
I owe you many thanks for so much kindness.

TARTUFFE
I do far less for you than you deserve.

ELMIRE
There is a matter that I wished to speak of
In private; I am glad there's no one here
To listen.

TARTUFFE
Madam, I am overjoyed.
'Tis sweet to find myself alone with you.
This is an opportunity I've asked
Of Heaven, many a time; till now, in vain.

ELMIRE
All that I wish, is just a word from you,
Quite frank and open, hiding nothing from me.

(DAMIS, without their seeing him, opens the closet door
halfway.)

TARTUFFE
I too could wish, as Heaven's especial favour,
To lay my soul quite open to your eyes,
And swear to you, the trouble that I made
About those visits which your charms attract,
Does not result from any hatred toward you,
But rather from a passionate devotion,
And purest motives . . .

ELMIRE
That is how I take it,
I think 'tis my salvation that concerns you.

TARTUFFE (pressing her finger tips)
Madam, 'tis so; and such is my devotion . . .

ELMIRE
Ouch! but you squeeze too hard.

TARTUFFE
Excess of zeal.
In no way could I ever mean to hurt you,
And I'd as soon . . .

(He puts his hand on her knee.)

ELMIRE
What's your hand doing there?

TARTUFFE
Feeling your gown; the stuff is very soft.

ELMIRE
Let be, I beg you; I am very ticklish.

(She moves her chair away, and Tartuffe brings his nearer.)

TARTUFFE (handling the lace yoke of Elmire's dress)
Dear me how wonderful in workmanship
This lace is! They do marvels, nowadays;
Things of all kinds were never better made.

ELMIRE
Yes, very true. But let us come to business.
They say my husband means to break his word.
And marry Mariane to you. Is't so?

TARTUFFE
He did hint some such thing; but truly, madam,
That's not the happiness I'm yearning after;
I see elsewhere the sweet compelling charms
Of such a joy as fills my every wish.

ELMIRE
You mean you cannot love terrestrial things.

TARTUFFE
The heart within my bosom is not stone.

ELMIRE
I well believe your sighs all tend to Heaven,
And nothing here below can stay your thoughts.

TARTUFFE

Love for the beauty of eternal things
Cannot destroy our love for earthly beauty;
Our mortal senses well may be entranced
By perfect works that Heaven has fashioned here.
Its charms reflected shine in such as you,
And in yourself, its rarest miracles;
It has displayed such marvels in your face,
That eyes are dazed, and hearts are rapt away;
I could not look on you, the perfect creature,
Without admiring Nature's great Creator,
And feeling all my heart inflamed with love
For you, His fairest image of Himself.
At first I trembled lest this secret love
Might be the Evil Spirit's artful snare;
I even schooled my heart to flee your beauty,
Thinking it was a bar to my salvation.
But soon, enlightened, O all lovely one,
I saw how this my passion may be blameless,
How I may make it fit with modesty,
And thus completely yield my heart to it.
'Tis I must own, a great presumption in me
To dare make you the offer of my heart;
My love hopes all things from your perfect goodness,
And nothing from my own poor weak endeavour.
You are my hope, my stay, my peace of heart;
On you depends my torment or my bliss;
And by your doom of judgment, I shall be
Blest, if you will; or damned, by your decree.

ELMIRE

Your declaration's turned most gallantly;
But truly, it is just a bit surprising.
You should have better armed your heart, methinks,
And taken thought somewhat on such a matter.
A pious man like you, known everywhere . . .

TARTUFFE
Though pious, I am none the less a man;
And when a man beholds your heavenly charms,
The heart surrenders, and can think no more.
I know such words seem strange, coming from me;
But, madam, I'm no angel, after all;
If you condemn my frankly made avowal
You only have your charming self to blame.
Soon as I saw your more than human beauty,
You were thenceforth the sovereign of my soul;
Sweetness ineffable was in your eyes,
That took by storm my still resisting heart,
And conquered everything, fasts, prayers, and tears,
And turned my worship wholly to yourself.
My looks, my sighs, have spoke a thousand times;
Now, to express it all, my voice must speak.
If but you will look down with gracious favour
Upon the sorrows of your worthless slave,
If in your goodness you will give me comfort
And condescend unto my nothingness,
I'll ever pay you, O sweet miracle,
An unexampled worship and devotion.
Then too, with me your honour runs no risk;
With me you need not fear a public scandal.
These court gallants, that women are so fond of,
Are boastful of their acts, and vain in speech;
They always brag in public of their progress;
Soon as a favour's granted, they'll divulge it;
Their tattling tongues, if you but trust to them,
Will foul the altar where their hearts have worshipped.
But men like me are so discreet in love,
That you may trust their lasting secrecy.
The care we take to guard our own good name
May fully guarantee the one we love;
So you may find, with hearts like ours sincere,

Love without scandal, pleasure without fear.

ELMIRE
I've heard you through — your speech is clear, at least.
But don't you fear that I may take a fancy
To tell my husband of your gallant passion,
And that a prompt report of this affair
May somewhat change the friendship which he bears you?

TARTUFFE
I know that you're too good and generous,
That you will pardon my temerity,
Excuse, upon the score of human frailty,
The violence of passion that offends you,
And not forget, when you consult your mirror,
That I'm not blind, and man is made of flesh.

ELMIRE
Some women might do otherwise, perhaps,
But I am willing to employ discretion,
And not repeat the matter to my husband;
But in return, I'll ask one thing of you:
That you urge forward, frankly and sincerely,
The marriage of Valere to Mariane;
That you give up the unjust influence
By which you hope to win another's rights;
And . . .

SCENE IV

ELMIRE, DAMIS, TARTUFFE

DAMIS (coming out of the closet-room where he had been hiding)

No, I say! This thing must be made public.
I was just there, and overheard it all;
And Heaven's goodness must have brought me there
On purpose to confound this scoundrel's pride
And grant me means to take a signal vengeance
On his hypocrisy and arrogance,
And undeceive my father, showing up
The rascal caught at making love to you.

ELMIRE
No, no; it is enough if he reforms,
Endeavouring to deserve the favour shown him.
And since I've promised, do not you belie me.
'Tis not my way to make a public scandal;
An honest wife will scorn to heed such follies,
And never fret her husband's ears with them.

DAMIS
You've reasons of your own for acting thus;
And I have mine for doing otherwise.
To spare him now would be a mockery;
His bigot's pride has triumphed all too long
Over my righteous anger, and has caused
Far too much trouble in our family.
The rascal all too long has ruled my father,
And crossed my sister's love, and mine as well.
The traitor now must be unmasked before him:
And Providence has given me means to do it.
To Heaven I owe the opportunity,
And if I did not use it now I have it,
I should deserve to lose it once for all.

ELMIRE
Damis . . .

DAMIS
No, by your leave; I'll not be counselled.
I'm overjoyed. You needn't try to tell me
I must give up the pleasure of revenge.
I'll make an end of this affair at once;
And, to content me, here's my father now.

SCENE V

ORGON, ELMIRE, DAMIS, TARTUFFE

DAMIS
Father, we've news to welcome your arrival,
That's altogether novel, and surprising.
You are well paid for your caressing care,
And this fine gentleman rewards your love
Most handsomely, with zeal that seeks no less
Than your dishonour, as has now been proven.
I've just surprised him making to your wife
The shameful offer of a guilty love.
She, somewhat over gentle and discreet,
Insisted that the thing should be concealed;
But I will not condone such shamelessness,
Nor so far wrong you as to keep it secret.

ELMIRE
Yes, I believe a wife should never trouble
Her husband's peace of mind with such vain gossip;
A woman's honour does not hang on telling;
It is enough if she defend herself;
Or so I think; Damis, you'd not have spoken,
If you would but have heeded my advice.

SCENE VI

ORGON, DAMIS, TARTUFFE

ORGON
Just Heaven! Can what I hear be credited?

TARTUFFE
Yes, brother, I am wicked, I am guilty,
A miserable sinner, steeped in evil,
The greatest criminal that ever lived.
Each moment of my life is stained with soilures;
And all is but a mass of crime and filth;
Heaven, for my punishment, I see it plainly,
Would mortify me now. Whatever wrong
They find to charge me with, I'll not deny it
But guard against the pride of self-defence.
Believe their stories, arm your wrath against me,
And drive me like a villain from your house;
I cannot have so great a share of shame
But what I have deserved a greater still.

ORGON (to his son)
You miscreant, can you dare, with such a falsehood,
To try to stain the whiteness of his virtue?

DAMIS
What! The feigned meekness of this hypocrite
Makes you discredit . . .

ORGON
Silence, cursed plague!

TARTUFFE
Ah! Let him speak; you chide him wrongfully;

You'd do far better to believe his tales.
Why favour me so much in such a matter?
How can you know of what I'm capable?
And should you trust my outward semblance, brother,
Or judge therefrom that I'm the better man?
No, no; you let appearances deceive you;
I'm anything but what I'm thought to be,
Alas! and though all men believe me godly,
The simple truth is, I'm a worthless creature.

(To Damis)
Yes, my dear son, say on, and call me traitor,
Abandoned scoundrel, thief, and murderer;
Heap on me names yet more detestable,
And I shall not gainsay you; I've deserved them;
I'll bear this ignominy on my knees,
To expiate in shame the crimes I've done.

ORGON (to Tartuffe)
Ah, brother, 'tis too much!

(To his son)
You'll not relent,
You blackguard?

DAMIS
What! His talk can so deceive you . . .

ORGON
Silence, you scoundrel!

(To Tartuffe)
Brother, rise, I beg you.

(To his son)
Infamous villain!

DAMIS
Can he . . .

ORGON
Silence!

DAMIS
What . . .

ORGON
Another word, I'll break your every bone.

TARTUFFE
Brother, in God's name, don't be angry with him!
I'd rather bear myself the bitterest torture
Than have him get a scratch on my account.

ORGON (to his son)
Ungrateful monster!

TARTUFFE
Stop. Upon my knees
I beg you pardon him . . .

ORGON (throwing himself on his knees too, and embracing
Tartuffe)
Alas! How can you?

(To his son)
Villain! Behold his goodness!

DAMIS
So . . .

ORGON

Be still.

DAMIS
What! I . . .

ORGON
Be still, I say. I know your motives
For this attack. You hate him, all of you;
Wife, children, servants, all let loose upon him,
You have recourse to every shameful trick
To drive this godly man out of my house;
The more you strive to rid yourselves of him,
The more I'll strive to make him stay with me;
I'll have him straightway married to my daughter,
Just to confound the pride of all of you.

DAMIS
What! Will you force her to accept his hand?

ORGON
Yes, and this very evening, to enrage you,
Young rascal! Ah! I'll brave you all, and show you
That I'm the master, and must be obeyed.
Now, down upon your knees this instant, rogue,
And take back what you said, and ask his pardon.

DAMIS
Who? I? Ask pardon of that cheating scoundrel . . . ?

ORGON
Do you resist, you beggar, and insult him?
A cudgel, here! a cudgel!

(To Tartuffe)
Don't restrain me.

(To his son)
Off with you! Leave my house this instant, sirrah,
And never dare set foot in it again.

DAMIS
Yes, I will leave your house, but . . .

ORGON
Leave it quickly.
You reprobate, I disinherit you,
And give you, too, my curse into the bargain.

SCENE VII

ORGON, TARTUFFE

ORGON
What! So insult a saintly man of God!

TARTUFFE
Heaven, forgive him all the pain he gives me! [4]

[Footnote 4: Some modern editions have adopted the reading, preserved
by tradition as that of the earliest stage version: Heaven, forgive
him even as I forgive him! Voltaire gives still another reading:
Heaven, forgive me even as I forgive him! Whichever was the original
version, it appears in none of the early editions, and Moliere
probably felt forced to change it on account of its too close
resemblance to the Biblical phrase.]

(To Orgon)

Could you but know with what distress I see
Them try to vilify me to my brother!

ORGON
Ah!

TARTUFFE
The mere thought of such ingratitude
Makes my soul suffer torture, bitterly . . .
My horror at it . . . Ah! my heart's so full
I cannot speak . . . I think I'll die of it.

ORGON (in tears, running to the door through which he drove away his
son)
Scoundrel! I wish I'd never let you go,
But slain you on the spot with my own hand.

(To Tartuffe)
Brother, compose yourself, and don't be angry.

TARTUFFE
Nay, brother, let us end these painful quarrels.
I see what troublous times I bring upon you,
And think 'tis needful that I leave this house.

ORGON
What! You can't mean it?

TARTUFFE
Yes, they hate me here,
And try, I find, to make you doubt my faith.

ORGON
What of it? Do you find I listen to them?

TARTUFFE
No doubt they won't stop there. These same reports
You now reject, may some day win a hearing.

ORGON
No, brother, never.

TARTUFFE
Ah! my friend, a woman
May easily mislead her husband's mind.

ORGON
No, no.

TARTUFFE
So let me quickly go away
And thus remove all cause for such attacks.

ORGON
No, you shall stay; my life depends upon it.

TARTUFFE
Then I must mortify myself. And yet,
If you should wish . . .

ORGON
No, never!

TARTUFFE
Very well, then;
No more of that. But I shall rule my conduct
To fit the case. Honour is delicate,
And friendship binds me to forestall suspicion,
Prevent all scandal, and avoid your wife.

ORGON

No, you shall haunt her, just to spite them all.
'Tis my delight to set them in a rage;
You shall be seen together at all hours
And what is more, the better to defy them,
I'll have no other heir but you; and straightway
I'll go and make a deed of gift to you,
Drawn in due form, of all my property.
A good true friend, my son-in-law to be,
Is more to me than son, and wife, and kindred.
You will accept my offer, will you not?

TARTUFFE
Heaven's will be done in everything!

ORGON
Poor man!
We'll go make haste to draw the deed aright,
And then let envy burst itself with spite!

ACT IV

SCENE I

CLEANTE, TARTUFFE

CLEANTE
Yes, it's become the talk of all the town,
And make a stir that's scarcely to your credit;
And I have met you, sir, most opportunely,
To tell you in a word my frank opinion.
Not to sift out this scandal to the bottom,
Suppose the worst for us — suppose Damis
Acted the traitor, and accused you falsely;
Should not a Christian pardon this offence,
And stifle in his heart all wish for vengeance?
Should you permit that, for your petty quarrel,
A son be driven from his father's house?
I tell you yet again, and tell you frankly,
Everyone, high or low, is scandalised;
If you'll take my advice, you'll make it up,
And not push matters to extremities.
Make sacrifice to God of your resentment;
Restore the son to favour with his father.

TARTUFFE
Alas! So far as I'm concerned, how gladly
Would I do so! I bear him no ill will;
I pardon all, lay nothing to his charge,
And wish with all my heart that I might serve him;
But Heaven's interests cannot allow it;
If he returns, then I must leave the house.
After his conduct, quite unparalleled,
All intercourse between us would bring scandal;
God knows what everyone's first thought would be!

They would attribute it to merest scheming
On my part — say that conscious of my guilt
I feigned a Christian love for my accuser,
But feared him in my heart, and hoped to win him
And underhandedly secure his silence.

CLEANTE
You try to put us off with specious phrases;
But all your arguments are too far-fetched.
Why take upon yourself the cause of Heaven?
Does Heaven need our help to punish sinners?
Leave to itself the care of its own vengeance,
And keep in mind the pardon it commands us;
Besides, think somewhat less of men's opinions,
When you are following the will of Heaven.
Shall petty fear of what the world may think
Prevent the doing of a noble deed?
No! — let us always do as Heaven commands,
And not perplex our brains with further questions.

TARTUFFE
Already I have told you I forgive him;
And that is doing, sir, as Heaven commands.
But after this day's scandal and affront
Heaven does not order me to live with him.

CLEANTE
And does it order you to lend your ear
To what mere whim suggested to his father,
And to accept gift of his estates,
On which, in justice, you can make no claim?

TARTUFFE
No one who knows me, sir, can have the thought
That I am acting from a selfish motive.
The goods of this world have no charms for me;

I am not dazzled by their treacherous glamour;
And if I bring myself to take the gift
Which he insists on giving me, I do so,
To tell the truth, only because I fear
This whole estate may fall into bad hands,
And those to whom it comes may use it ill
And not employ it, as is my design,
For Heaven's glory and my neighbours' good.

CLEANTE
Eh, sir, give up these conscientious scruples
That well may cause a rightful heir's complaints.
Don't take so much upon yourself, but let him
Possess what's his, at his own risk and peril;
Consider, it were better he misused it,
Than you should be accused of robbing him.
I am astounded that unblushingly
You could allow such offers to be made!
Tell me — has true religion any maxim
That teaches us to rob the lawful heir?
If Heaven has made it quite impossible
Damis and you should live together here,
Were it not better you should quietly
And honourably withdraw, than let the son
Be driven out for your sake, dead against
All reason? 'Twould be giving, sir, believe me,
Such an example of your probity . . .

TARTUFFE
Sir, it is half-past three; certain devotions
Recall me to my closet; you'll forgive me
For leaving you so soon.

CLEANTE (alone)
Ah!

SCENE II

ELMIRE, MARIANE, CLEANTE, DORINE

DORINE (to Cleante)
Sir, we beg you
To help us all you can in her behalf;
She's suffering almost more than heart can bear;
This match her father means to make to-night
Drives her each moment to despair. He's coming.
Let us unite our efforts now, we beg you,
And try by strength or skill to change his purpose.

SCENE III

ORGON, ELMIRE, MARIANE, CLEANTE, DORINE

ORGON
So ho! I'm glad to find you all together.

(To Mariane)
Here is the contract that shall make you happy,
My dear. You know already what it means.

MARIANE (on her knees before Orgon)
Father, I beg you, in the name of Heaven
That knows my grief, and by whate'er can move you,
Relax a little your paternal rights,
And free my love from this obedience!
Oh, do not make me, by your harsh command,
Complain to Heaven you ever were my father;
Do not make wretched this poor life you gave me.

If, crossing that fond hope which I had formed,
You'll not permit me to belong to one
Whom I have dared to love, at least, I beg you
Upon my knees, oh, save me from the torment
Of being possessed by one whom I abhor!
And do not drive me to some desperate act
By exercising all your rights upon me.

ORGON (a little touched)
Come, come, my heart, be firm! no human weakness!

MARIANE
I am not jealous of your love for him;
Display it freely; give him your estate,
And if that's not enough, add all of mine;
I willingly agree, and give it up,
If only you'll not give him me, your daughter;
Oh, rather let a convent's rigid rule
Wear out the wretched days that Heaven allots me.

ORGON
These girls are ninnies! — always turning nuns
When fathers thwart their silly love-affairs.
Get on your feet! The more you hate to have him,
The more 'twill help you earn your soul's salvation.
So, mortify your senses by this marriage,
And don't vex me about it any more.

DORINE
But what . . . ?

ORGON
You hold your tongue, before your betters.
Don't dare to say a single word, I tell you.

CLEANTE
If you will let me answer, and advise . . .

ORGON
Brother, I value your advice most highly;
'Tis well thought out; no better can be had;
But you'll allow me — not to follow it.

ELMIRE (to her husband)
I can't find words to cope with such a case;
Your blindness makes me quite astounded at you.
You are bewitched with him, to disbelieve
The things we tell you happened here to-day.

ORGON
I am your humble servant, and can see
Things, when they're plain as noses on folks' faces,
I know you're partial to my rascal son,
And didn't dare to disavow the trick
He tried to play on this poor man; besides,
You were too calm, to be believed; if that
Had happened, you'd have been far more disturbed.

ELMIRE
And must our honour always rush to arms
At the mere mention of illicit love?
Or can we answer no attack upon it
Except with blazing eyes and lips of scorn?
For my part, I just laugh away such nonsense;
I've no desire to make a loud to-do.
Our virtue should, I think, be gentle-natured;
Nor can I quite approve those savage prudes
Whose honour arms itself with teeth and claws
To tear men's eyes out at the slightest word.
Heaven preserve me from that kind of honour!
I like my virtue not to be a vixen,

And I believe a quiet cold rebuff
No less effective to repulse a lover.

ORGON
I know . . . and you can't throw me off the scent.

ELMIRE
Once more, I am astounded at your weakness;
I wonder what your unbelief would answer,
If I should let you see we've told the truth?

ORGON
See it?

ELMIRE
Yes.

ORGON
Nonsense.

ELMIRE
Come! If I should find
A way to make you see it clear as day?

ORGON
All rubbish.

ELMIRE
What a man! But answer me.
I'm not proposing now that you believe us;
But let's suppose that here, from proper hiding,
You should be made to see and hear all plainly;
What would you say then, to your man of virtue?

ORGON
Why, then, I'd say . . . say nothing. It can't be.

ELMIRE
Your error has endured too long already,
And quite too long you've branded me a liar.
I must at once, for my own satisfaction,
Make you a witness of the things we've told you.

ORGON
Amen! I take you at your word. We'll see
What tricks you have, and how you'll keep your promise.

ELMIRE (to Dorine)
Send him to me.

DORINE (to Elmire)
The man's a crafty codger,
Perhaps you'll find it difficult to catch him.

ELMIRE (to Dorine)
Oh no! A lover's never hard to cheat,
And self-conceit leads straight to self-deceit.
Bid him come down to me.

(To Cleante and Mariane)
And you, withdraw.

SCENE IV

ELMIRE, ORGON

ELMIRE
Bring up this table, and get under it.

ORGON

What?

ELMIRE
One essential is to hide you well.

ORGON
Why under there?

ELMIRE
Oh, dear! Do as I say;
I know what I'm about, as you shall see.
Get under, now, I tell you; and once there
Be careful no one either sees or hears you.

ORGON
I'm going a long way to humour you,
I must say; but I'll see you through your scheme.

ELMIRE
And then you'll have, I think, no more to say.

(To her husband, who is now under the table.)
But mind, I'm going to meddle with strange matters;
Prepare yourself to be in no wise shocked.
Whatever I may say must pass, because
'Tis only to convince you, as I promised.
By wheedling speeches, since I'm forced to do it,
I'll make this hypocrite put off his mask,
Flatter the longings of his shameless passion,
And give free play to all his impudence.
But, since 'tis for your sake, to prove to you
His guilt, that I shall feign to share his love,
I can leave off as soon as you're convinced,
And things shall go no farther than you choose.
So, when you think they've gone quite far enough,
It is for you to stop his mad pursuit,

To spare your wife, and not expose me farther
Than you shall need, yourself, to undeceive you.
It is your own affair, and you must end it
When . . . Here he comes. Keep still, don't show yourself.

SCENE V

TARTUFFE, ELMIRE; ORGON (under the table)

TARTUFFE
They told me that you wished to see me here.

ELMIRE
Yes. I have secrets for your ear alone.
But shut the door first, and look everywhere
For fear of spies.

(Tartuffe goes and closes the door, and comes back.)
We surely can't afford
Another scene like that we had just now;
Was ever anyone so caught before!
Damis did frighten me most terribly
On your account; you saw I did my best
To baffle his design, and calm his anger.
But I was so confused, I never thought
To contradict his story; still, thank Heaven,
Things turned out all the better, as it happened,
And now we're on an even safer footing.
The high esteem you're held in, laid the storm;
My husband can have no suspicion of you,
And even insists, to spite the scandal-mongers,
That we shall be together constantly;
So that is how, without the risk of blame,
I can be here locked up with you alone,

And can reveal to you my heart, perhaps
Only too ready to allow your passion.

TARTUFFE
Your words are somewhat hard to understand,
Madam; just now you used a different style.

ELMIRE
If that refusal has offended you,
How little do you know a woman's heart!
How ill you guess what it would have you know,
When it presents so feeble a defence!
Always, at first, our modesty resists
The tender feelings you inspire us with.
Whatever cause we find to justify
The love that masters us, we still must feel
Some little shame in owning it; and strive
To make as though we would not, when we would.
But from the very way we go about it
We let a lover know our heart surrenders,
The while our lips, for honour's sake, oppose
Our heart's desire, and in refusing promise.
I'm telling you my secret all too freely
And with too little heed to modesty.
But — now that I've made bold to speak — pray tell me.
Should I have tried to keep Damis from speaking,
Should I have heard the offer of your heart
So quietly, and suffered all your pleading,
And taken it just as I did — remember —
If such a declaration had not pleased me,
And, when I tried my utmost to persuade you
Not to accept the marriage that was talked of,
What should my earnestness have hinted to you
If not the interest that you've inspired,
And my chagrin, should such a match compel me

To share a heart I want all to myself?

TARTUFFE
'Tis, past a doubt, the height of happiness,
To hear such words from lips we dote upon;
Their honeyed sweetness pours through all my senses
Long draughts of suavity ineffable.
My heart employs its utmost zeal to please you,
And counts your love its one beatitude;
And yet that heart must beg that you allow it
To doubt a little its felicity.
I well might think these words an honest trick
To make me break off this approaching marriage;
And if I may express myself quite plainly,
I cannot trust these too enchanting words
Until the granting of some little favour
I sigh for, shall assure me of their truth
And build within my soul, on firm foundations,
A lasting faith in your sweet charity.

ELMIRE (coughing to draw her husband's attention)
What! Must you go so fast? — and all at once
Exhaust the whole love of a woman's heart?
She does herself the violence to make
This dear confession of her love, and you
Are not yet satisfied, and will not be
Without the granting of her utmost favours?

TARTUFFE
The less a blessing is deserved, the less
We dare to hope for it; and words alone
Can ill assuage our love's desires. A fate
Too full of happiness, seems doubtful still;
We must enjoy it ere we can believe it.
And I, who know how little I deserve
Your goodness, doubt the fortunes of my daring;

So I shall trust to nothing, madam, till
You have convinced my love by something real.

ELMIRE
Ah! How your love enacts the tyrant's role,
And throws my mind into a strange confusion!
With what fierce sway it rules a conquered heart,
And violently will have its wishes granted!
What! Is there no escape from your pursuit?
No respite even? — not a breathing space?
Nay, is it decent to be so exacting,
And so abuse by urgency the weakness
You may discover in a woman's heart?

TARTUFFE
But if my worship wins your gracious favour,
Then why refuse me some sure proof thereof?

ELMIRE
But how can I consent to what you wish,
Without offending Heaven you talk so much of?

TARTUFFE
If Heaven is all that stands now in my way,
I'll easily remove that little hindrance;
Your heart need not hold back for such a trifle.

ELMIRE
But they affright us so with Heaven's commands!

TARTUFFE
I can dispel these foolish fears, dear madam;
I know the art of pacifying scruples
Heaven forbids, 'tis true, some satisfactions;
But we find means to make things right with Heaven.

('Tis a scoundrel speaking.) [5]

[Footnote 5: Moliere's note, in the original edition.]

There is a science, madam, that instructs us
How to enlarge the limits of our conscience
According to our various occasions,
And rectify the evil of the deed
According to our purity of motive.
I'll duly teach you all these secrets, madam;
You only need to let yourself be guided.
Content my wishes, have no fear at all;
I answer for't, and take the sin upon me.

(Elmire coughs still louder.)
Your cough is very bad.

ELMIRE
Yes, I'm in torture.

TARTUFFE
Would you accept this bit of licorice?

ELMIRE
The case is obstinate, I find; and all
The licorice in the world will do no good.

TARTUFFE
'Tis very trying.

ELMIRE
More than words can say.

TARTUFFE
In any case, your scruple's easily
Removed. With me you're sure of secrecy,

And there's no harm unless a thing is known.
The public scandal is what brings offence,
And secret sinning is not sin at all.

ELMIRE (after coughing again)
So then, I see I must resolve to yield;
I must consent to grant you everything,
And cannot hope to give full satisfaction
Or win full confidence, at lesser cost.
No doubt 'tis very hard to come to this;
'Tis quite against my will I go so far;
But since I must be forced to it, since nothing
That can be said suffices for belief,
Since more convincing proof is still demanded,
I must make up my mind to humour people.
If my consent give reason for offence,
So much the worse for him who forced me to it;
The fault can surely not be counted mine.

TARTUFFE
It need not, madam; and the thing itself . . .

ELMIRE
Open the door, I pray you, and just see
Whether my husband's not there, in the hall.

TARTUFFE
Why take such care for him? Between ourselves,
He is a man to lead round by the nose.
He's capable of glorying in our meetings;
I've fooled him so, he'd see all, and deny it.

ELMIRE
No matter; go, I beg you, look about,
And carefully examine every corner.

SCENE VI

ORGON, ELMIRE

ORGON (crawling out from under the table)
That is, I own, a man . . . abominable!
I can't get over it; the whole thing floors me.

ELMIRE
What? You come out so soon? You cannot mean it!
Get back under the table; 'tis not time yet;
Wait till the end, to see, and make quite certain,
And don't believe a thing on mere conjecture.

ORGON
Nothing more wicked e'er came out of Hell.

ELMIRE
Dear me! Don't go and credit things too lightly.
No, let yourself be thoroughly convinced;
Don't yield too soon, for fear you'll be mistaken.

(As Tartuffe enters, she makes her husband stand behind her.)

SCENE VII

TARTUFFE, ELMIRE, ORGON

TARTUFFE (not seeing Orgon)
All things conspire toward my satisfaction,
Madam, I've searched the whole apartment through.

There's no one here; and now my ravished soul . . .

ORGON (stopping him)
Softly! You are too eager in your amours;
You needn't be so passionate. Ah ha!
My holy man! You want to put it on me!
How is your soul abandoned to temptation!
Marry my daughter, eh? — and want my wife, too?
I doubted long enough if this was earnest,
Expecting all the time the tone would change;
But now the proof's been carried far enough;
I'm satisfied, and ask no more, for my part.

ELMIRE (to Tartuffe)
'Twas quite against my character to play
This part; but I was forced to treat you so.

TARTUFFE
What? You believe . . . ?

ORGON
Come, now, no protestations.
Get out from here, and make no fuss about it.

TARTUFFE
But my intent . . .

ORGON
That talk is out of season.
You leave my house this instant.

TARTUFFE
You're the one
To leave it, you who play the master here!
This house belongs to me, I'll have you know,
And show you plainly it's no use to turn

To these low tricks, to pick a quarrel with me,
And that you can't insult me at your pleasure,
For I have wherewith to confound your lies,
Avenge offended Heaven, and compel
Those to repent who talk to me of leaving.

SCENE VIII

ELMIRE, ORGON

ELMIRE
What sort of speech is this? What can it mean?

ORGON
My faith, I'm dazed. This is no laughing matter.

ELMIRE
What?

ORGON
From his words I see my great mistake;
The deed of gift is one thing troubles me.

ELMIRE
The deed of gift . . .

ORGON
Yes, that is past recall.
But I've another thing to make me anxious.

ELMIRE
What's that?

ORGON

You shall know all. Let's see at once
Whether a certain box is still upstairs.

ACT V

SCENE I

ORGON, CLEANTE

CLEANTE
Whither away so fast?

ORGON
How should I know?

CLEANTE
Methinks we should begin by taking counsel
To see what can be done to meet the case.

ORGON
I'm all worked up about that wretched box.
More than all else it drives me to despair.

CLEANTE
That box must hide some mighty mystery?

ORGON
Argas, my friend who is in trouble, brought it
Himself, most secretly, and left it with me.
He chose me, in his exile, for this trust;
And on these documents, from what he said,
I judge his life and property depend.

CLEANTE
How could you trust them to another's hands?

ORGON
By reason of a conscientious scruple.

I went straight to my traitor, to confide
In him; his sophistry made me believe
That I must give the box to him to keep,
So that, in case of search, I might deny
My having it at all, and still, by favour
Of this evasion, keep my conscience clear
Even in taking oath against the truth.

CLEANTE
Your case is bad, so far as I can see;
This deed of gift, this trusting of the secret
To him, were both — to state my frank opinion —
Steps that you took too lightly; he can lead you
To any length, with these for hostages;
And since he holds you at such disadvantage,
You'd be still more imprudent, to provoke him;
So you must go some gentler way about.

ORGON
What! Can a soul so base, a heart so false,
Hide neath the semblance of such touching fervour?
I took him in, a vagabond, a beggar! . . .
'Tis too much! No more pious folk for me!
I shall abhor them utterly forever,
And henceforth treat them worse than any devil.

CLEANTE
So! There you go again, quite off the handle!
In nothing do you keep an even temper.
You never know what reason is, but always
Jump first to one extreme, and then the other.
You see your error, and you recognise
That you've been cozened by a feigned zeal;
But to make up for't, in the name of reason,
Why should you plunge into a worse mistake,
And find no difference in character

Between a worthless scamp, and all good people?
What! Just because a rascal boldly duped you
With pompous show of false austerity,
Must you needs have it everybody's like him,
And no one's truly pious nowadays?
Leave such conclusions to mere infidels;
Distinguish virtue from its counterfeit,
Don't give esteem too quickly, at a venture,
But try to keep, in this, the golden mean.
If you can help it, don't uphold imposture;
But do not rail at true devoutness, either;
And if you must fall into one extreme,
Then rather err again the other way.

SCENE II

DAMIS, ORGON, CLEANTE

DAMIS
What! father, can the scoundrel threaten you,
Forget the many benefits received,
And in his base abominable pride
Make of your very favours arms against you?

ORGON
Too true, my son. It tortures me to think on't.

DAMIS
Let me alone, I'll chop his ears off for him.
We must deal roundly with his insolence;
'Tis I must free you from him at a blow;
'Tis I, to set things right, must strike him down.

CLEANTE
Spoke like a true young man. Now just calm down,
And moderate your towering tantrums, will you?
We live in such an age, with such a king,
That violence can not advance our cause.

SCENE III

MADAME PERNELLE, ORGON, ELMIRE, CLEANTE,
MARIANE, DAMIS, DORINE

MADAME PERNELLE
What's this? I hear of fearful mysteries!

ORGON
Strange things indeed, for my own eyes to witness;
You see how I'm requited for my kindness,
I zealously receive a wretched beggar,
I lodge him, entertain him like my brother,
Load him with benefactions every day,
Give him my daughter, give him all my fortune:
And he meanwhile, the villain, rascal, wretch,
Tries with black treason to suborn my wife,
And not content with such a foul design,
He dares to menace me with my own favours,
And would make use of those advantages
Which my too foolish kindness armed him with,
To ruin me, to take my fortune from me,
And leave me in the state I saved him from.

DORINE
Poor man!

MADAME PERNELLE
My son, I cannot possibly
Believe he could intend so black a deed.

ORGON
What?

MADAME PERNELLE
Worthy men are still the sport of envy.

ORGON
Mother, what do you mean by such a speech?

MADAME PERNELLE
There are strange goings-on about your house,
And everybody knows your people hate him.

ORGON
What's that to do with what I tell you now?

MADAME PERNELLE
I always said, my son, when you were little:
That virtue here below is hated ever;
The envious may die, but envy never.

ORGON
What's that fine speech to do with present facts?

MADAME PERNELLE
Be sure, they've forged a hundred silly lies . . .

ORGON
I've told you once, I saw it all myself.

MADAME PERNELLE
For slanderers abound in calumnies . . .

ORGON
Mother, you'd make me damn my soul. I tell you
I saw with my own eyes his shamelessness.

MADAME PERNELLE
Their tongues for spitting venom never lack,
There's nothing here below they'll not attack.

ORGON
Your speech has not a single grain of sense.
I saw it, harkee, saw it, with these eyes
I saw — d'ye know what saw means? — must I say it
A hundred times, and din it in your ears?

MADAME PERNELLE
My dear, appearances are oft deceiving,
And seeing shouldn't always be believing.

ORGON
I'll go mad.

MADAME PERNELLE
False suspicions may delude,
And good to evil oft is misconstrued.

ORGON
Must I construe as Christian charity
The wish to kiss my wife!

MADAME PERNELLE
You must, at least,
Have just foundation for accusing people,
And wait until you see a thing for sure.

ORGON
The devil! How could I see any surer?
Should I have waited till, before my eyes,
He . . . No, you'll make me say things quite improper.

MADAME PERNELLE
In short, 'tis known too pure a zeal inflames him;
And so, I cannot possibly conceive
That he should try to do what's charged against him.

ORGON
If you were not my mother, I should say
Such things! . . . I know not what, I'm so enraged!

DORINE (to Orgon)
Fortune has paid you fair, to be so doubted;
You flouted our report, now yours is flouted.

CLEANTE
We're wasting time here in the merest trifling,
Which we should rather use in taking measures
To guard ourselves against the scoundrel's threats.

DAMIS
You think his impudence could go far?

ELMIRE
For one, I can't believe it possible;
Why, his ingratitude would be too patent.

CLEANTE
Don't trust to that; he'll find abundant warrant
To give good colour to his acts against you;
And for less cause than this, a strong cabal
Can make one's life a labyrinth of troubles.
I tell you once again: armed as he is

You never should have pushed him quite so far.

ORGON
True; yet what could I do? The rascal's pride
Made me lose all control of my resentment.

CLEANTE
I wish with all my heart that some pretence
Of peace could be patched up between you two

ELMIRE
If I had known what weapons he was armed with,
I never should have raised such an alarm,
And my . . .

ORGON (to Dorine, seeing Mr. Loyal come in)
Who's coming now? Go quick, find out.
I'm in a fine state to receive a visit!

SCENE IV

ORGON, MADAME PERNELLE, ELMIRE, MARIANE,
CLEANTE, DAMIS, DORINE, MR. LOYAL

MR. LOYAL (to Dorine, at the back of the stage)
Good day, good sister. Pray you, let me see
The master of the house.

DORINE
He's occupied;
I think he can see nobody at present.

MR. LOYAL
I'm not by way of being unwelcome here.

My coming can, I think, nowise displease him;
My errand will be found to his advantage.

DORINE
Your name, then?

MR. LOYAL
Tell him simply that his friend
Mr. Tartuffe has sent me, for his goods . . .

DORINE (to Orgon)
It is a man who comes, with civil manners,
Sent by Tartuffe, he says, upon an errand
That you'll be pleased with.

CLEANTE (to Orgon)
Surely you must see him,
And find out who he is, and what he wants.

ORGON (to Cleante)
Perhaps he's come to make it up between us:
How shall I treat him?

CLEANTE
You must not get angry;
And if he talks of reconciliation
Accept it.

MR. LOYAL (to Orgon)
Sir, good-day. And Heaven send
Harm to your enemies, favour to you.

ORGON (aside to Cleante)
This mild beginning suits with my conjectures
And promises some compromize already.

MR. LOYAL
All of your house has long been dear to me;
I had the honour, sir, to serve your father.

ORGON
Sir, I am much ashamed, and ask your pardon
For not recalling now your face or name.

MR. LOYAL
My name is Loyal. I'm from Normandy.
My office is court-bailiff, in despite
Of envy; and for forty years, thank Heaven,
It's been my fortune to perform that office
With honour. So I've come, sir, by your leave
To render service of a certain writ . . .

ORGON
What, you are here to . . .

MR. LOYAL
Pray, sir, don't be angry.
'Tis nothing, sir, but just a little summons: —
Order to vacate, you and yours, this house,
Move out your furniture, make room for others,
And that without delay or putting off,
As needs must be . . .

ORGON
I? Leave this house?

MR. LOYAL
Yes, please, sir
The house is now, as you well know, of course,
Mr. Tartuffe's. And he, beyond dispute,
Of all your goods is henceforth lord and master
By virtue of a contract here attached,

Drawn in due form, and unassailable.

DAMIS (to Mr. Loyal)
Your insolence is monstrous, and astounding!

MR. LOYAL (to Damis)
I have no business, sir, that touches you;

(Pointing to Orgon)
This is the gentleman. He's fair and courteous,
And knows too well a gentleman's behaviour
To wish in any wise to question justice.

ORGON
But . . .

MR. LOYAL
Sir, I know you would not for a million
Wish to rebel; like a good citizen
You'll let me put in force the court's decree.

DAMIS
Your long black gown may well, before you know it,
Mister Court-bailiff, get a thorough beating.

MR. LOYAL (to Orgon)
Sir, make your son be silent or withdraw.
I should be loath to have to set things down,
And see your names inscribed in my report.

DORINE (aside)
This Mr. Loyal's looks are most disloyal.

MR. LOYAL
I have much feeling for respectable

And honest folk like you, sir, and consented
To serve these papers, only to oblige you,
And thus prevent the choice of any other
Who, less possessed of zeal for you than I am
Might order matters in less gentle fashion.

ORGON
And how could one do worse than order people
Out of their house?

MR. LOYAL
Why, we allow you time;
And even will suspend until to-morrow
The execution of the order, sir.
I'll merely, without scandal, quietly,
Come here and spend the night, with half a score
Of officers; and just for form's sake, please,
You'll bring your keys to me, before retiring.
I will take care not to disturb your rest,
And see there's no unseemly conduct here.
But by to-morrow, and at early morning,
You must make haste to move your least belongings;
My men will help you — I have chosen strong ones
To serve you, sir, in clearing out the house.
No one could act more generously, I fancy,
And, since I'm treating you with great indulgence,
I beg you'll do as well by me, and see
I'm not disturbed in my discharge of duty.

ORGON
I'd give this very minute, and not grudge it,
The hundred best gold louis I have left,
If I could just indulge myself, and land
My fist, for one good square one, on his snout.

CLEANTE (aside to Orgon)
Careful! — don't make things worse.

DAMIS
Such insolence!
I hardly can restrain myself. My hands
Are itching to be at him.

DORINE
By my faith,
With such a fine broad back, good Mr. Loyal,
A little beating would become you well.

MR. LOYAL
My girl, such infamous words are actionable.
And warrants can be issued against women.

CLEANTE (to Mr. Loyal)
Enough of this discussion, sir; have done.
Give us the paper, and then leave us, pray.

MR. LOYAL
Then /au revoir/. Heaven keep you from disaster!

ORGON
May Heaven confound you both, you and your master!

SCENE V

ORGON, MADAME PERNELLE, ELMIRE, CLEANTE,
MARIANE, DAMIS, DORINE

ORGON
Well, mother, am I right or am I not?

This writ may help you now to judge the matter.
Or don't you see his treason even yet?

MADAME PERNELLE
I'm all amazed, befuddled, and beflustered!

DORINE (to Orgon)
You are quite wrong, you have no right to blame him;
This action only proves his good intentions.
Love for his neighbour makes his virtue perfect;
And knowing money is a root of evil,
In Christian charity, he'd take away
Whatever things may hinder your salvation.

ORGON
Be still. You always need to have that told you.

CLEANTE (to Orgon)
Come, let us see what course you are to follow.

ELMIRE
Go and expose his bold ingratitude.
Such action must invalidate the contract;
His perfidy must now appear too black
To bring him the success that he expects.

SCENE VI

VALERE, ORGON, MADAME PERNELLE, ELMIRE,
CLEANTE, MARIANE, DAMIS,
DORINE

VALERE
'Tis with regret, sir, that I bring bad news;

But urgent danger forces me to do so.
A close and intimate friend of mine, who knows
The interest I take in what concerns you,
Has gone so far, for my sake, as to break
The secrecy that's due to state affairs,
And sent me word but now, that leaves you only
The one expedient of sudden flight.
The villain who so long imposed upon you,
Found means, an hour ago, to see the prince,
And to accuse you (among other things)
By putting in his hands the private strong-box
Of a state-criminal, whose guilty secret,
You, failing in your duty as a subject,
(He says) have kept. I know no more of it
Save that a warrant's drawn against you, sir,
And for the greater surety, that same rascal
Comes with the officer who must arrest you.

CLEANTE
His rights are armed; and this is how the scoundrel
Seeks to secure the property he claims.

ORGON
Man is a wicked animal, I'll own it!

VALERE
The least delay may still be fatal, sir.
I have my carriage, and a thousand louis,
Provided for your journey, at the door.
Let's lose no time; the bolt is swift to strike,
And such as only flight can save you from.
I'll be your guide to seek a place of safety,
And stay with you until you reach it, sir.

ORGON
How much I owe to your obliging care!

Another time must serve to thank you fitly;
And I pray Heaven to grant me so much favour
That I may some day recompense your service.
Good-bye; see to it, all of you . . .

CLEANTE
Come hurry;
We'll see to everything that's needful, brother.

SCENE VII

TARTUFFE, AN OFFICER, MADAME PERNELLE,
ORGON, ELMIRE, CLEANTE,
MARIANE, VALERE, DAMIS, DORINE

TARTUFFE (stopping Orgon)
Softly, sir, softly; do not run so fast;
You haven't far to go to find your lodging;
By order of the prince, we here arrest you.

ORGON
Traitor! You saved this worst stroke for the last;
This crowns your perfidies, and ruins me.

TARTUFFE
I shall not be embittered by your insults,
For Heaven has taught me to endure all things.

CLEANTE
Your moderation, I must own, is great.

DAMIS
How shamelessly the wretch makes bold with Heaven!

TARTUFFE
Your ravings cannot move me; all my thought
Is but to do my duty.

MARIANE
You must claim
Great glory from this honourable act.

TARTUFFE
The act cannot be aught but honourable,
Coming from that high power which sends me here.

ORGON
Ungrateful wretch, do you forget 'twas I
That rescued you from utter misery?

TARTUFFE
I've not forgot some help you may have given;
But my first duty now is toward my prince.
The higher power of that most sacred claim
Must stifle in my heart all gratitude;
And to such puissant ties I'd sacrifice
My friend, my wife, my kindred, and myself.

ELMIRE
The hypocrite!

DORINE
How well he knows the trick
Of cloaking him with what we most revere!

CLEANTE
But if the motive that you make parade of
Is perfect as you say, why should it wait
To show itself, until the day he caught you
Soliciting his wife? How happens it

You have not thought to go inform against him
Until his honour forces him to drive you
Out of his house? And though I need not mention
That he'd just given you his whole estate,
Still, if you meant to treat him now as guilty,
How could you then consent to take his gift?

TARTUFFE (to the Officer)
Pray, sir, deliver me from all this clamour;
Be good enough to carry out your order.

THE OFFICER
Yes, I've too long delayed its execution;
'Tis very fitting you should urge me to it;
So therefore, you must follow me at once
To prison, where you'll find your lodging ready.

TARTUFFE
Who? I, sir?

THE OFFICER
You.

TARTUFFE
By why to prison?

THE OFFICER
You
Are not the one to whom I owe account.
You, sir (to Orgon), recover from your hot alarm.
Our prince is not a friend to double dealing,
His eyes can read men's inmost hearts, and all
The art of hypocrites cannot deceive him.
His sharp discernment sees things clear and true;
His mind cannot too easily be swayed,
For reason always holds the balance even.

He honours and exalts true piety,
But knows the false, and views it with disgust.
This fellow was by no means apt to fool him,
Far subtler snares have failed against his wisdom,
And his quick insight pierced immediately
The hidden baseness of this tortuous heart.
Accusing you, the knave betrayed himself,
And by true recompense of Heaven's justice
He stood revealed before our monarch's eyes
A scoundrel known before by other names,
Whose horrid crimes, detailed at length, might fill
A long-drawn history of many volumes.
Our monarch — to resolve you in a word —
Detesting his ingratitude and baseness,
Added this horror to his other crimes,
And sent me hither under his direction
To see his insolence out-top itself,
And force him then to give you satisfaction.
Your papers, which the traitor says are his,
I am to take from him, and give you back;
The deed of gift transferring your estate
Our monarch's sovereign will makes null and void;
And for the secret personal offence
Your friend involved you in, he pardons you:
Thus he rewards your recent zeal, displayed
In helping to maintain his rights, and shows
How well his heart, when it is least expected,
Knows how to recompense a noble deed,
And will not let true merit miss its due,
Remembering always rather good than evil.

DORINE
Now Heaven be praised!

MADAME PERNELLE
At last I breathe again.

ELMIRE
A happy outcome!

MARIANE
Who'd have dared to hope it?

ORGON (to Tartuffe, who is being led by the officer)
There traitor! Now you're . . .

SCENE VIII

MADAME PERNELLE, ORGON, ELMIRE, MARIANE,
CLEANTE, VALERE, DAMIS,
DORINE

CLEANTE
Brother, hold! — and don't
Descend to such indignities, I beg you.
Leave the poor wretch to his unhappy fate,
And let remorse oppress him, but not you.
Hope rather that his heart may now return
To virtue, hate his vice, reform his ways,
And win the pardon of our glorious prince;
While you must straightway go, and on your knees
Repay with thanks his noble generous kindness.

ORGON
Well said! We'll go, and at his feet kneel down,
With joy to thank him for his goodness shown;
And this first duty done, with honours due,
We'll then attend upon another, too.
With wedded happiness reward Valere,
And crown a lover noble and sincere.

The Middle Classe Gentleman
JEAN BAPTISTE POQUELIN MOLIÈRE

THE CAST

Monsieur Jourdain, bourgeois
Madame Jourdain, his wife
Lucile, their daughter
Nicole, maid.
Cleonte, suitor of Lucile
Covielle, Cleonte's valet
Dorante, Count, suitor of Dorimene
Dorimene, Marchioness
Music Master
Pupil of the Music Master
Dancing Master
Fencing Master
Master of Philosophy
Tailor
Tailor's apprentice
Two lackeys
Many male and female musicians, instrumentalists, dancers, cooks,
tailor's apprentices, and others necessary for the interludes

The scene is Monsieur Jourdain's house in Paris.

ACT I

SCENE I

Music Master, Dancing Master, Musicians, and Dancers

The play opens with a great assembly of instruments, and in the middle of the stage is a pupil of the Music Master seated at a table composing a melody which Monsieur Jourdain has ordered for a serenade.

MUSIC MASTER
(To Musicians) Come, come into this room, sit there and wait until he comes.

DANCING MASTER
(To dancers) And you too, on this side.

MUSIC MASTER
(To Pupil) Is it done?

PUPIL
Yes.

MUSIC MASTER
Let's see. . . This is good.

DANCING MASTER
Is it something new?

MUSIC MASTER
Yes, it's a melody for a serenade that I set him to composing here, while waiting for our man to awake.

DANCING MASTER
May I see it?

MUSIC MASTER
You'll hear it, with the dialogue, when he comes. He won't be long.

DANCING MASTER
Our work, yours and mine, is not trivial at present.

MUSIC MASTER
This is true. We've found here such a man as we both need. This is a nice source of income for us — this Monsieur Jourdain, with the visions of nobility and gallantry that he has gotten into his head. You and I should hope that everyone resembled him.

DANCING MASTER
Not entirely; I could wish that he understood better the things that we give him.

MUSIC MASTER
It's true that he understands them poorly, but he pays well, and that's what our art needs now more than anything else.

DANCING MASTER
As for me, I admit, I feed a little on glory. Applause touches me; and I hold that, in all the fine arts, it is painful to produce for dolts, to endure the barbarous opinions of a fool about my choreography. It is a pleasure, don't tell me otherwise, to work for people who can appreciate the fine points of an art, who know how to give a sweet reception to the beauties of a work and, by pleasurable approbations, gratify us for our labor. Yes, the most agreeable recompense we can receive for the things we do is to see them recognized and flattered by an applause that honors us. There is nothing, in my opinion, that pays us better for all our fatigue; and it is an exquisite delight to receive the praises of the well-informed.

MUSIC MASTER
I agree, and I enjoy them as you do. There is surely nothing more agreeable than the applause you speak of; but that incense does not provide a living. Pure praises do not provide a comfortable existence; it is necessary to add something solid, and the best way to praise is to praise with cash-in-hand. He's a man, it's true, whose insight is very slight, who talks nonsense about everything and applauds only for the wrong reasons but his money makes up for his judgments. He has discernment in his purse. His praises are in cash, and this ignorant bourgeois is worth more to us, as you see, than the educated nobleman who introduced us here.

DANCING MASTER
There is some truth in what you say; but I find that you lean a little too heavily on money; and material interest is something so base that a man of good taste should never show an attachment to it.

MUSIC MASTER
You are ready enough to receive the money our man gives you.

DANCING MASTER
Assuredly; but I don't place all my happiness in it, and I could wish that together with his fortune he had some good taste in things.

MUSIC MASTER
I could wish it too, that's what both of us are working for as much as we can. But, in any case, he gives us the means to make ourselves known in the world; and he will pay others if they will praise him.

DANCING MASTER
Here he comes.

SCENE II

Monsieur Jourdain, Two Lackeys, Music Master, Dancing Master, Pupil, Musicians, and Dancers

MONSIEUR JOURDAIN
Well gentlemen? What's this? Are you going to show me your little skit?

DANCING MASTER
How? What little skit?

MONSIEUR JOURDAIN
Well, the. . . What-do-you-call it? Your prologue or dialogue of songs and dances.

DANCING MASTER
Ha, ha!

MUSIC MASTER
You find us ready for you.

MONSIEUR JOURDAIN
I kept you waiting a little, but it's because I'm having myself dressed today like the people of quality, and my tailor sent me some silk stockings that I thought I would never get on.

MUSIC MASTER
We are here only to wait upon your leisure.

MONSIEUR JOURDAIN
I want you both to stay until they have brought me my suit, so that you may see me.

DANCING MASTER
Whatever you would like.

MONSIEUR JOURDAIN
You will see me fitted out properly, from head to foot.

MUSIC MASTER
We have no doubt of it.

MONSIEUR JOURDAIN
I had this robe made for me.

DANCING MASTER
It's very attractive.

MONSIEUR JOURDAIN
My tailor told me the people of quality dress like this in the mornings.

MUSIC MASTER
It's marvelously becoming.

MONSIEUR JOURDAIN
Hey lackeys! My two lackeys!

FIRST LACKEY
What do you wish, Sir?

MONSIEUR JOURDAIN
Nothing. I just wanted to see if you were paying attention. (To the two masters) What say you of my liveries?

DANCING MASTER
They're magnificent.

MONSIEUR JOURDAIN
(Half opening his gown, showing a pair of tight red velvet breeches, and a green velvet vest, that he is wearing) Here again is a sort of lounging dress to perform my morning exercises in.

MUSIC MASTER
It is elegant.

MONSIEUR JOURDAIN
Lackey!

FIRST LACKEY
Sir?

MONSIEUR JOURDAIN
The other lackey!

SECOND LACKEY
Sir?

MONSIEUR JOURDAIN
Hold my robe. (To the Masters) Do you think I look good?

DANCING MASTER
Very well. No one could look better.

MONSIEUR JOURDAIN
Now let's have a look at your little show. MUSIC MASTER
I would like very much for you to listen to a melody he (indicating his student)has just composed for the serenade that you ordered from me. He's one of my pupils who has an admirable talent for these kinds of things.

MONSIEUR JOURDAIN
Yes, but you should not have had that done by a pupil; you yourself were none too good for that piece of work.

MUSIC MASTER
You must not let the name of pupil fool you, sir. Pupils of this
sort know as much as the greatest masters, and the melody is as
fine as could be made. Just listen.

MONSIEUR JOURDAIN
(To Lackeys) Give me my robe so I can listen better . . . Wait, I
believe I would be better without a robe. . . No, give it back, that
will be better.

MUSICIAN
(Singing) I languish night and day, my suffering is extreme Since
to your control your lovely eyes subjected me; If you thus treat,
fair Iris, those you love, Alas, how would you treat an enemy?

MONSIEUR JOURDAIN
This song seems to me a little mournful, it lulls to sleep, and I
would like it if you could liven it up a little, here and there.

MUSIC MASTER
It is necessary, Sir, that the tune be suited to the words.

MONSIEUR JOURDAIN
Someone taught me a perfectly pretty one some time ago. Listen .
. . Now . . . how does it go?

DANCING MASTER
By my faith, I don't know.

MONSIEUR JOURDAIN
There are sheep in it.

DANCING MASTER
Sheep?

MONSIEUR JOURDAIN
Yes. Ah! (He sings) I thought my Jeanneton As beautiful as sweet; I thought my Jeanneton Far sweeter than a sheep. Alas! Alas! She is a hundred times, A thousand times, more cruel Than tigers in the woods! Isn't it pretty?

MUSIC MASTER
The prettiest in the world.

DANCING MASTER
And you sing it well.

MONSIEUR JOURDAIN
It's without having learned music.

MUSIC MASTER
You ought to learn it, Sir, as you are learning dancing. They are two arts which have a close connection.

DANCING MASTER
And which open the mind of a man to fine things.

MONSIEUR JOURDAIN
And do people of quality learn music, too?

MUSIC MASTER
Yes sir.

MONSIEUR JOURDAIN
I'll learn it then. But I don't know when I can find time; for besides the Fencing Master who's teaching me, I have also engaged a master of philosophy who is to begin this morning.

MUSIC MASTER
Philosophy is something; but music, sir, music . . .

DANCING MASTER
Music and dancing, music and dancing, that's all that's necessary.

MUSIC MASTER
There's nothing so useful in a State as music.

DANCING MASTER
There's nothing so necessary to men as dancing.

MUSIC MASTER
Without music, a State cannot subsist.

DANCING MASTER
Without the dance, a man can do nothing.

MUSIC MASTER
All the disorders, all the wars one sees in the world happen only from not learning music.

DANCING MASTER
All the misfortunes of mankind, all the dreadful disasters that fill the history books, the blunders of politicians and the faults of omission of great commanders, all this comes from not knowing how to dance.

MONSIEUR JOURDAIN
How is that?

MUSIC MASTER
Does not war result from a lack of agreement between men?

MONSIEUR JOURDAIN
That is true.

MUSIC MASTER
And if all men learned music, wouldn't that be a means of bringing about harmony and of seeing universal peace in the world?

MONSIEUR JOURDAIN
You are right.

DANCING MASTER
When a man has committed a mistake in his conduct, in family affairs, or in affairs of government of a state, or in the command of an army, do we not always say, "He took a bad step in such and such an affair?"

MONSIEUR JOURDAIN
Yes, that's said.

DANCING MASTER
And can taking a bad step result from anything but not knowing how to dance?

MONSIEUR JOURDAIN
It's true, you are both right.

DANCING MASTER
It makes you see the excellence and usefulness of music and the dance.

MONSIEUR JOURDAIN
I understand that, now.

MUSIC MASTER
Do you wish to see our pieces?

MONSIEUR JOURDAIN
Yes.

MUSIC MASTER
I have already told you that this is a little attempt I have made to show the different passions that music can express.

MONSIEUR JOURDAIN
Very good.

MUSIC MASTER (To musicians) Here, come forward. (To Monsieur Jourdain) You must imagine that they are dressed as shepherds.

MONSIEUR JOURDAIN
Why always as shepherds? You see nothing but that everywhere.

MUSIC MASTER
When we have characters that are to speak in music, it's necessary, for believability, to make them pastoral. Singing has always been assigned to shepherds; and it is scarcely natural dialogue for princes or merchants to sing their passions.

MONSIEUR JOURDAIN
Alright, alright. Let's see.

DIALOGUE IN MUSIC
(A Woman and Two Men)

ALL THREE
A heart, under the domination of love, Is always with a thousand cares oppressed. It is said that we gladly languish, gladly sigh; But, despite what can be said, There is nothing so sweet as our liberty!

FIRST MAN
There is nothing so sweet as the loving fires That make two hearts beat as one. One cannot live without amorous desires; Take love from life, you take away the pleasures.

SECOND MAN
It would be sweet to submit to love's rule, If one could find faithful love, But, alas! oh cruel rule! No faithful shepherdess is to be seen, And that inconstant sex, much too unworthy, Must renounce love eternally.

FIRST MAN
Pleasing ardor!

WOMAN
Happy liberty!

SECOND MAN
Deceitful woman!

FIRST MAN
How precious you are to me!

WOMAN
How you please my heart!

SECOND MAN
How horrible you are to me!

FIRST MAN
Ah, leave, for love, that mortal hate!

WOMAN
We can, we can show you a faithful shepherdess!

SECOND MAN
 Alas! Where to find her?

WOMAN
 In order to defend our reputation, I want to offer you my heart!

FIRST MAN
 But, shepherdess, can I believe That it will not be deceitful?

WOMAN
 We'll see through experience, Who of the two loves best.

SECOND MAN
 Who lacks constancy, May the gods destroy!

ALL THREE
 With ardors so beautiful Let us be inflamed! Ah, how sweet it is to love, When two hearts are faithful!

MONSIEUR JOURDAIN
Is that all?

MUSIC MASTER
Yes.

MONSIEUR JOURDAIN
I find it well-done, and there are some pretty enough sayings in it.

DANCING MASTER
Here, for my presentation, is a little display of the loveliest movements and the most beautiful attitudes with which a dance can possibly be varied.

MONSIEUR JOURDAIN
Are these shepherds too?

DANCING MASTER

They're whatever you please. Let's go! (Four dancers execute all the different movements and all the kinds of steps that the Dancing Master commands; and this dance makes the First Interlude.)

ACT II

SCENE I

Monsieur Jourdain, Music Master, Dancing Master, Lackeys

MONSIEUR JOURDAIN
That's not all that bad, and those people there hop around well.

MUSIC MASTER
When the dance is combined with the music, it will have even better effect, and you will see something quite good in the little ballet we have prepared for you.

MONSIEUR JOURDAIN
That's for later, when the person I ordered all this for is to do me the honor of coming here to dine.

DANCING MASTER
Everything is ready.

MUSIC MASTER
However, sir, this is not enough. A person like you, who lives magnificently, and who are inclined towards fine things, should have a concert of music here every Wednesday or every Thursday.

MONSIEUR JOURDAIN
Is that what people of quality do?

MUSIC MASTER
Yes, Sir.

MONSIEUR JOURDAIN
Then I'll have them. Will it be fine?

MUSIC MASTER
Without doubt. You must have three voices — a tenor, a soprano, and a bass, who will be accompanied by a bass-viol, a theorbo, and a clavecin for the chords, with two violins to play the ritournelles.

MONSIEUR JOURDAIN
You must also add a trumpet marine. The trumpet marine is an instrument that pleases me and it's harmonious.

MUSIC MASTER
Leave it to us to manage things.

MONSIEUR JOURDAIN
At least, don't forget to send the musicians to sing at table.

MUSIC MASTER
You will have everything you should have.

MONSIEUR JOURDAIN
But above all, let the ballet be fine.

MUSIC MASTER
You will be pleased with it, and, among other things, with certain minuets you will find in it.

MONSIEUR JOURDAIN
Ah! Minuets are my dance, and I would like you to see me dance them. Come, my Dancing Master.

DANCING MASTER
A hat, sir, if you please. La, la, la, la. La, la, la, la. In cadence please. La, la, la, la. Your right leg. La, la, la, la. Don't move your shoulders so. La, la, la, la. Your arms are wrong. La, la, la, la. Raise your head. Turn the toe out. La, la, la, la. Straighten your body up.

MONSIEUR JOURDAIN
How was that? (Breathlessly)

MUSIC MASTER
The best.

MONSIEUR JOURDAIN
By the way, teach me how to bow to salute a marchioness; I shall need to know soon.

DANCING MASTER
How you must bow to salute a marchioness?

MONSIEUR JOURDAIN
Yes, a marchioness named Dorimene.

DANCING MASTER
Give me your hand.

MONSIEUR JOURDAIN
No. You only have to do it, I'll remember it well.

DANCING MASTER
If you want to salute her with a great deal of respect, you must first bow and step back, then bow three times as you walk towards her, and at the last one bow down to her knees.

MONSIEUR JOURDAIN
(After the Dancing Master has illustrated) Do it some. Good!

LACKEY
Sir, your Fencing Master is here. MONSIEUR JOURDAIN
Tell him to come in here for my lesson. I want you to see me perform.

SCENE II

Fencing Master, Music Master, Dancing Master, Monsier Jourdain, a Lackey

FENCING MASTER
(After giving a foil to Monsieur Jourdain) Come, sir, the salute. Your body straight. A little inclined upon the left thigh. Your legs not so wide apart. Your feet both in a line. Your wrist opposite your hip. The point of your sword even with your shoulder. The arm not so much extended. The left hand at the level of the eye. The left shoulder more squared. The head up. The expression bold. Advance. The body steady. Beat carte, and thrust. One, two. Recover. Again, with the foot firm. Leap back. When you make a pass, Sir, you must first disengage, and your body must be well turned. One, two. Come, beat tierce and thrust. Advance. Stop there. One, two. Recover. Repeat. Leap back. On guard, Sir, on guard. (The fencing master touches him two or three times with the foil while saying, "On guard.")

MONSIEUR JOURDAIN
How was that? (Breathlessly)

MUSIC MASTER
You did marvelously!

FENCING MASTER
As I have told you, the entire secret of fencing lies in two things to give and not to receive; and as I demonstrated to you the other day, it is impossible for you to receive, if you know how to turn your opponent's sword from the line of your body. This depends solely on a slight movement of the wrist, either inward or outward.

MONSIEUR JOURDAIN
In this way then, a man, without courage, is sure to kill his man and not be killed himself?

FENCING MASTER
Without doubt. Didn't you see the demonstration?

MONSIEUR JOURDAIN
Yes.

FENCING MASTER
And thus you have seen how men like me should be considered by the State, and how the science of fencing is more important than all the other useless sciences, such as dancing, music, ...

DANCING MASTER
Careful there, Monsieur swordsman! Speak of the dance only with respect.

MUSIC MASTER
I beg you to speak better of the excellence of music.

FENCING MASTER
You are amusing fellows, to want to compare your sciences with mine!

MUSIC MASTER
See the self-importance of the man!

FENCING MASTER
My little Dancing Master, I'll make you dance as you ought. And you, my little musician, I'll make you sing in a pretty way.

DANCING MASTER
Monsieur Clanger-of-iron, I'll teach you your trade.

MONSIEUR JOURDAIN
(To the Dancing Master) Are you crazy to quarrel with him, who knows tierce and quarte, and who can kill a man by demonstration?

DANCING MASTER
I disdain his demonstrations, and his tierce, and his quarte.

MONSIEUR JOURDAIN
Careful, I tell you.

FENCING MASTER
What? You little impertinent!

MONSIEUR JOURDAIN
Oh! My Fencing Master.

DANCING MASTER
What? You big workhorse!

MONSIEUR JOURDAIN
Oh! My Dancing Master.

FENCING MASTER
If I throw myself on you …

MONSIEUR JOURDAIN
Careful.

DANCING MASTER
If I get my hands on you …

MONSIEUR JOURDAIN
Be nice!

FENCING MASTER
I'll go over you with a curry-comb, in such a way...

MONSIEUR JOURDAIN
Mercy!

DANCING MASTER
I'll give you a beating such as ...

MONSIEUR JOURDAIN
I beg of you!

MUSIC MASTER
Let us teach him a little how to talk!

MONSIEUR JOURDAIN
Oh Lord! Stop.

SCENE III

Philosophy Master, Music Master, Dancing Master, Fencing Master, Monsieur Jourdain, Lackeys

MONSIEUR JOURDAIN
Aha! Monsieur Philosopher, you come just in time with your philosophy. Come, make a little peace among these people.

PHILOSOPHY MASTER
What's happening? What's the matter, gentlemen.

MONSIEUR JOURDAIN
They have got into a rage over the superiority of their professions to the point of injurious words and of wanting to come to blows.

PHILOSOPHY MASTER
What! Gentlemen, must you act this way? Haven't you read the learned treatise that Seneca composed on anger? Is there anything more base and more shameful than this passion, which turns a man into a savage beast? And shouldn't reason be the mistress of all our activities?

DANCING MASTER
Well! Sir, he has just abused both of us by, despising the dance, which I practice, and music, which is his profession.

PHILOSOPHY MASTER
A wise man is above all the insults that can be spoken to him; and the grand reply one should make to such outrages is moderation and patience.

FENCING MASTER
They both had the audacity of trying to compare their professions with mine.

PHILOSOPHY MASTER
Should that disturb you? Men should not dispute amongst themselves about vainglory and rank; that which perfectly distinguishes one from the other is wisdom and virtue.

DANCING MASTER
I insist to him that dance is a science to which one cannot do enough honor.

MUSIC MASTER
And I, that music is something that all the ages have revered.

FENCING MASTER
And I insist to them that the science of fencing is the finest and the most necessary of all sciences.

PHILOSOPHY MASTER
And where then will philosophy be? I find you all very impertinent to speak with this arrogance in front of me, and impudently to give the name of science to things that one should not even honor with the name of art, and that cannot be classified except under the name of miserable gladiator, singer, and buffoon!

FENCING MASTER
Get out, you dog of a philosopher!

MUSIC MASTER
Get out, you worthless pedant!

DANCING MASTER
Get out, you ill-mannered cur!

PHILOSOPHY MASTER
What! Rascals that you are ... (The philosopher flings himself at them, and all three go out fighting).

MONSIEUR JOURDAIN
Monsieur Philosopher!

PHILOSOPHY MASTER
Rogues! Scoundrels! Insolent dogs!

MONSIEUR JOURDAIN
Monsieur Philosopher!

FENCING MASTER
A pox on the beast!

MONSIEUR JOURDAIN
Gentlemen!

PHILOSOPHY MASTER
Impudent rogues!

MONSIEUR JOURDAIN
Monsieur Philosopher!

DANCING MASTER
The devil take the jackass!

MONSIEUR JOURDAIN
Gentlemen!

PHILOSOPHY MASTER
Villains!

MONSIEUR JOURDAIN
Monsieur Philosopher!

MUSIC MASTER
To the devil with the impertinent fellow!

MONSIEUR JOURDAIN
Gentlemen!

PHILOSOPHY MASTER
Rascals! Beggars! Traitors! Impostors! (They leave).

MONSIEUR JOURDAIN
Monsieur Philosopher, Gentlemen! Monsieur Philosopher!
Gentlemen! Monsieur Philosopher! Oh! Fight as much as you
like. I don't know what to do, and I'll not spoil my robe to
separate you. I would be a fool to go among them and receive
some damaging blow.

SCENE IV

Philosophy Master, Monsieur Jourdain

PHILOSOPHY MASTER
(Straightening the collar that indicates he is a Philosopher) Now to our lesson.

MONSIEUR JOURDAIN
Oh! Sir, I am distressed by the blows they gave you.

PHILOSOPHY MASTER
It's nothing. A philosopher knows how to take these things and I'll compose a satire against them, in the style of Juvenal, which will fix them nicely. Let it be. What would you like to learn?

MONSIEUR JOURDAIN
Everything I can, for I have every desire in the world to be educated, and I'm furious that my father and mother did not make me study all the sciences when I was young.

PHILOSOPHY MASTER
This is a reasonable sentiment. Nam sine doctrina vita est quasi mortis imago. You understand that, and you doubtless know Latin?

MONSIEUR JOURDAIN
Yes, but act as if I did not know it. Tell me what it says.

PHILOSOPHY MASTER
It says that without science life is almost an image of death.

MONSIEUR JOURDAIN
That Latin is right.

PHILOSOPHY MASTER
Don't you know some principles, some basics of the sciences?

MONSIEUR JOURDAIN
Oh yes! I can read and write.

PHILOSOPHY MASTER
Where would it please you for us to begin? Would you like me to teach you logic?

MONSIEUR JOURDAIN
What is this logic?

PHILOSOPHY MASTER
It is that which teaches the three operations of the mind.

MONSIEUR JOURDAIN
What are these three operations of the mind?

PHILOSOPHY MASTER
The first, the second, and the third. The first is to conceive well by means of the universals; the second is to judge well by means of the categories; and the third is to draw well a conclusion by means of figures. Barbara, Celarent, Darii, Ferio, Baralipton, etc.

MONSIEUR JOURDAIN
Those words are too ugly. This logic doesn't suit me at all. Let's learn something else that's prettier.

PHILOSOPHY MASTER
Would you like to learn morality?

MONSIEUR JOURDAIN
Morality?

PHILOSOPHY MASTER
Yes.

MONSIEUR JOURDAIN
What does it say, this morality?

PHILOSOPHY MASTER
It treats of happiness, teaches men to moderate their passions, and
...

MONSIEUR JOURDAIN
No, let's leave that. I'm as choleric as all the devils and there's no
morality that sticks, I want to be as full of anger as I want
whenever I like.

PHILOSOPHY MASTER
Would you like to learn physics?

MONSIEUR JOURDAIN
What's it about, this physics?

PHILOSOPHY MASTER
Physics explains the principles of natural things and the
properties of the material world; it discourses on the nature of the
elements, of metals, minerals, of stones, of plants and animals,
and teaches the causes of all the meteors, the rainbow, the will o'
the wisps, the comets, lightning, thunder, thunderbolts, rain,
snow, hail, winds, and whirlwinds.

MONSIEUR JOURDAIN
There's too much commotion in it, too much confusion.

PHILOSOPHY MASTER
Then what do you want me to teach you?

MONSIEUR JOURDAIN
Teach me how to spell.

PHILOSOPHY MASTER
Very gladly.

MONSIEUR JOURDAIN
Afterwards, you may teach me the almanack, to know when there is a moon and when not.

PHILOSOPHY MASTER
So be it. Following your thought and treating this matter as a philosopher, it is necessary to begin according to the order of things, by an exact knowledge of the nature of letters and the different ways of pronouncing them all. And thereupon I must tell you letters are divided into vowels, called vowels because they express the voice; and into consonants because they sound with the vowels and only mark the diverse articulations of the voice. There are five vowels or voices
A, E, I, O, U.

MONSIEUR JOURDAIN
I understand all that.

PHILOSOPHY MASTER
The vowel A is formed by opening the mouth widely
A. Its vowels are to be given the sounds used in vocalizing
Ah-aye-ee-o-ou.

MONSIEUR JOURDAIN
A, A. Yes.

PHILOSOPHY MASTER
The vowel E is formed by approaching the lower jaw to the upper
A, E.

MONSIEUR JOURDAIN
A, E; A, E. By my faith, yes. Ah! How fine! PHILOSOPHY
MASTER
And the vowel I, by bringing the jaws still nearer each other and
stretching the two corners of the mouth towards the ears
A, E, I.

MONSIEUR JOURDAIN
A, E, I. I. I. I. That's true. Long live science!

PHILOSOPHY MASTER
The vowel O is formed by opening the jaws and drawing together
the two corners of the lips, upper and lower
O.

MONSIEUR JOURDAIN
O, O. There's nothing truer. A, E, I, O,I O.. That's admirable! I,
O, I, O.

PHILOSOPHY MASTER
The opening of the mouth happens to make a little circle which
represents an O.

MONSIEUR JOURDAIN
O, O, O. You are right! O. Ah! What a fine thing it is to know
something!

PHILOSOPHY MASTER
The vowel U is formed by bringing the teeth nearly together
without completely joining them, and thrusting the two lips
outward, also bringing them nearly together without completely
joining them
U.

MONSIEUR JOURDAIN
U, U. There's nothing truer. U.

PHILOSOPHY MASTER
Your two lips thrust out as if you were making a face, whence it results that if you want to make a face at someone and mock him, you have only to say to him "U."

MONSIEUR JOURDAIN
U, U. That's true. Ah! Why didn't I study sooner in order to know all that!

PHILOSOPHY MASTER
Tomorrow we shall look at the other letters, which are the consonants.

MONSIEUR JOURDAIN
Are there things as curious about them as about these?

PHILOSOPHY MASTER
Without a doubt. The consonant D, for example, is pronounced by clapping the tongue above the upper teeth
D.

MONSIEUR JOURDAIN
D, D, Yes. Ah! What fine things! Fine things!

PHILOSOPHY MASTER
The F, by pressing the upper teeth against the lower lip
F.

MONSIEUR JOURDAIN
F, F. That's the truth. Ah! My father and my mother, how I wish you ill!

PHILOSOPHY MASTER
And the R, by carrying the tip of the tongue to the top of the palate, so that being grazed by the air that comes out with force, it yields to it and comes back always to the same place, making a kind of trill
R. AR.

MONSIEUR JOURDAIN
R, R, AR. R, R, R, R, R, RA. That's true. Ah! What a clever man you are! And how I have lost time! R, R, R, AR.

PHILOSOPHY MASTER
I'll explain to you all these strange things to their very depths.

MONSIEUR JOURDAIN
Please do. But now, I must confide in you. I'm in love with a lady of great quality, and I wish that you would help me write something to her in a little note that I will let fall at her feet.

PHILOSOPHY MASTER
Very well.

MONSIEUR JOURDAIN
That will be gallant, yes?

PHILOSOPHY MASTER
Without doubt. Is it verse that you wish to write her?

MONSIEUR JOURDAIN
No, no. No verse.

PHILOSOPHY MASTER
Do you want only prose?

MONSIEUR JOURDAIN
No, I don't want either prose or verse.

PHILOSOPHY MASTER
It must be one or the other.

MONSIEUR JOURDAIN
Why?

PHILOSOPHY MASTER
Because, sir, there is no other way to express oneself than with prose or verse.

MONSIEUR JOURDAIN
There is nothing but prose or verse?

PHILOSOPHY MASTER
No, sir, everything that is not prose is verse, and everything that is not verse is prose.

MONSIEUR JOURDAIN
And when one speaks, what is that then?

PHILOSOPHY MASTER
Prose.

MONSIEUR JOURDAIN
What! When I say, "Nicole, bring me my slippers, and give me my nightcap," that's prose?

PHILOSOPHY MASTER
Yes, Sir.

MONSIEUR JOURDAIN
By my faith! For more than forty years I have been speaking prose without knowing anything about it, and I am much obliged to you for having taught me that. I would like then to put into a note to her

"Beautiful marchioness, your lovely eyes make me die of love," but I want that put in a gallant manner and be nicely turned.

PHILOSOPHY MASTER
Put it that the fires of her eyes reduce your heart to cinders; that you suffer night and day for her the torments of a . . .

MONSIEUR JOURDAIN
No, no, no. I want none of that; I only want you to say "Beautiful marchioness, your lovely eyes make me die of love."

PHILOSOPHY MASTER
The thing requires a little lengthening.

MONSIEUR JOURDAIN
No, I tell you, I want only those words in the note, but turned stylishly, well arranged, as is necessary. Please tell me, just to see, the diverse ways they could be put.

PHILOSOPHY MASTER
One could put them first of all as you said them
"Beautiful marchioness, your lovely eyes make me die of love." Or else
"Of love to die make me, beautiful marchioness, your beautiful eyes." Or else
"Your lovely eyes, of love make me, beautiful marchioness, die." Or else
"Die, your lovely eyes, beautiful marchioness, of love make me." Or else
"Me make your lovely eyes die, beautiful marchioness, of love."

MONSIEUR JOURDAIN
But, of all those ways, which is the best?

PHILOSOPHY MASTER
The way you said it

"Beautiful marchioness, your lovely eyes make me die of love."

MONSIEUR JOURDAIN
I never studied, and yet I made the whole thing up at the first try. I thank you with all my heart, and I ask you to come tomorrow early.

PHILOSOPHY MASTER
I shall not fail to do so. (He leaves).

MONSIEUR JOURDAIN
What? Hasn't my suit come yet?

THE LACKEY
No, Sir.

MONSIEUR JOURDAIN
That cursed tailor makes me wait all day when I have so much to do! I'm enraged. May the quartan fever shake that tormentor of a tailor! To the devil with the tailor! May the plague choke the tailor! If I had him here now, that detestable tailor, that dog of a tailor, that traitor of a tailor, I . . .

SCENE V

Master Tailor, Apprentice Tailor carrying suit, Monsieur Jourdain, Lackeys

MONSIEUR JOURDAIN
Ah! You're here! I was getting into a rage against you.

MASTER TAILOR
I could not come sooner, and I put twenty men to work on your suit.

MONSIEUR JOURDAIN

You sent me some silk hose so small that I had all the difficulty in the world putting them on, and already there are two broken stitches.

MASTER TAILOR
They get bigger, too much so.

MONSIEUR JOURDAIN
Yes, if I always break the stitches. You also had made for me a pair of shoes that pinch furiously.

MASTER TAILOR
Not at all, sir.

MONSIEUR JOURDAIN
How, not at all!

MASTER TAILOR
No, they don't pinch you at all.

MONSIEUR JOURDAIN
I tell you, they pinch me.

MASTER TAILOR
You imagine that.

MONSIEUR JOURDAIN
I imagine it because I feel it. That's a good reason for you!

MASTER TAILOR
Wait, here is the finest court-suit, and the best matched. It's a masterpiece to have invented a serious suit that is not black. And I give six attempts to the best tailors to equal it.

MONSIEUR JOURDAIN
What's this? You've put the flowers upside down.

MASTER TAILOR
You didn't tell me you wanted them right side up.

MONSIEUR JOURDAIN
Did I have to tell you that?

MASTER TAILOR
Yes, surely. All the people of quality wear them this way.

MONSIEUR JOURDAIN
The people of quality wear the flowers upside down?

MASTER TAILOR
Yes, Sir.

MONSIEUR JOURDAIN
Oh! It's alright then.

MASTER TAILOR
If you like, I'll put them right side up.

MONSIEUR JOURDAIN
No, no.

MASTER TAILOR
You have only to say so.

MONSIEUR JOURDAIN
No, I tell you. You've made it very well. Do you think the suit is going to look good on me?

MASTER TAILOR
What a question! I defy a painter with his brush to do anything that would fit you better. I have a worker in my place who is the

greatest genius in the world at mounting a rhinegrave, and another who is the hero of the age at assembling a doublet.

MONSIEUR JOURDAIN
The perruque and the plumes
are they correct?

MASTER TAILOR
Everything's good.

MONSIEUR JOURDAIN
(Looking at the tailor's suit) Ah! Ah! Monsieur Tailor, here's the material from the last suit you made for me. I know it well.

MASTER TAILOR
You see, the material seemed so fine that I wanted a suit made of it for myself.

MONSIEUR JOURDAIN
Yes, but you should not have cut it out of mine.

MASTER TAILOR
Do you want to put on your suit?

MONSIEUR JOURDAIN
Yes, give it to me.

MASTER TAILOR
Wait. That's not the way it's done. I have brought men to dress you in a cadence; these kinds of suits are put on with ceremony. Hey there! Come in, you! Put this suit on the gentleman the way you do with people of quality.

(Four APPRENTICE TAILORS enter, two of them pull off Monsieur Jourdain's breeches made for his morning exercises, and two others pull off his waistcoat; then they put on his new suit;

Monsieur Jourdain promenades among them and shows them his suit for their approval. All this to the cadence of instrumental music.)

APPRENTICE TAILOR
My dear gentleman, please to give the apprentices a small tip.

MONSIEUR JOURDAIN
What did you call me?

APPRENTICE TAILOR
My dear gentleman.

MONSIEUR JOURDAIN
My dear gentleman! That's what it is to dress like people of quality! Go all your life dressed like a bourgeois and they'll never call you "My dear gentleman." Here, take this for the "My dear gentleman."

APPRENTICE TAILOR
My Lord, we are very much obliged to you.

MONSIEUR JOURDAIN
"My Lord!" Oh! Oh! "My Lord!" Wait, my friend. "My Lord" deserves something, and it's not a little word, this "My Lord." Take this. That's what "My Lord" gives you.

APPRENTICE TAILOR
My Lord, we will drink to the health of Your Grace.

MONSIEUR JOURDAIN
"Your Grace!" Oh! Oh! Oh! Wait, don't go. To me, "Your Grace!" My faith, if he goes as far as "Highness," he will have all my purse. Wait. That's for "My Grace."

APPRENTICE TAILOR
My Lord, we thank you very humbly for your liberality.

MONSIEUR JOURDAIN
He did well, I was going to give him everything. (The four Apprentice Tailors celebrate with a dance, which comprises the Second Interlude.)

ACT III

SCENE I

Monsieur Jourdain and his two Lackeys

MONSIEUR JOURDAIN
Follow me, I am going to show off my clothes a little about town. And above all both of you take care to walk close at my heels, so people can see that you are with me.

LACKEYS
Yes, Sir.

MONSIEUR JOURDAIN
Call Nicole for me, so I can give her some orders. Don't bother, there she is.

ACT THREE

SCENE II

Nicole, Monsieur Jourdain, two Lackeys

MONSIEUR JOURDAIN
Nicole!

NICOLE
Yes, sir?

MONSIEUR JOURDAIN
Listen.

NICOLE
He, he, he, he, he!

MONSIEUR JOURDAIN
What are you laughing about?

NICOLE
He, he, he, he, he, he!

MONSIEUR JOURDAIN
What does the hussy mean by this?

NICOLE
He, he, he! Oh, how you are got up! He, he, he!

MONSIEUR JOURDAIN
How's that?

NICOLE
Ah! Ah! Oh Lord! He, he, he, he, he!

MONSIEUR JOURDAIN
What kind of little baggage is this? Are you mocking me?

NICOLE
Certainly not, sir, I should be very sorry to do so. He, he, he, he, he!

MONSIEUR JOURDAIN
I'll give you a smack on the nose if you go on laughing.

NICOLE
Sir, I can't help it. He, he, he, he, he, he!

MONSIEUR JOURDAIN
You are not going to stop?

NICOLE
Sir, I beg pardon. But you are so funny that I couldn't help laughing. He, he, he!

MONSIEUR JOURDAIN
What insolence!

NICOLE
You're so funny like that. He, he!

MONSIEUR JOURDAIN
I'll . . .

NICOLE
Please excuse me. He, he, he, he!

MONSIEUR JOURDAIN
Listen. If you go on laughing the least bit, I swear I'll give you the biggest slap ever given.

NICOLE
Alright, sir, it's done, I won't laugh any more.

MONSIEUR JOURDAIN
Take good care not to. Presently you must clean . . .

NICOLE
He, he!

MONSIEUR JOURDAIN
You must clean . . .

NICOLE
He, he!

MONSIEUR JOURDAIN

You must, I say, clean the room and . . .

NICOLE
He, he!

MONSIEUR JOURDAIN
Again! NICOLE
(Falling down with laughter) Then beat me sir, and let me have my laugh out, it will do me more good. He, he, he, he, he!

MONSIEUR JOURDAIN
I'm furious.

NICOLE
Have mercy, sir! I beg you to let me laugh. He, he, he!

MONSIEUR JOURDAIN
If I catch you . . .

NICOLE
Sir! I shall burst . . . Oh! if I don't laugh. He, he, he!

MONSIEUR JOURDAIN
But did anyone ever see such a hussy as that, who laughs in my face instead of receiving my, orders?

NICOLE
What would you have me do, sir?

MONSIEUR JOURDAIN
That you consider getting my house ready for the company that's coming soon, you hussy.

NICOLE
Ah, by my faith, I don't feel like laughing any more. All your guests make such a disorder here that the word "company" is enough to put me in a bad humor.

MONSIEUR JOURDAIN
Why, should I shut my door to everyone for your sake?

NICOLE
You should at least shut it to some people.

SCENE III

Madame Jourdain, Monsieur Jourdain, Nicole, Lackeys

MADAME JOURDAIN
Ah, ah! Here's a new story! What's this, what's this, husband, this outfit you have on there? Don't you care what people think of you when you are got up like that? And do you want yourself laughed at everywhere?

MONSIEUR JOURDAIN
None but fools and dolts will laugh at me wife.

MADAME JOURDAIN
Truly, they haven't waited until now, your antics have long given a laugh to everyone.

MONSIEUR JOURDAIN
Who's everyone, if you please?

MADAME JOURDAIN
Everyone is everyone who is right and who is wiser than you. For my part, I am scandalized at the life you lead. I no longer recognize our house. One would say it's the beginning of Carnival here, every day; and beginning early in the morning, so it won't be

forgotten, one hears nothing but the racket of fiddles and singers which disturbs the whole neighborhood.

NICOLE
Madame speaks well. I'll never be able to get my housework done properly with that gang you have come here. They have feet that hunt for mud in every part of town to bring it here; and poor Franoise almost has her teeth on the floor, scrubbing the boards that your fine masters come to dirty up every day.

MONSIEUR JOURDAIN
What, our servant Nicole, you have quite a tongue for a peasant.

MADAME JOURDAIN
Nicole is right, and she has more sense than you. I'd like to know what you think you're going to do with a Dancing Master, at your age?

NICOLE
And with a hulking Fencing Master who comes stamping his feet, shaking the whole house and tearing up all the floorboards in our drawing-room.

MONSIEUR JOURDAIN
Be quiet, both servant and wife!

MADAME JOURDAIN
Is it that you're learning to dance for the time when you'll have no legs to dance on?

NICOLE
Do you want to kill someone?

MONSIEUR JOURDAIN
Quiet, I tell you! You are ignorant women, both of you, and you don't know the advantages of all this.

MADAME JOURDAIN
You should instead be thinking of marrying off your daughter, who is of an age to be provided for.

MONSIEUR JOURDAIN
I'll think of marrying off my daughter when a suitable match comes along, but I also want to learn about fine things.

NICOLE
I heard said, Madame, that today he took a Philosophy Master to thicken the soup!

MONSIEUR JOURDAIN
Very well. I have a wish to have wit and to reason about things with decent people.

MADAME JOURDAIN
Don't you intend, one of these days, to go to school and have yourself whipped at your age?

MONSIEUR JOURDAIN
Why not? Would to God I were whipped this minute in front of everyone, if I only knew what they learn at school!

NICOLE
Yes, my faith! That would get you into better shape.

MONSIEUR JOURDAIN
Without doubt.

MADAME JOURDAIN
All this is very important to the management of your house.

MONSIEUR JOURDAIN

Assuredly. You both talk like beasts, and I'm ashamed of your ignorance. For example, do you know what are you speaking just now?

MADAME JOURDAIN
Yes, I know that what I'm saying is well said and that you ought to be considering living in another way.

MONSIEUR JOURDAIN
I'm not talking about that. I'm asking if you know what the words are that you are saying here?

MADAME JOURDAIN
They are words that are very sensible, and your conduct is scarcely so.

MONSIEUR JOURDAIN
I'm not talking about that, I tell you. I'm asking you
what is it that I'm speaking to you this minute, what is it?

MADAME JOURDAIN
Nonsense.

MONSIEUR JOURDAIN
No, no! That's not it. What is it we are both saying, what language is it that we are speaking right now?

MADAME JOURDAIN
Well?

MONSIEUR JOURDAIN
What is it called?

MADAME JOURDAIN
It's called whatever you want.

MONSIEUR JOURDAIN
It's prose, you ignorant creature.

MADAME JOURDAIN
Prose?

MONSIEUR JOURDAIN
Yes, prose. Everything is prose that is not verse; and everything that's not verse is prose. There! This is what it is to study! And you (to Nicole), do you know what you must do to say U?

NICOLE
What?

MONSIEUR JOURDAIN
Say U, in order to see.

NICOLE
Oh Well, U.

MONSIEUR JOURDAIN
What do you do?

NICOLE
I say U.

MONSIEUR JOURDAIN
Yes, but, when you say U, what do you do?

NICOLE
I do what you tell me to.

MONSIEUR JOURDAIN
Oh, how strange it is to have to deal with morons! You thrust your lips out and bring your lower jaw to your upper jaw

U, see? U. Do you see? I make a pout
U.

NICOLE
Yes, that's beautiful.

MADAME JOURDAIN
How admirable.

MONSIEUR JOURDAIN
But it's quite another thing, if you have seen O, and D, D, and F,
F.

MADAME JOURDAIN
What is all this rigmarole?

NICOLE
What does all this do for us?

MONSIEUR JOURDAIN
It enrages me when I see these ignorant women.

MADAME JOURDAIN
Go, go, you ought to send all those people packing with their
foolishness.

NICOLE
And above all, that great gawk of a Fencing Master, who ruins all
my work with dust.

MONSIEUR JOURDAIN
Well! This Fencing Master seems to get under your skin. I'll soon
show you how impertinent you are.(He has the foils brought and
gives one to Nicole). There. Demonstration
The line of the body. When your opponent thrusts in quarte, you
need only do this, and when they thrust in tierce, you need only

do this. That is the way never to be killed, and isn't it fine to be assured of what one does, when fighting against someone? There, thrust at me a little, to see.

NICOLE
Well then, what? (Nicole thrusts, giving him several hits).

MONSIEUR JOURDAIN
Easy! Wait! Oh! Gently! Devil take the hussy!

NICOLE
You told me to thrust.

MONSIEUR JOURDAIN
Yes, but you thrust in tierce, before you thrust in quarte, and you didn't have the patience to let me parry.

MADAME JOURDAIN
You are a fool, husband, with all your fantasies, and this has come to you since you took a notion to associate with the nobility.

MONSIEUR JOURDAIN
When I associate with the nobility, I show my good judgment; and that's better than associating with your shopkeepers.

MADAME JOURDAIN
Oh yes, truly! There's a great deal to gain by consorting with your nobles, and you did so well with your fine Count you were so taken with!

MONSIEUR JOURDAIN
Peace! Think what you're saying. You know very well, wife, that you don't know who you're talking about, when you talk about him! He's a more important person than you think
a great Lord, respected at court, and who talks to the King just as I talk to you. Is it not a thing which does me great honor, that a

person of this quality is seen to come so often to my house, who calls me his dear friend and treats me as if I were his equal? He has more regard for me than one would ever imagine; and, in front of everyone, he shows me so much affection that I am embarrassed myself.

MADAME JOURDAIN
Yes, he has a kindness for you, and shows his affection, but he borrows your money.

MONSIEUR JOURDAIN
So! Isn't it an honor for me to lend money to a man of that condition? And can I do less for a lord who calls me his dear friend?

MADAME JOURDAIN
And this lord, what does he do for you?

MONSIEUR JOURDAIN
Things that would astonish you if you knew them.

MADAME JOURDAIN
Like what?

MONSIEUR JOURDAIN
Blast! I cannot explain myself. It must suffice that if I have lent him money, he'll pay it back fully, and before long.

MADAME JOURDAIN
Yes. You are waiting for that.

MONSIEUR JOURDAIN
Assuredly. Didn't he tell me so?

MADAME JOURDAIN
Yes, yes, he won't fail to do it.

MONSIEUR JOURDAIN
He swore it on the faith of a gentleman.

MADAME JOURDAIN
Nonsense!

MONSIEUR JOURDAIN
Well! You are very obstinate, wife. I tell you he will keep his word, I'm sure of it.

MADAME JOURDAIN
And I'm sure he will not, and that all his show of affection is only to flatter you.

MONSIEUR JOURDAIN
Be still. Here he is.

MADAME JOURDAIN
That's all we needed! He's come again perhaps to borrow something from you. The very sight of him spoils my appetite.

MONSIEUR JOURDAIN
Be still, I tell you.

SCENE IV

Count Dorante, Monsieur Jourdain, Madame Jourdain, Nicole

DORANTE
My dear friend, Monsieur Jourdain, how do you do?

MONSIEUR JOURDAIN
Very well, sir, to render you my small services.

DORANTE

And Madame Jourdain there, how is she?

MADAME JOURDAIN
Madame Jourdain is as well as she can be.

DORANTE
Well! Monsieur Jourdain, you are excellently well dressed!

MONSIEUR JOURDAIN
You see.

DORANTE
You have a fine air in that suit, and we have no young men at court who are better made than you.

MONSIEUR JOURDAIN
Well! well!

MADAME JOURDAIN
(Aside) He scratches him where it itches.

DORANTE
Turn around. It's positively elegant.

MADAME JOURDAIN
(Aside) Yes, as big a fool behind as in front.

DORANTE
My faith, Monsieur Jourdain, I was strangely impatient to see you. You are the man in the world I esteem most, and I was speaking of you again this morning in the bedchamber of the King.

MONSIEUR JOURDAIN
You do me great honor, sir. (To Madame Jourdain) In the King's bedchamber!

DORANTE
Come, put on . . .

MONSIEUR JOURDAIN
Sir, I know the respect I owe you.

DORANTE
Heavens! Put on your hat; I pray you, no ceremony between us.

MONSIEUR JOURDAIN
Sir . . .

DORANTE
Put it on, I tell you, Monsieur Jourdain
you are my friend.

MONSIEUR JOURDAIN
Sir, I am your humble servant.

DORANTE
I won't be covered if you won't.

MONSIEUR JOURDAIN
(Putting on his hat) I would rather be uncivil than troublesome.

DORANTE
I am in your debt, as you know.

MADAME JOURDAIN
Yes, we know it all too well.

DORANTE
You have generously lent me money upon several occasions, and
you have obliged me with the best grace in the world, assuredly.

MONSIEUR JOURDAIN
Sir, you jest with me.

DORANTE
But I know how to repay what is lent me, and to acknowledge the favors rendered me.

MONSIEUR JOURDAIN
I have no doubt of it, sir.

DORANTE
I want to settle this matter with you, and I came here to make up our accounts together.

MONSIEUR JOURDAIN
There wife! You see your impertinence!

DORANTE
I am a man who likes to repay debts as soon as I can.

MONSIEUR JOURDAIN
(Aside to Madame Jourdain) I told you so.

DORANTE
Let's see how much do I owe you.

MONSIEUR JOURDAIN
(Aside to Madame Jourdain) There you are, with your ridiculous suspicions.

DORANTE
Do you remember well all the money you have lent me?

MONSIEUR JOURDAIN
I believe so. I made a little note of it. Here it is. Once you were given two hundred louis d'or.

DORANTE
That's true.

MONSIEUR JOURDAIN
Another time, six-score.

DORANTE
Yes. MONSIEUR JOURDAIN
And another time, a hundred and forty.

DORANTE
You're right.

MONSIEUR JOURDAIN
These three items make four hundred and sixty louis d'or, which comes to five thousand sixty livres.

DORANTE
The account is quite right. Five thousand sixty livres.

MONSIEUR JOURDAIN
One thousand eight hundred thirty-two livres to your plume-maker.

DORANTE
Exactly.

MONSIEUR JOURDAIN
Two thousand seven hundred eighty livres to your tailor.

DORANTE
It's true.

MONSIEUR JOURDAIN
Four thousand three hundred seventy-nine livres twelve sols eight deniers to your tradesman.

DORANTE
Quite right. Twelve sols eight deniers. The account is exact.

MONSIEUR JouRDAIN
And one thousand seven hundred forty-eight livres seven sols four deniers to your saddler.

DORANTE
All that is true. What does that come to?

MONSIEUR JOURDAIN
Sum total, fifteen thousand eight hundred livres.

DORANTE
The sum total is exact
fifteen thousand eight hundred livres. To which add two hundred pistoles that you are going to give me, which will make exactly eighteen thousand francs, which I shall pay you at the first opportunity.

MADAME JOURDAIN
(Aside) Well, didn't I predict it?

MONSIEUR JOURDAIN
Peace!

DORANTE
Will that inconvenience you, to give me the amount I say?

MONSIEUR JOURDAIN
Oh, no!

MADAME JOURDAIN
(Aside) That man is making a milk-cow out of you!

MONSIEUR JOURDAIN
Be quiet!

DORANTE
If that inconveniences you, I will seek it somewhere else.

MONSIEUR JOURDAIN
NO, Sir.

MADAME JOURDAIN
(Aside) He won't be content until he's ruined you.

MONSIEUR JOURDAIN
Be quiet, I tell you.

DORANTE
You have only to tell me if that embarrasses you.

MONSIEUR JOURDAIN
Not at all, sir.

MADAME JOURDAIN
(Aside) He's a real wheedler!

MONSIEUR JOURDAIN
Hush.

MADAME JOURDAIN
(Aside) He'll drain you to the last sou.

MONSIEUR JOURDAIN
Will you be quiet?

DORANTE
I have a number of people who would gladly lend it to me; but since you are my best friend, I believed I might do you wrong if I asked someone else for it.

MONSIEUR JOURDAIN
It's too great an honor, sir, that you do me. I'll go get it for you.

MADAME JOURDAIN
(Aside) What! You're going to give it to him again?

MONSIEUR JOURDAIN
What can I do? Do you want me to refuse a man of this station, who spoke about me this morning in the King's bedchamber?

MADAME JOURDAIN
(Aside) Go on, you're a true dupe.

ACT THREE

SCENE V

Dorante, Madame Jourdain, Nicole

DORANTE
You appear to be very melancholy. What is wrong, Madame Jourdain?

MADAME JOURDAIN
I have a head bigger than my fist, even if it's not swollen.

DORANTE
Mademoiselle, your daughter, where is she that I don't see her?

MADAME JOURDAIN
Mademoiselle my daughter is right where she is.

DORANTE
How is she getting on?

MADAME JOURDAIN
She "gets on" on her two legs.

DORANTE
Wouldn't you like to come with her one of these days to see the
ballet and the comedy they are putting on at court?

MADAME JOURDAIN
Yes truly, we have a great desire to laugh, a very great desire to
laugh.

DORANTE
I think, Madame Jourdain, that you must have had many admirers
in your youth, beautiful and good humored as you were.

MADAME JOURDAIN
By Our Lady! Sir, is Madame Jourdain decrepit, and does her
head already shake with palsy?

DORANTE
Ah! My faith, Madame Jourdain, I beg pardon. I did not
remember that you are young. I am often distracted. Pray excuse
my impertinence.

SCENE VI

Monsieur Jourdain, Madame Jourdain, Dorante, Nicole)

MONSIEUR JOURDAIN
There are two hundred louis d'or.

DORANTE

I assure you, Monsieur Jourdain, that I am completely yours, and that I am eager to render you a service at court.

MONSIEUR JOURDAIN

I'm much obliged to you.

DORANTE

If Madame Jourdain desires to see the royal entertainment, I will have the best places in the ballroom given to her.

MADAME JOURDAIN

Madame Jourdain kisses your hands [but declines].

DORANTE

(Aside to Monsieur Jourdain) Our beautiful marchioness, as I sent word to you, in my note, will come here soon for the ballet and refreshments; I finally brought her to consent to the entertainment you wish to give her.

MONSIEUR JOURDAIN

Let us move a little farther away, for a certain reason.

DORANTE

It has been eight days since I saw you, and I have sent you no news regarding the diamond you put into my hands to present to her on your behalf; but it's because I had the greatest difficulty in conquering her scruples, and it's only today that she resolved to accept it.

MONSIEUR JOURDAIN

How did she judge it?

DORANTE
Marvelous. And I am greatly deceived if the beauty of that diamond does not produce for you an admirable effect on her spirit.

MONSIEUR JOURDAIN
Would to Heaven!

MADAME JOURDAIN
(To Nicole) Once he's with him he cannot leave him.

DORANTE
I made her value as she should the richness of that present and the grandeur of your love.

MONSIEUR JOURDAIN
These are, sir, favors which overwhelm me; and I am in the very greatest confusion at seeing a person of your quality demean himself for me as you do.

DORANTE
Are you joking? Among friends, does one stop at these sorts of scruples? And wouldn't you do the same thing for me, if the occasion offered?

MONSIEUR JOURDAIN
Oh! Certainly, and with all my heart.

MADAME JOURDAIN
(To Nicole) His presence weighs me down!

DORANTE
As for me, I never mind anything when it is necessary to serve a friend; and when you confided in me about the ardent passion you have formed for that delightful marchioness with whom I

have contacts, you saw that I volunteered immediately to assist your love.

MONSIEUR JOURDAIN
It's true, these are favors that confound me.

MADAME JOURDAIN
(To Nicole) Will he never go?

NICOLE
They enjoy being together.

DORANTE
You took the right tack to touch her heart. Women love above all the expenses we go to for them; and your frequent serenades, your continual bouquets, that superb fireworks for her over the water, the diamond she has received from you, and the entertainment you are preparing for her, all this speaks much better in favor of your love than all the words you might have spoken yourself.

MONSIEUR JOURDAIN
There are no expenditures I would not make if by that means I might find the road to her heart. A woman of quality has ravishing charms for me and it's an honor I would purchase at any price.

MADAME JOURDAIN
(To Nicole) What can they talk about so much? Steal over and listen a little.

DORANTE
Soon enough you will enjoy at your ease the pleasure of seeing her, and your eyes will have a long time to satisfy themselves.

MONSIEUR JOURDAIN
To be completely free, I have arranged for my wife to go to dinner at her sister's, where she'll spend all the after-dinner hours.

DORANTE
You have done prudently, as your wife might have embarrassed us. I have given the necessary orders to the cook for you, and for the ballet. It is of my own invention; and, provided the execution corresponds to the idea, I am sure it will be found . . .

MONSIEUR JOURDAIN
(Sees that Nicole is listening, and gives her a slap) Say! You're very impertinent! (To Dorante) Let's go, if you please.

SCENE VII

Madame Jourdain, Nicole

NICOLE
My faith, Madame, curiosity has cost me; but I believe something's afoot, since they were talking of some event where they did not want you to be.

MADAME JOURDAIN
Today's not the first time, Nicole, that I've had suspicions about my husband. I'm the most mistaken woman in the world, or there's some love-affair in the making. But let us see to my daughter. You know the love Cleonte has for her. He's a man who appeals to me, and I want to help his suit and give him Lucile, if I can.

NICOLE
Truly, Madame, I'm the most delighted creature in the world to see that you feel this way, since, if the master appeals to you, his valet appeals to me no less, and I could wish our marriage made under the shadow of theirs.

MADAME JOURDAIN
Go speak to Cleonte about it for me, and tell him to come to me
soon so we can present his request to my husband for my
daughter in marriage.

NICOLE
I hasten, Madame, with joy, for I could not receive a more
agreeable commission. (Alone) I shall, I think, make them very
happy.

SCENE VIII

Cleonte, Covielle, Nicole

NICOLE
Ah! I'm glad to have found you. I'm an ambassadress of joy, and I
come . . .

CLEONTE
Get out, traitor, and don't come to amuse me with your
treacherous words.

NICOLE
Is this how you receive me . . .

CLEONTE
Get out, I tell you, and go tell your faithless mistress that she will
never again in her life deceive the too trusting Cleonte.

NICOLE
What caprice is this? My dear Covielle, explain a little what you
are trying to say.

COVIELLE

Your dear Covielle, little hussy? Go, quickly, out of my sight, villainess , and leave me in peace.

NICOLE

What! You come to me too. . . COVIELLE

Out of my sight, I tell you, and never speak to me again.
NICOLE

My word! What fly has bitten those two? Let's go tell this pretty story to my mistress.

SCENE IX

Cleonte, Covielle

CLEONTE

What! Treat a lover in this way? And a lover who is the most faithful and passionate of lovers?

COVIELLE

It is a frightful thing that they have done to us both.

CLEONTE

I show a woman all the ardor and tenderness that can be imagined; I love nothing in the world but her, and I have nothing but her in my thoughts; she is all I care for, all my desire, all my joy; I talk of nothing but her, I think of nothing but her, I have no dreams but of her, I breathe only because of her, my heart lives wholly in her; and see how so much love is well repaid! I have been two days without seeing her, which are for me two frightful centuries; I meet her by chance; my heart, at that sight, is completely transported, my joy shines on my face; I fly with ecstasy towards her — and the faithless one averts her eyes and hurries by as if she had never seen me in her life!

COVIELLE
I say the same things as you.

CLEONTE
Covielle, can one see anything to equal this perfidy of the ungrateful Lucile?

COVIELLE
And that, Monsieur, of the treacherous Nicole?

CLEONTE
After so many ardent homages, sighs, and vows that I have made to her charms!

COVIELLE
After so many assiduous compliments, cares, and services that I rendered her in the kitchen!

CLEONTE
So many tears I have shed at her knees!

COVIELLE
So many buckets of water I have drawn for her!

CLEONTE
So much passion I have shown her in loving her more than myself!

COVIELLE
So much heat I have endured in turning the spit for her!

CLEONTE
She flies from me in disdain!

COVIELLE
She turns her back on me!

CLEONTE
It is perfidy worthy of the greatest punishments.

COVIELLE
It is treachery that merits a thousand slaps.

CLEONTE
Don't think, I beg you, of ever speaking in her favor to me.

COVIELLE
I, sir? God forbid!

CLEONTE
Never come to excuse the action of this faithless woman.

COVIELLE
Have no fear.

CLEONTE; No, you see, all your speeches in her defense will serve no purpose.

COVIELLE
Who even thinks of that?

CLEONTE
I want to conserve my resentment against her and end all contact with her.

COVIELLE
I agree.

CLEONTE
This Count who goes to her house is perhaps pleasant in her view; and her mind, I well see, allows itself to be dazzled by social standing. But it is necessary for me, for my honor, to prevent the

scandal of her inconstancy. I want to break off with her first and not leave her all the glory of dumping me. COVIELLE
That's very well said, and I agree, for my part, with all your feelings.

CLEONTE
Strengthen my resentment and aid my resolve against all the remains of love that could speak in her behalf. Tell me, I order you, all the bad you can of her; make for me a painting of her that will render her despicable; and show well, in order to disgust me, all the faults that you can see in her.

COVIELLE
Her, sir? There's a pretty fool, a well made flirt for you to give so much love! I see only mediocrity in her, and you will find a hundred women who will be more worthy of you. First of all, she has small eyes.

CLEONTE
That's true, she has small eyes; but they are full of fire, the brightest, the keenest in the world, the most touching eyes that one can see.

COVIELLE
She has a big mouth.

CLEONTE
Yes; but upon it one sees grace that one never sees on other mouths; and the sight of that mouth, which is the most attractive, the most amorous in the world, inspires desire.

COVIELLE
As for her figure, she's not tall.

CLEONTE
No, but she is graceful and well made.

COVIELLE
She affects a nonchalance in her speech and in her actions.

CLEONTE
That's true; but she may be forgiven all that, for her manners are so engaging, they have an irresistible charm.

COVIELLE
As to her wit . . .

CLEONTE
Ah! She has that, Covielle, the finest, the most delicate!

COVIELLE
Her conversation . . .

CLEONTE
Her conversation is charming.

COVIELLE
She is always serious . . .

CLEONTE; Would you have grinning playfulness, constant open merriment? And do you see anything more impertinent than those women who laugh all the time?

COVIELLE
But finally she is as capricious as any woman in the world.

CLEONTE
Yes, she is capricious, I concede; but everything becomes beautiful ladies well, one suffers everything for beauty.

COVIELLE
I see clearly how it goes, you want to go on loving her.

CLEONTE
Me, I'd like better to die; and I am going to hate her as much as I loved her.

COVIELLE
How, if you find her so perfect?

CLEONTE
That's how my vengeance will be more striking, in that way I'll show better the strength of my heart, by hating her, by quitting her, with all her beauty, all her charms, and as lovable as I find her. Here she is.

SCENE X

Cleonte, Lucile, Covielle, Nicole

NICOLE
For my part, I was completely shocked at it.

LUCILE
It can only be, Nicole, what I told you. But there he is.

CLEONTE
I don't even want to speak to her.

COVIELLE
I'll imitate you.

LUCILE
What's the matter Cleonte? What's wrong with you?

NICOLE
What's the matter with you, Covielle?

LUCILE
What grief possesses you?

NICOLE
What bad humor holds you?

LUCILE
Are you mute, Cleonte?

NICOLE
Have you lost your voice, Covielle?

CLEONTE
Is this not villainous!

COVIELLE
It's a Judas!

LUCILE
I clearly see that our recent meeting has troubled you.

CLEONTE
Ah! Ah! She sees what she's done.

NICOLE
Our greeting this morning has annoyed you. COVIELLE
She has guessed the problem.

LUCILE
Isn't it true, Cleonte, that this is the cause of your resentment?

CLEONTE
Yes, perfidious one, it is, since I must speak; and I must tell that
you shall not triumph in your faithlessness as you think, I want to
be the first to break with you, and you won't have the advantage
of driving me away. I will have difficulty in conquering the love I

have for you; it will cause me pain; I will suffer for a while. But I'll come through it, and I would rather stab myself through the heart than have the weakness to return to you.

COVIELLE
Me too.

LUCILE
What an uproar over nothing. I want to tell you, Cleonte, what made me avoid joining you this morning.

CLEONTE
No, I don't want to listen to anything . . .

NICOLE
I want to tell you what made us pass so quickly.

COVIELLE
I don't want to hear anything.

LUCILE
(Following Cleonte) Know that this morning . . .

CLEONTE
No, I tell you.

NICOLE
(Following Covielle) Learn that . . .

COVIELLE
No, traitor.

LUCILE
Listen.

CLEONTE
I won't listen.

NICOLE
Let me speak.

COVIELLE
I'm deaf.

LUCILE
Cleonte! CLEONTE
No.

NICOLE
Covielle!

COVIELLE
I won't listen.

LUCILE
Stop.

CLEONTE
Gibberish!

NICOLE
Listen to me.

COVIELLE
Rubbish!

LUCILE
One moment.

CLEONTE
Never.

NICOLE
A little patience.

COVIELLE
Not interested!

LUCILE
Two words.

CLEONTE
No, you've had them.

NICOLE
One word.

COVIELLE
No more talking.

LUCILE
Alright! Since you don't want to listen to me, think what you like, and do what you want.

NICOLE
Since you act like that, make whatever you like of it all.

CLEONTE
Let us know the reason, then, for such a fine reception.

LUCILE
It no longer pleases me to say.

COVIELLE
Let us know something of your story.

NICOLE
I ,myself, no longer want to tell you.

CLEONTE
Tell me . . .

LUCILE
No, I don't want to say anything.

COVIELLE
Tell it . . .

NICOLE
No, I'll tell nothing.

CLEONTE
For pity . . .

LUCILE
No, I say.

COVIELLE
Have mercy.

NICOLE
It's no use.

CLEONTE
I beg you.

LUCILE
Leave me . . .

COVIELLE
I plead with you.

NICOLE
Get out of here.

CLEONTE
Lucile!

LUCILE
No.

COVIELLE
Nicole!

NICOLE
Never.

CLEONTE
In the name of God! . . .

LUCILE
I don't want to.

COVIELLE
Talk to me.

NICOLE
Definitely not.

CLEONTE
Clear up my doubts.

LUCILE
No, I'll do nothing.

COVIELLE
Relieve my mind!

NICOLE
No, I don't care to.

CLEONTE
Alright! since you are so little concerned to take me out of my
pain and to justify yourself for the shameful treatment you gave
to my passion, you are seeing me, ingrate, for the last time, and I
am going far from you to die of sorrow and love.

COVIELLE
And I — I will follow in his steps.

LUCILE
Cleonte!

NICOLE
Covielle!

CLEONTE
What?

COVIELLE
Yes?

LUCILE
Where are you going?

CLEONTE
Where I told you.

COVIELLE
We are going to die.

LUCILE
You are going to die, Cleonte?

CLEONTE
Yes, cruel one, since you wish it.

LUCILE
Me! I wish you to die?

CLEONTE
Yes, you wish it.

LUCILE
Who told you that?

CLEONTE
Is it not wishing it when you don't wish to clear up my suspicions?

LUCILE
Is it my fault? And, if you had wished to listen to me, would I not have told you that the incident you complain of was caused this morning by the presence of an old aunt who insists that the mere approach of a man dishonors a woman — an aunt who constantly delivers sermons to us on this text, and tells us that all men are like devils we must flee?

NICOLE
There's the key to the entire affair.

CLEONTE
Are you sure you're not deceiving me, Lucile?

COVIELLE
Aren't you making this up?

LUCILE
There's nothing more true.

NICOLE
It's the absolute truth.

COVIELLE
Are we going to give in to this?

CLEONTE
Ah! Lucile, how with a word from your lips you are able to appease the things in my heart, and how easily one allows himself to be persuaded by the people one loves!

COVIELLE
How easily we are manipulated by these blasted minxes!

SCENE XI

Madame Jourdain, Cleonte, Lucile, Covielle, Nicole

MADAME JOURDAIN
I am very glad to see you, Cleonte and you are here at just the right time. My husband is coming, seize the opportunity to ask for Lucile in marriage.

CLEONTE
Ah! Madame, how sweet that word is to me, and how it flatters my desires! Could I receive an order more charming, a favor more precious?

SCENE XII

Monsieur Jourdain, Madame Jourdain, Cleonte, Lucile, Covielle, Nicole

CLEONTE

Sir, I did not want to use anyone to make a request of you that I have long considered. It affects me enough for me to take charge of it myself; and, without further ado, I will say to you that the honor of being your son-in-law is a glorious favor that I beg you to grant me.

MONSIEUR JOURDAIN

Before giving you a reply, sir, I beg to ask if you are a gentleman.

CLEONTE

Sir, most people don't hesitate much over this question. They use the word carelessly. They take the name without scruple, and the usage of today seems to validate the theft. As for me, I confess to you, I have a little more delicate feelings on this matter. I find all imposture undignified for an honest man, and that there is cowardice in disguising what Heaven made us at birth; to present ourselves to the eyes of the world with a stolen title; to wish to give a false impression. I was born of parents who, without doubt, held honorable positions. I have six years of service in the army, and I find myself established well enough to maintain a tolerable rank in the world; but despite all that I certainly have no wish to give myself a name to which others in my place might believe they could pretend, and I will tell you frankly that I am not a gentleman.

MONSIEUR JOURDAIN

Shake hands, Sir! My daughter is not for you.

CLEONTE

What?

MONSIEUR JOURDAIN

You are not a gentleman. You will not have my daughter.

MADAME JOURDAIN
What are you trying to say with your talk of gentleman? Are we ourselves of the line of St. Louis?

MONSIEUR JOURDAIN
Quiet, wife, I see what you are up to.

MADAME JOURDAIN
Aren't we both descended from good bourgeois families?

MONSIEUR JOURDAIN
There's that hateful word!

MADAME JOURDAIN
And wasn't your father a merchant just like mine?

MONSIEUR JOURDAIN
Plague take the woman! She never fails to do this! If your father was a merchant, so much the worse for him! But, as for mine, those who say that are misinformed. All that I have to say to you is, that I want a gentleman for a son-in-law.

MADAME JOURDAIN
It's necessary for your daughter to have a husband who is worthy of her, and it's better for her to have an honest rich man who is well made than an impoverished gentleman who is badly built.

NICOLE
That's true. We have the son of a gentleman in our village who is the most ill formed and the greatest fool I have ever seen.

MONSIEUR JOURDAIN
Hold your impertinent tongue! You always butt into the conversation. I have enough money for my daughter, I need only honor, and I want to make her a marchioness.

MADAME JOURDAIN
A marchioness?

MONSIEUR JOURDAIN
Yes, marchioness.

MADAME JOURDAIN
Alas! God save me from it!

MONSIEUR JOURDAIN
It's a thing I have resolved.

MADAME JOURDAIN
As for me, it's a thing I'll never consent to. Marriages above one's
station are always subject to great inconveniences. I have
absolutely no wish for a son-in-law who can reproach her parents
to my daughter, and I don't want her to have children who will be
ashamed to call me their grandmother. If she arrives to visit me in
the equipage of a great lady and if she fails, by mischance, to greet
someone of the neighborhood, they wouldn't fail immediately to
say a hundred stupidities. "Do you see," they would say, "this
madam marchioness who gives herself such glorious airs? It's the
daughter of Monsieur Jourdain, who was all too glad, when she
was little, to play house with us; she's not always been so haughty
as she now is; and her two grandfathers sold cloth near St.
Innocent's Gate. They amassed wealth for their children, they're
paying dearly perhaps for it now in the other world, and one can
scarcely get that rich by being honest." I certainly don't want all
that gossip, and I want, in a word, a man who will be obliged to
me for my daughter and to whom I can say, "Sit down there, my
son-in-law, and have dinner with me."

MONSIEUR JOURDAIN
Surely those are the sentiments of a little spirit, to want to remain
always in a base condition. Don't talk back to me

my daughter will be a marchioness in spite of everyone. And, if you make me angrier, I'll make a duchess of her.

MADAME JOURDAIN
Cleonte, don't lose courage yet. Follow me, my daughter, and tell your father resolutely that, if you can't have him, you don't want to marry anyone.

SCENE XIII

Cleonte, Covielle

COVIELLE
You've made a fine business, with your pretty sentiments.

CLEONTE
What do you want? I have a scruple about that which precedent cannot conquer.

COVIELLE
Don't you make a fool of yourself by taking it seriously with a man like that? Don't you see that he is a fool? And would it cost you anything to accommodate yourself to his fantasies?

CLEONTE
You're right. But I didn't believe it necessary to prove nobility in order to be Monsieur Jourdain's son-in-law.

COVIELLE
Ha, ha, ha!

CLEONTE
What are you laughing at?

COVIELLE
At a thought that just occurred to me of how to play our man a trick and help you obtain what you desire.

CLEONTE
How?

COVIELLE
The idea is really funny.

CLEONTE
What is it?

COVIELLE
A short time ago there was a certain masquerade which fits here better than anything, and that I intend to make part of a prank I want to play on our fool. It all seems a little phony; but, with him, one can try anything, there is hardly any reason to be subtle, and he is the man to play his role marvelously and to swallow easily any fabrication we want to tell him. I have the actors, I have the costumes ready, just leave it to me.

CLEONTE
But tell me . . .

COVIELLE
I am going to instruct you in everything. Let's go, there he is, returning.

SCENE XIV

Monsieur Jourdain, Lackey

MONSIEUR JOURDAIN
What the devil is this? They have nothing other than the great lords to reproach me with, and as for me, I see nothing so fine as

to associate with the great lords; there is only honor and civility among them, and I would have given two fingers of a hand to have been born a count or a marquis.

LACKEY
Sir, here's the Count, and he has a lady with him. MONSIEUR JOURDAIN
What! My Goodness, I have some orders to give. Tell them I'll be back here soon.

SCENE XV

Dorimene, Dorante, Lackey

LACKEY
Monsieur says that he'll be here very soon.

DORANTE
That's fine.

DORIMENE
I don't know, Dorante; I feel strange allowing you to bring me to this house where I know no one.

DORANTE
Then where would you like, Madame, for me to express my love with an entertainment, since you will allow neither your house nor mine for fear of scandal?

DORIMENE
But you don't mention that every day I am gradually preparing myself to receive too great proofs of your passion? As good a defense as I have put up, you wear down my resistance, and you have a polite persistence which makes me come gently to whatever you like. The frequent visits began, declarations followed, after them came serenades and amusements in their train, and presents

followed them. I withstood all that, but you don't give up at all and step by step you are overcoming my resolve. As for me, I can no longer answer for anything, and I believe that in the end you will bring me to marriage, which I have so far avoided.

DORANTE
My faith! Madame, you should already have come to it. You are a widow, and you answer only to yourself. I am my own master and I love you more than my life. Why shouldn't you be all my happiness from today onward?

DORIMENE
Goodness! Dorante, for two people to live happily together both of them need particular qualities; and two of the most reasonable persons in the world often have trouble making a union satisfactory to them both.

DORANTE
You're fooling yourself, Madame, to imagine so many difficulties, and the experience you had with one marriage doesn't determine anything for others.

DORIMENE
Finally I always come back to this. The expenses that I see you go to for me disturb me for two reasons
one is that they get me more involved than I would like; and the other is that I am sure — meaning no offense — that you cannot do this without financially inconveniencing yourself, and I certainly don't want that.

DORANTE
Ah! Madame, they are trifles, and it isn't by that . . .

DORIMENE
I know what I'm talking about; and among other gifts, the diamond you forced me to take is worth ...

DORANTE
Oh! Madame, mercy, don't put any value on a thing that my love finds unworthy of you, and allow ... Here's the master of the house.

SCENE XVI

Monsieur Jourdain, Dorimene, Dorante, Lackey

MONSIEUR JOURDAIN
(After having made two bows, finding himself too near Dorimene) A little farther, Madame.

DORIMENE
What?

MONSIEUR JOURDAIN
One step, if you please.

DORIMENE
What is it?

MONSIEUR JOURDAIN
Step back a little for the third.

DORANTE
Madame, Monsieur Jourdain is very knowledgeable.

MONSIEUR JOURDAIN
Madame, it is a very great honor to me to be fortunate enough to be so happy as to have the joy that you should have had the goodness to accord me the graciousness of doing me the honor of honoring me with the favor of your presence; and, if I also had the merit to merit a merit such as yours, and if Heaven . . .

envious of my luck . . . should have accorded me . . . the advantage of seeing me worthy . . . of the . . .

DORANTE
Monsieur Jourdain, that is enough. Madame doesn't like grand compliments, and she knows that you are a man of wit. (Aside to Dorimene) As you can see, this good bourgeois is ridiculous enough in all his manners.

DORIMENE
It isn't difficult to see it.

DORANTE
Madame, he is the best of my friends.

MONSIEUR JOURDAIN
You do me too much honor.

DORANTE
A completely gallant man.

DORIMENE
I have great esteem for him.

MONSIEUR JOURDAIN
I have done nothing yet, Madame, to merit this favor.

DORANTE
(Aside to Monsieur Jourdain) Take care, nonetheless, to say absolutely nothing to her about the diamond that you gave her.

MONSIEUR JOURDAIN
Can't I even ask her how she likes it?

DORANTE
What? Take care that you don't. That would be loutish of you;
and, to act as a gallant man, you must act as though it were not
you who made her this present. (Aloud) Monsieur Jourdain,
Madame, says he is delighted to see you in his home.

DORIMENE
He honors me greatly.

MONSIEUR JOURDAIN
How obliged I am to you, sir, for speaking thus to her for me!

DORANTE
I have had frightful trouble getting her to come here.

MONSIEUR JOURDAIN
I don't know how to thank you enough.

DORANTE
He says, Madame, that he finds you the most beautiful woman in
the world.

DORIMENE
He does me a great favor.

MONSIEUR JOURDAIN
Madame, it is you who does the favors, and . . .

DORANTE
Let's consider eating.

LACKEY
Everything is ready, sir.

DORANTE
Come then let us sit at the table. And bring on the musicians.

(Six cooks, who have prepared the feast, dance together and make the third interlude; after which, they carry in a table covered with many dishes.)

ACT IV

SCENE I

Dorimene, Monsieur Jourdain, Dorante, two Male Musicians, a Female Musician, Lackeys

DORIMENE
Why, Dorante, that is really a magnificent repast!

MONSIEUR JOURDAIN
You jest, Madame; I wish it were worthy of being offered to you. (All sit at the table).

DORANTE
Monsieur Jourdain is right, Madame, to speak so, and he obliges me by making you so welcome. I agree with him that the repast is not worthy of you. Since it was I who ordered it, and since I do not have the accomplishments of our friends in this matter, you do not have here a very sophisticated meal, and you will find some incongruities in the combinations and some barbarities of taste. If Damis, our friend, had been involved, everything would have been according to the rules; everything would have been elegant and appropriate, and he would not have failed to impress upon you the significance of all the dishes of the repast, and to make you see his expertise when it comes to good food; he would have told you about hearth-baked bread, with its golden brown crust, crunching tenderly between the teeth; of a smooth, full-bodied wine, fortified with a piquancy not too strong, of a loin of mutton improved with parsley, of a cut of specially-raised veal as long as this, white and delicate, and which is like an almond paste between the teeth, of partridges complimented by a surprisingly flavorful sauce, and, for his masterpiece, a soup accompanied by a fat young turkey surrounded by pigeons and crowned with white onions mixed with chicory. But, as for me, I declare my ignorance;

and, as Monsieur Jourdain has said so well, I only wish that the repast were more worthy of being offered to you.

DORIMENE
I reply to this compliment only by eating.

MONSIEUR JOURDAIN
Ah! What beautiful hands!

DORIMENE
The hands are mediocre, Monsieur Jourdain; but you wish to speak of the diamond, which is very beautiful.

MONSIEUR JOURDAIN
Me, Madame? God forbid that I should wish to speak of it; that would not be acting gallantly, and the diamond is a very small thing.

DORIMENE
You are very particular.

MONSIEUR JOURDAIN
You are too kind. . .

DORANTE
Let's have some wine for Monsieur Jourdain and for these gentlemen and ladies who are going to favor us with a drinking song.

DORIMENE
It is marvelous to season good food, by mixing it with music, and I see I am being admirably entertained.

MONSIEUR JOURDAIN
Madame, it isn't . .

DORANTE
Monsieur Jourdain, let us remain silent for these gentlemen and ladies; what they have for us to hear is of more value than anything we could say. (The male singers and the woman singer take the glasses, sing two drinking songs, and are accompanied by all the instrumental ensemble.)

FIRST DRINKING SONG Drink a little, Phyllis, to start the glass round. Ah! A glass in your hands is charmingly agreeable! You and the wine arm each other, And I redouble my love for you both Let us three — wine, you, and me — Swear, my beauty, to an eternal passion. Your lips are made yet more attractive by wetting with wine! Ah! The one and the other inspire me with desire And both you and it intoxicate me Let us three — wine, you, and me — Swear, my beauty, to an eternal passion.

SECOND DRINKING SONG Let us drink, dear friends, let us drink; Time that flies beckons us to it! Let us profit from life as much as we can. Once we pass under the black shadow, Goodbye to wine, our loves; Let us drink while we can, One cannot drink forever. Let fools speculate On the true happiness of life. Our philosophy Puts it among the wine-pots. Possessions, knowledge and glory Hardly make us forget troubling cares, And it is only with good drink That one can be happy. Come on then, wine for all, pour, boys, pour, Pour, keep on pouring, until they say, "Enough."

DORIMENE
I don't believe it's possible to sing better, and that is positively beautiful.

MONSIEUR JOURDAIN
I see something here, Madame, yet more beautiful.

DORIMENE
Aha! Monsieur Jourdain is more gallant than I thought.

DORANTE
What! Madame, what did you take Monsieur Jourdain for?

MONSIEUR JOURDAIN
I would like for her to take me at my word.

DORIMENE
Again!

DORANTE
You don't know him.

MONSIEUR JOURDAIN
She may know me whenever it pleases her.

DORIMENE
Oh! I am overwhelmed.

DORANTE
He is a man who is always ready with a repartee. But don't you see that Monsieur Jourdain, Madame, eats all the pieces of food you have touched?

DORIMENE
I am captivated by Monsieur Jourdain . . .

MONSIEUR JOURDAIN
If I could captivate your heart, I would be . . .

SCENE II

Madame Jourdain, Monsieur Jourdain, Dorimene, Dorante, Musicians, Lackeys

MADAME JOURDAIN
Aha! I find good company here, and I see that I was not expected.
Was it for this pretty affair, Monsieur Husband, that you were so
eager to send me to dinner at my sister's? I just saw stage
decorations downstairs, and here I see a banquet fit for a wedding.
That is how you spend your money, and this is how you entertain
the ladies in my absence, and you give them music and
entertainment while sending me on my way.

DORANTE
What are you saying, Madame Jourdain? And what fantasies are
you getting into your head that your husband spends his money,
and that it is he who is giving this entertainment to Madame?
Please know that it is I; that he only lends me his house, and that
you ought to think more about the things you say.

MONSIEUR JOURDAIN
Yes, what impertinence. It is the Count who presents all this to
Madame, who is a person of quality. He does me the honor of
using my house and of wishing me to be with him.

MADAME JOURDAIN
All that's nonsense. I know what I know.

DORANTE
Come Madame Jourdain, put on better glasses.

MADAME JOURDAIN
I don't need glasses, sir, I see well enough; I have had suspicions
for a long time, and I'm not a fool. This is very low of you, of a
great lord, to lend a hand as you do to the follies of my husband.
And you, Madame, for a great lady, it is neither fine nor honest of
you to cause dissension in a household and to allow my husband
to be in love with you.

DORIMENE
What is she trying to say with all this? Goodness Dorante! You have outdone yourself by exposing me to the absurd fantasies of this ridiculous woman.

DORANTE
Madame, wait! Madame, where are you going?

MONSIEUR JOURDAIN
Madame! Monsieur Count, make excuses to her and try to bring her back. Ah! You impertinent creature, this is a fine way to act! You come and insult me in front of everybody, and you drive from me people of quality.

MADAME JOURDAIN
I laugh at their quality.

MONSIEUR JOURDAIN
I don't know who holds me back, evil creature, from breaking your head with the remains of the repast you came to disrupt. (The table is removed).

MADAME JOURDAIN
(Leaving) I'm not concerned. These are my rights that I defend, and I'll have all wives on my side.

MONSIEUR JOURDAIN
You do well to avoid my rage. She arrived very inopportunely. I was in the mood to say pretty things, and I had never felt so witty. What's that?

SCENE III

Covielle, disguised; Monsieur Jourdain, Lackey

COVIELLE
Sir, I don't know if I have the honor to be known to you?

MONSIEUR JOURDAIN
No, sir.

COVIELLE
I saw you when you were no taller than that.

MONSIEUR JOURDAIN
Me?

COVIELLE
Yes. You were the most beautiful child in the world, and all the ladies took you in their arms to kiss you.

MONSIEUR JOURDAIN
To kiss me?

COVIELLE
Yes, I was a great friend of your late father.

MONSIEUR JOURDAIN
Of my late father?

COVIELLE
Yes. He was a very honorable gentleman.

MONSIEUR JOURDAIN
What did you say?

COVIELLE
I said that he was a very honorable gentleman.

MONSIEUR JOURDAIN
My father?

COVIELLE
Yes.

MONSIEUR JOURDAIN
You knew him very well?

COVIELLE
Assuredly.

MONSIEUR JOURDAIN
And you knew him as a gentleman?

COVIELLE
Without doubt.

MONSIEUR JOURDAIN
Then I don't know what is going on!

COVIELLE
What?

MONSIEUR JOURDAIN
There are some fools who want to tell me that he was a tradesman.

COVIELLE
Him, a tradesman! It's pure slander, he never was one. All that he did was to be very obliging, very ready to help; and, since he was a connoisseur in cloth, he went all over to choose them, had them brought to his house, and gave them to his friends for money.

MONSIEUR JOURDAIN
I'm delighted to know you, so you can testify to the fact that my father was a gentleman.

COVIELLE
I'll attest to it before all the world.

MONSIEUR JOURDAIN
You'll oblige me. What business brings you here?

COVIELLE
Since knowing your late father, honorable gentleman, as I told you, I have traveled through all the world.

MONSIEUR JOURDAIN
Through all the world!

COVIELLE
Yes.

MONSIEUR JOURDAIN
I imagine it's a long way from here to there.

COVIELLE
Assuredly. I returned from all my long voyages only four days ago; and because of the interest I take in all that concerns you, I come to announce to you the best news in the world.

MONSIEUR JOURDAIN
What?

COVIELLE
You know that the son of the Grand Turk is here?

MONSIEUR JOURDAIN
Me? No.

COVIELLE
What! He has a very magnificent retinue; everybody goes to see it, and he has been received in this country as an important lord.

MONSIEUR JOURDAIN
By my faith! I didn't know that.

COVIELLE
The advantage to you in this is that he is in love with your daughter.

MONSIEUR JOURDAIN
The son of the Grand Turk?

COVIELLE
Yes. And he wants to be your son-in-law.

MONSIEUR JOURDAIN
My son-in-law, the son of the Grand Turk?

COVIELLE
The son of the Grand Turk your son-in-law. As I went to see him, and as I perfectly understand his language, he conversed with me; and, after some other discourse, he said to me, "Acciam croc soler ouch alla moustaph gidelum amanahem varahini oussere carbulath," that is to say, "Haven't you seen a beautiful young person who is the daughter of Monsieur Jourdain, gentleman of Paris?"

MONSIEUR JOURDAIN
The son of the Grand Turk said that of me?

COVIELLE
Yes. Inasmuch as I told him in reply that I knew you particularly well and that I had seen your daughter
"Ah!" he said to me, "marababa sahem;" Which is to say, "Ah, how I am enamored of her!"

MONSIEUR JOURDAIN

"Marababa sahem" means "Ah, how I am enamored of her"?

COVIELLE
Yes.

MONSIEUR JOURDAIN
By my faith, you do well to tell me, since, as for me, I would never have believed that "marababa sahem" could have meant to say "Oh, how I am enamored of her!" What an admirable language Turkish is!

COVIELLE
More admirable than one can believe. Do you know what Cacaracamouchen means?

MONSIEUR JOURDAIN
Cacaracamouchen? No.

COVIELLE
It means
It means, "My dear soul."

MONSIEUR JOURDAIN
Cacaracamouchen means "My dear soul?"

COVIELLE
Yes.

MONSIEUR JOURDAIN
That's marvelous! Cacaracamouchen, my dear soul. Who would have thought? I'm dumbfounded.

COVIELLE
Finally, to complete my assignment, he comes to ask for your daughter in marriage; and in order to have a father-in-law who

should be worthy of him, he wants to make you a Mamamouchi, which is a certain high rank in his country.

MONSIEUR JOURDAIN
Mamamouchi?'

COVIELLE
Yes, Mamamouchi; that is to say, in our language, a Paladin. Paladin is one of those ancient . . . Well, Paladin! There is none nobler than that in the world, and you will be equal to the greatest lords of the earth.

MONSIEUR JOURDAIN
The son of the Grand Turk honors me greatly. Please take me to him in order to express my thanks.

COVIELLE
What! He is going to come here.

MONSIEUR JOURDAIN
He's coming here?

COVIELLE
Yes. And he is bringing everything for the ceremony of bestowing your rank.

MONSIEUR JOURDAIN
That seems very quick.

COVIELLE
His love can suffer no delay.

MONSIEUR JOURDAIN
All that embarrasses me here is that my daughter is a stubborn one who has gotten into her head a certain Cleonte, and she swears she'll marry no one but him.

COVIELLE
She'll change her mind when she sees the son of the Grand Turk; and then there is a remarkable coincidence here, it is that the son of the Grand Turk resembles this Cleonte very closely. I just saw him, someone showed him to me; and the love she has for the one can easily pass to the other, and . . . I hear him coming. There he is.

SCENE IV

Cleonte, as a Turk, with three Pages carrying his outer clothes, Monsieur Jourdain, Covielle, disguised

CLEONTE
Ambousahim oqui boraf, Iordina, salamalequi.

COVIELLE
That is to say
"Monsieur Jourdain, may your heart be all the year like a flowering rosebush." This is the way of speaking politely in those countries.

MONSIEUR JOURDAIN
I am the most humble servant of His Turkish Highness.

COVIELLE
Carigar camboto oustin moraf .

CLEONTE
Oustin yoc catamalequi basum base alla moran.

COVIELLE
He says
"Heaven gives you the strength of lions and the wisdom of serpents."

MONSIEUR JOURDAIN
His Turkish Highness honors me too much, and I wish him all sorts of good fortune.

COVIELLE
Ossa binamen sadoc bahally oracaf ouram.

CLEONTE
Bel-men.

COVIELLE
He says that you should go with him quickly to prepare yourself for the ceremony; then you can see your daughter and conclude the marriage.

MONSIEUR JOURDAIN
So many things in two words?

COVIELLE
Yes; the Turkish language is like that, it says much in few words. Go quickly where he wants.

SCENE V

Dorante, Covielle

COVIELLE
Ha, ha, ha! My faith, that was hilarious. What a dupe! If he had learned his role by heart, he could not have played it better. Ah! Ah! Excuse me, Sir, Wouldn't you like to help us here in an affair that is taking place.

DORANTE
Ah! Ah! Covielle, who would have recognized you? How you are made up!

COVIELLE
You see, ha, ha!

DORANTE
What are you laughing at?

COVIELLE
At a thing, Sir, that well deserves it.

DORANTE
What?

COVIELLE
I'll give you many chances, Sir, to guess the stratagem we are using on Monsieur Jourdain to get him to give his daughter to my master.

DORANTE
I can't begin to guess the stratagem, but I guess it will not fail in its effect, since you are undertaking it.

COVIELLE
I see, Sir, that you know me too well.

DORANTE
Tell me what it is.

COVIELLE
Come over here a little to make room for what I see coming. You can see part of the story, while I tell you the rest.

(The Turkish ceremony for ennobling Monsieur Jourdain is performed in dance and music, and comprises the Fourth Interlude.) [The ceremony is a burlesque full of comic gibberish in pseudo-Turkish and nonsensical French, in which Monsieur

Jourdain is made to appear ludicrous and during which he is outfitted with an extravagant costume, turban, and sword.]

ACT V

SCENE I

Madame Jourdaine, Monsieur Jourdain

MADAME JOURDAIN
Ah, My God! Mercy! What is all of this? What a spectacle! Are you dressed for a masquerade, and is this a time to go masked? Speak then, what is this? Who has bundled you up like that?

MONSIEUR JOURDAIN
See the impertinent woman, to speak in this way to a Mamamouchi!

MADAME JOURDAIN
How's that?

MONSIEUR JOURDAIN
Yes, you must show me respect now, as I've just been made a Mamamouchi.

MADAME JOURDAIN
What are you trying to say with your Mamamouchi?

MONSIEUR JOURDAIN
Mamamouchi, I tell you. I'm a Mamamouchi.

MADAME JOURDAIN
What animal is that?

MONSIEUR JOURDAIN
Mamamouchi, that is to say, in our language, Paladin.

MADAME JOURDAIN
Baladin! Are you of an age to dance in ballets?

MONSIEUR JOURDAIN
What an ignorant woman! I said Paladin. It's a dignity which has just been bestowed upon me in a ceremony.

MADAME JOURDAIN
What ceremony then?

MONSIEUR JOURDAIN
Mahometa-per-Jordina.

MADAME JOURDAIN
What does that mean?

MONSIEUR JOURDAIN
Jordina, that is to say, Jourdain.

MADAME JOURDAIN
Very well, what of Jourdain?

MONSIEUR JOURDAIN
Voler far un Paladina de Jordina.

MADAME JOURDAIN
What?

MONSIEUR JOURDAIN
Dar turbanta con galera.

MADAME JOURDAIN
Which is to say what? MONSIEUR JOURDAIN
Per deffender Palestina.

MADAME JOURDAIN
What are you trying to say?

MONSIEUR JOURDAIN
Dara, dara, bastonnara.

MADAME JOURDAIN
What jargon is this?

MONSIEUR JOURDAIN
Non tener honta, questa star l'ultima affronta.

MADAME JOURDAIN
What in the world is all that?

MONSIEUR JOURDAIN
(Dancing and singing). Hou la ba, Ba la chou, ba la ba, ba la da.

MADAME JOURDAIN
Alas! Oh Lord, my husband has gone mad.

MONSIEUR JOURDAIN
(Leaving) Peace, insolent woman! Show respect to the Monsieur
Mamamouchi.

MADAME JOURDAIN
Has he lost his mind? I must hurry to stop him from going out.
Ah! Ah! This is the last straw! I see nothing but shame on all
sides. (She leaves.)

SCENE II

Dorante, Dorimene

DORANTE
Yes, Madame, you are going to see the most amusing thing
imaginable. I don't believe it would be possible to find in all the
world another man as crazy as that one is. And then too,

Madame, we must try to help Cleonte's plan by supporting his masquerade. He's a very gallant man and deserves our help.

DORIMENE
I think highly of him and he deserves happiness.

DORANTE
Besides that, we have here, Madame, another ballet performance that we shouldn't miss, and I want to see if my idea will succeed.

DORIMENE
I saw magnificent preparations, and I can no longer permit this Dorante. Yes, I finally want to end your extravagances and to stop all these expenses that I see you go to for me, I have decided to marry you right away. This is the truth of it, that all these sorts of things end with marriage, as you know.

DORANTE
Ah! Madame, is it possible that you should have taken such a sweet decision in my favor?

DORIMENE
It is only to impede you from ruining yourself; without that, I see very well that before long you would not have a penny.

DORANTE
How obliged I am to you, Madame, for the care you have to conserve my money! It is entirely yours, as well as my heart, and you may use them in whatever fashion you please.

DORIMENE
I'll make use of them both. But here is your man
his costume is wonderful.

SCENE III

Monsieur Jourdain, Dorante, Dorimene

DORANTE
Sir, we come to pay homage, Madame and I, to your new dignity, and to rejoice with you at the marriage between your daughter and the son of the Grand Turk.

MONSIEUR JOURDAIN
(After bowing in the Turkish way) Sir, I wish you the strength of serpents and the wisdom of lions.

DORIMENE,
I was very glad, Sir, to be among the first to come to congratulate you upon rising to such a high degree of honor.

MONSIEUR JOURDAIN
Madame, I wish your rosebush to flower all year long; I am infinitely obliged to you for taking part in the honors bestowed upon me; and I am very happy to see you returned here, so I can make very humble excuses for the ridiculous behavior of my wife.

DORIMENE
That's nothing. I excuse her jumping to conclusions your heart must be precious to her, and it isn't strange that the possession of such a man as you should inspire some jealousy.

MONSIEUR JOURDAIN
The possession of my heart is a thing that has been entirely gained by you.

DORANTE
You see, Madame, that Monsieur Jourdain is not one of those men that good fortune blinds, and that he still knows, even in his glory, how to recognize his friends.

DORIMENE
It is the mark of a completely generous soul.

DORANTE
Where then is His Turkish Highness? We want, as your friends, to pay him our respects.

MONSIEUR JOURDAIN
There he comes, and I have sent for my daughter in order to give him her hand.

SCENE IV

Cleonte, Covielle, Monsieur Jourdain, etc.

DORANTE
Sir, we come to bow to Your Highness as friends of the gentleman who is your father-in-law, and to assure you with respect of our very humble services.

MONSIEUR JOURDAIN
Where's the interpreter to tell him who you are and to make him understand what you say? You will see that he will reply, and that he speaks Turkish marvelously. Hey there! Where the devil has he gone? (To Cleonte). Strouf, strif, strof, straf. The gentleman is a grande Segnore, grande Segnore, grande Segnore. And Madame is a Dama granda Dama, granda. Ahi! He, Monsieur, he French Mamamauchi, and Madame also French Mamamouchie. I can't say it more clearly. Good, here's the interpreter. Where are you going? We won't know how to say anything without you. Tell him, that Monsieur and Madame are persons of high rank, who have come to pay their respects to him, as my friends, and to assure him of their services. You'll see how he will reply.

COVIELLE
Alabala crociam acci boram alabamen.

CLEONTE
Catalequi tubal ourin soter amalouchan.

MONSIEUR JOURDAIN
See?

COVIELLE
He says that the rain of prosperity should water the garden of your family in all seasons.

MONSIEUR JOURDAIN
I told you that he speaks Turkish!

DORANTE
That's wonderful.

SCENE V

Lucile, Monsieur Jourdain, Dorante, Dorimene, etc.

MONSIEUR JOURDAIN
Come, my daughter; come here and give your hand to the gentleman who does you the honor of asking for you in marriage.

LUCILE
What! Father, look at you! Are you playing in a comedy?

MONSIEUR JOURDAIN
No, no, this is not a comedy, it's a very serious matter, and as full of honor for you as possible. There is the husband I give you.

LUCILE
To me, father?

MONSIEUR JOURDAIN
Yes, to you. Come, put your hand in his, and give thanks to Heaven for your happiness.

LUCILE
I have absolutely no wish to marry.

MONSIEUR JOURDAIN
I wish it, I, who am your father.

LUCILLE
I'll do nothing of the sort.

MONSIEUR JOURDAIN
Ah! What a nuisance! Come, I tell you. Give your hand.

LUCILE
No, my father, I told you, there is no power on earth that can make me take any husband other than Cleonte. And I will go to extreme measures rather than . . . (Recognizes Cleonte) It is true that you are my father; I owe you complete obedience; and it is for you to dispose of me according to your wishes.

MONSIEUR JOURDAIN
Ah! I am delighted to see you return so promptly to your duty, and it pleases me to have an obedient daughter.

SCENE VI

Madame Jourdain, Monsieur Jourdain, Cleonte, etc.

MADAME JOURDAIN
What now? What's this? They say that you want to give your daughter in marriage to a someone in a Carnival costume?

MONSIEUR JOURDAIN
Will you be quiet, impertinent woman? You always throw your absurdities into everything, and there's no teaching you to be reasonable.

MADAME JOURDAIN
It's you that there is no way of making wise, and you go from folly to folly. What is your plan, and what do you want to do with this assemblage of people?

MONSIEUR JOURDAIN
I want to marry our daughter to the son of the Grand Turk.

MADAME JOURDAIN
To the son of the Grand Turk?

MONSIEUR JOURDAIN
Yes. Greet him through the interpreter there.

MADAME JOURDAIN
I don't need an interpreter; and I'll tell him straight out myself, to his face, that there is no way he will have my daughter.

MONSIEUR JOURDAIN
I ask again, will you be quiet?

DORANTE
What! Madame Jourdain, do you oppose such good fortune as that? You refuse His Turkish Highness as your son-in-law?

MADAME JOURDAIN
My Goodness, Sir, mind your own business.

DORIMENE
It's a great glory, which is not to be rejected.

MADAME JOURDAIN
Madame, I beg you also not to concern yourself with what does
not affect you.

DORANTE
It's the friendship we have for you that makes us involve ourselves
in your interest.

MADAME JOURDAIN
I can get along quite well without your friendship.

DORANTE
Your daughter here agrees to the wishes of her father.

MADAME JOURDAIN
My daughter consents to marry a Turk?

DORANTE
Without doubt.

MADAME JOURDAIN
She can forget Cleonte?

DORANTE
What wouldn't one do to be a great lady?

MADAME JOURDAIN
I would strangle her with my own hands if she did something like
that.

MONSIEUR JOURDAIN
That is just so much talk. I tell you, this marriage shall take place.

MADAME JOURDAIN
And I say there is no way that it will happen.

MONSIEUR JOURDAIN
Oh, what a row!

LUCILE
Mother!

MADAME JOURDAIN
Go away, you are a hussy.

MONSIEUR JOURDAIN
What! You quarrel with her for obeying me?

MADAME JOURDAIN
Yes. She is mine as much as yours.

COVIELLE
Madame!

MADAME JOURDAIN
What do you want to tell me?

COVIELLE
A word.

MADAME JOURDAIN
I want nothing to do with your word.

COVIELLE
(To Monsieur Jourdain) Sir, if she will hear a word in private, I promise you to make her consent to what you want.

MADAME JOURDAIN
I will never consent to it.

COVIELLE
Only listen to me.

MADAME JOURDAIN
No.

MONSIEUR JOURDAIN
Listen to him.

MADAME JOURDAIN
No, I don't want to listen to him.

MONSIEUR JOURDAIN
He is going tell you . . .

MADAME JOURDAIN
I don't want him to tell me anything whatsoever.

MONSIEUR JOURDAIN
There is the great stubbornness of a woman! How can it hurt you to listen to him?

COVIELLE
Just listen to me; after that you can do as you please.

MADAME JOURDAIN
Alright! What?

COVIELLE
(Aside to Madame Jourdain) For an hour, Madame, we've been signaling to you. Don't you see that all this is done only to accommodate ourselves to the fantasies of your husband, that we are fooling him under this disguise and that it is Cleonte himself who is the son of the Grand Turk?

MADAME JOURDAIN
Ah! Ah!

COVIELLE
And I, Covielle, am the interpreter?

MADAME JOURDAIN
Ah! If this is the case then, I surrender.

COVIELLE
Don't let on.

MADAME JOURDAIN
Yes, it's done, I agree to the marriage.

MONSIEUR JOURDAIN
Ah! Now everyone's reasonable. You didn't want to hear it. I knew he would explain to you what it means to be the son of the Grand Turk.

MADAME JOURDAIN
He explained it to me very well, and I am satisfied. Let us send for a notary.

DORANTE
This is very well said. And finally, Madame Jourdain, in order to relieve your mind completely, and that you may lose today all the jealousy that you may have conceived of your husband, we shall have the same notary marry us, Madame and me.

MADAME JOURDAIN
I agree to that also.

MONSIEUR JOURDAIN
Is this to make her believe our story?

DORANTE
(Aside to Monsieur Jourdain) It is necessary to amuse her with this pretence.

MONSIEUR JOURDAIN
Good, good! Someone go for the notary.

DORANTE
While we wait for him to come and while he draws up the contracts, let us see our ballet, and divert His Turkish Highness with it.

MONSIEUR JOURDAIN
That is very well advised. Come, let's take our places.

MADAME JOURDAIN
And Nicole?

MONSIEUR JOURDAIN
I give her to the interpreter; and my wife to whoever wants her.

COVIELLE
Sir, I thank you. (Aside) If one can find a greater fool, I'll go to Rome to tell it.

(The comedy ends with a ballet)

www.ingramcontent.com/pod-product-compliance
Lightning Source LLC
Chambersburg PA
CBHW060813030726
47503CB00002B/470